SOMEONE BEFORE US

George Frederick Clarke, July 1967

SOMEONE BEFORE US

BURIED HISTORY IN CENTRAL NEW BRUNSWICK

FOURTH EDITION

GEORGE FREDERICK CLARKE

EDITED BY MARY BERNARD

CHAPEL STREET EDITIONS

4th edition by
Chapel Street Editions
Edited by Mary Bernard
© The Estate of George Frederick Clarke 2016

Published by Chapel Street Editions
150 Chapel Street
Woodstock, NB Canada E7M 1H4
chapelstreeteditions@gmail.com

Library and Archives Canada Cataloguing in Publication

Clarke, George Frederick, 1883-1974, author

    Someone before us : buried history in central New Brunswick / George Frederick Clarke ; edited by Mary Bernard. -- 4th edition.

Includes bibliographical references and index.
ISBN 978-1-988299-05-1 (paperback)

    1. Indians of North America--New Brunswick--Antiquities. 2. Nova Scotia--History--To 1784. 3. New Brunswick--Antiquities. 4. Excavations (Archaeology)--New Brunswick. I. Bernard, Mary, 1941-, editor II. Title.

E78.N46C54 2016   971.5'101   C2016-906939-7

The type is set in Minion Pro designed by Robert Slimbach for Adobe Systems

Cover painting, *Noel Bear Smoking Meat,* by Edwin Tappan Adney

Book design by Brendan Helmuth

To my Indian friends in the Maritime provinces, and especially to Peter Paul, of the Reserve below Woodstock, who has made so many contributions in the fields of folklore and the dialects of the northeastern Indians. To the memory of my Indian friend, Noel Moulton, my companion on many an important exploration of prehistoric campsites. To Robert A. Tweedie, Director of the New Brunswick Tourist Bureau and Fred Phillips, Assistant Director, both of whom many times during the last twenty years urged me to put my knowledge of our Indians in permanent form. And lastly to the memory of Edwin Tappan Adney, who knew more about the bark canoes of the North American Indian than any one else in the world, and in his many other activities was the most remarkable genius I have ever known, this book is affectionately dedicated.

CONTENTS

LIST OF ILLUSTRATIONS

Initials in parentheses are those of the photographer:

Photo credits follow the list of illustrations.

Sources of Illustrations

Front cover: reproduced with the kind permission of the owners of "Noel Bear", Frank and Brenda Creighton.

In the first three editions of *Someone Before Us* GFC described the painting as: "Noel Bear (Mooin) famous hunter, trapper and guide, of Maliseet, Tobique River."

In 1893 Noel Bear was probably in his late nineties, according to the entry "Noel Bear," by Andrea Bear Nicholas, in vol 13 of The Dictionary of Canadian Biography.

Figures 7, 12-15 and 46 were photographed by Michael Saunders in 1964.

The photographs in figure 3 were taken by Jane Bernard, c. 1961. The negatives are in the editor's collection.

Figures 6, 10, 16, 18-19, 21-24, 27-28, 30-31, 34-35, 37, 40 e-f and 43 were photographed by Rob Blanchard in 2016.

Figures B, C, 33, 40 a-b and 41 a-d were scanned by Rob Blanchard in 2016 from photographs once owned by GFC, now in the Archaeological Research Laboratory, Department of Anthropology, University of New Brunswick, Fredericton.

Figures 2, 5, 7, 9, 12, 14-15, 20, 25-26, 36, 38, and 51-52 were scanned by Rob Blanchard in 2016 from large-format negatives once owned by GFC, now in the Archaeological Research Laboratory at UNB.

Figure 39 was taken by David Sanger in the late 1960s or early 1970s. GFC had a copy of the print; it is now in the UNB Archaeological Research Laboratory, GFC Paper Archive, item # GFC-093.

Figure 8 comes from the Vincent Erickson Collection, MG H 117, Negative AC10276-28, Image courtesy of Archives & Special Collections, Harriet Irving Library, University of New Brunswick. (I have cropped and edited the photograph.)

Figure E comes from the Stephen Homer collection.

Figures 1, 13, 42, 48-50 and 53 were scanned by the editor from the first edition of *Someone Before Us.*

Figures A, 29, 32, 44, 46, 47 a-b and 55, were scanned from prints in the editor's collection.

Figure 11 comes from a snapshot once owned by GFC and photographed by the editor in 1983.

The front cover photograph (2015), frontispiece (1967) and figures D (2015), 17 (2009), 45 a-d (2002) and 54 (2002) were photographed by the editor.

The back cover photograph (1972) and figures 4 (1979) and 40 e (1972) were photographed by Ian Fleming.

I have digitally edited all photographs and illustrations.

Editor's Preface

A Family Affair

I am in a deep trench. My grandfather is at the other end, making it longer. I am trying to see over the top. The smell of earth fills my nostrils. I can see a fringe of grass and sunlight, but down here it is dark. Now and then, when I remember to, I scrape the side of the trench with a small trowel, carefully, delicately, as my grandfather has told me to, alert for the chink of stone against metal. I want to be an archaeologist like him when I grow up.

I am four years old. My grandfather is George Frederick Clarke; I am the daughter of his elder daughter, Jane. It is 1946, and he is excavating on a farm he recently bought for his younger daughter, Dees, on the flat above Lane's Creek in Upper Woodstock,

A few days later he wrote to Dees, who was in Boston:

> Little Mary and I were up to the farm the other afternoon, and she wanted me to promise, today, that I'd take her up tomorrow. She wants to dig arrowheads. Her favourite story is one I told her about "Thumblatch" and "Mirandy" going on a digging expedition to your farm. Already she is an ardent archaeologist, and will pore over the books containing pictures of the different artifacts, asking me what this and that is for.

We all dug with him at one time or another. When Jane was little he took her digging on the Meductic intervale; in this book he describes her "bounding over a ploughed field towards me, holding a hand high above her head while she cried exultantly: 'I've found one! I've found one!'—a beautiful red jasper arrowhead." In her teens she often went on digging trips with him; she remembered "walking down through a field, then climbing down a sort of ravine, sliding, hanging onto trees," to get to a site on Eel River. Sometimes the whole family went with him, taking a picnic, and relaxed while he dug— on the Bert Shaw farm, for instance, with its "great ledges, paths winding down to the ledges, sheep nibbling."

His nephew Roy came to visit in 1939, and got hauled off to dig. His son-in-law Ken often dug with him in the 1940s (Fig. A, p 52). Any outing with GFC could turn into a dig.[1] If we walked across a ploughed field, he poked the furrows with the tip of his cane, and sometimes turned up an arrowhead. He always carried spade and trowel in the trunk of the car. He took them on fishing trips as well. He may be the only salmon

---

1 I call him GFC here and in the notes because his full name is a mouthful.

fisherman in New Brunswick who has ever given up an expensive day's angling to dig for artefacts—usually roping in his guides as helpers.

In my teens I lost my enthusiasm for excavation, but by then my brother, Ian, and my cousin Stephen had caught the bug. They were still children when he first took them digging. Ian dug with him at Meductic in his teens, in the early 1960s, when GFC was digging there as much as possible, to rescue what he could before Mactaquac flooded the flat. Once in those years he took Ian to Grand Lake with a man from the Field Institute of Chicago. When they got there, says Ian, GFC "scouted around, and scouted around, and scouted around, and finally said, 'I think we should dig here.' We dug, and we found artefacts. The man from the Field Institute was astonished."

GFC loved the solitude of digging, but he also liked company—and help. In the 1930s and 1940s he employed as a helper his Maliseet friend Noel Moulton, who figures largely in this book; sometimes he hired Levi Grant, son of his old woodsman friend Fred Grant.[2] In the 1950s and 1960s he was lucky enough to find a young man from Woodstock, John McClement, who wanted to hunt for artefacts just as much as he did.[3]

GFC's Archaeological Avocation

GFC had found an arrowhead at French Lake in 1902, but he didn't start seriously hunting for artefacts till 1923. That summer, noticing broken arrowheads in the earth beside his camp at the Forks of the Miramichi, he set to with a spade—and excavated so enthusiastically that he undermined the puncheons holding up the camp. All at once he was an archaeologist. The avocation lasted the rest of his life.

It is not surprising that archaeology became such a passion. It spoke to his interest in First Nations people and their crafts, which had been strong since 1907, when he met two of the most important men in his life—Noel Polchies, who had become his dearest friend, and Tappan Adney, who was engrossed in the ethnology of First Nations and had already begun his great life's work of preserving the knowledge of how their bark canoes were constructed. It spoke to the romantic in him, to his sense of being "swept back face-to-face with our own prehistoric ancestors;" and to his love of history, which grew throughout his life: to him, history included prehistory. It appealed likewise to his scientific side, which was stronger than he usually let on; and to his practical curiosity. When he wondered how something was made or what it was used for, he experimented: using a flint stone to manufacture a "reasonably good" stone knife; or rotating "so-called plummets" on cords to prove that they could be used to weave cloth or twist rope. Finally, he was good at it. He found artefacts on the beach that Adney missed; he had an instinct about where to dig for buried artefacts, an instinct he called the result of "long and intensive detective work," of working out where he would camp if he were a Native American.

2 I describe both men at greater length in my book *The Last Romantic: the Life of George Frederick Clarke, Master Storyteller of New Brunswick* (Chapel Street Editions, 2015).

3 In 1964 McClement wrote a paper, "Excavations at Meductic," for the Carleton County Historical Society.

Curiously, GFC does not describe his digging technique in *Someone Before Us* in detail; but he does so in an interview recorded in 1964:

> When I discovered a campsite, I dug a trench about 2 feet deep, and then I worked along the perpendicular side with a hand trowel, or, having dug my trench, I took off the topsoil, the grass, just down to the grass-roots, and then gradually trowelled away the top of the soil. The trowel is very sensitive, and if it strikes a bit of flint or an arrowhead, it gives forth an unmistakable clinking sound.
>
> I prefer working down the perpendicular side of the trench. I can sit down in the trench and work very carefully, and establish at the same time the different levels of occupation, if there are any. Sometimes there is only one level of occupation, but other times there are two or sometimes three.

B GFC digging at the Forks of the Miramichi, 1971

The year after that interview he cracked his knee. From then on he could only just lower himself gingerly into a trench John McClement had dug. His last major excavations were on the Meductic flat in 1964; after that he wrote about artefacts in this book rather than digging for them. But he couldn't altogether resist the lure of a good site. His digging career ended in the summer of 1971, at his camp at the Forks of the Miramichi. Finding the shore soft after high water, he fetched a spade and started excavating, only a few yards from the spot where his adventures in archaeology began, back in 1923 (Fig. B, p ix).

Composition History

Many collectors of prehistoric stone artefacts collect artefacts much as stamp-collectors collect stamps. GFC's interest was always broader than that. From early on (with a little prodding from Tappan Adney) he recorded some details about horizontal and vertical relationships among artefacts, though far less than a modern professional would consider minimally adequate; and he was always interested in the context of his pieces: in who had made and used them; and why, and when; in the whole human culture that had produced them. The breadth of his interest can be seen even in an article, "Indian Relics," written in about 1925, only two years after he started digging. It starts as an account of the "allurement" in the simple pastime of hunting artefacts, but quickly moves to the history of humankind: "Geology and archaeology are the alphabet whereby we slowly spell out and piece together the remote history of the cultural progress of man." The article is as much about the makers of his artefacts as about the artefacts themselves, and he characteristically ends it with a cry for justice for the first inhabitants of the continent:

> ...the strong and virile race that once peopled this continent of North America has been herded together on reservations, the beneficiary of governments which know little and care less about the history of this once free and proud people. We have absorbed his material culture in the canoe, the snowshoe, the moccasin; many of his medicinal cures; we have imitated his league of nations; and for his passing we have not even given a sigh.

He wrote other articles in the late 1930s,[4] not surprisingly: all his life he wrote about anything that interested him. Then in 1945 an historian associated with the New Brunswick Museum urged him to write a monograph about his discoveries. He set to work and finished *Archaeology of Central New Brunswick* in early 1946. He was proud, he told Dees, of having written it in "a discursive style...along the line of the English essay," rather than the "dry as dust" style of the academics who he knew would be its primary audience.

The monograph got as far as page proofs, but it was never published (Fig. C, p 53). The story behind that failure is the story of GFC's betrayal by his friend Tappan Adney. I have told it in detail in *The Last Romantic*, so I shall not tell it again here, except to say that GFC never knew what Adney had done. He accepted the excuses of Museum officials at face value and put the manuscript aside. No publisher outside New Brunswick would be interested in publishing it; and there were then no book publishers in New Brunswick.

Then in the early 1960s, encouraged by the publishing success of his two angling memoirs, he rewrote it for the general reader, adding material that brought the story of his archaeological life up to date. The dam fight slowed him up, but once that was lost, he went full speed ahead. Jane and I corrected a late typescript in the summer of 1967, and the Brunswick Press had it by early fall. They were slow; it didn't come out till a year later.

---

4   MMS in the GFC Collection at UNB and in the editor's collection.

Only a few pages of the 1946 monograph survived an attic fire in GFC's house in 2001, twenty-seven years after his death. They are now in the George Frederick Clarke collection at UNB (see below), along with many other textual materials related to his life in archaeology.

The Fate of the Collection

However much history and romance GFC read from his artefacts, he loved them themselves, as things of beauty all the more beautiful for being also things of utility; and as his collection grew, he became concerned that it should find a home in a museum after he died. He had several large, handsome cases of artefacts on display in the L.P. Fisher Library in Woodstock, but he could not trust it permanently with his entire collection. For a while the New Brunswick Museum seemed like the right place.

But in the 1960s the fate of the artefacts became tangled with the politics of the Mactaquac dam. GFC was one of the most outspoken and best-known opponents of the dam, and the bitterness of that fight spilled over into what even ostensibly non-political people said about his artefacts. By the time he was writing *Someone Before Us* in its present form, between 1963 and 1967, a rumour was afloat that no reputable institution would be interested in them, because they hadn't been excavated in a manner that met modern standards of documentation. (Neither had Tutankhamun's tomb.) GFC was given to understand that the New Brunswick Museum would not be interested in acquiring them for the province. He died in 1974 not knowing where the collection would go. Thirty years later his heirs still didn't know whether we would find a suitable institution to take it.

D Plaque on the door of the GFC Teaching Lab, Anthropology Department, UNB, 2012

E GFC showing double-pointed blade, 1974

Two men rescued the collection. The first was our friend David Myles. In 2005 he approached David Black, of the Department of Anthropology at the University of New Brunswick—who, says David Myles, "saw it as an opportunity and immediately took steps to secure the collection for UNB… His report to the Board convinced them immediately that these items were an essential component for the archaeology program. He was the man with the vision." (David Myles is unduly modest. Both Davids had the vision.)

Within a couple of years the collection was at UNB, except for two display cases of artefacts on long-term loan, one in the Fisher Library and a small one in the Atlantic Salmon Museum in Doaktown. The George Frederick Clarke Artifact Collection is now in the Department of Anthropology at the University of New Brunswick, being used for teaching and research.[5] (Fig. D, p xi)

GFC always delighted in showing his artefacts to visitors, especially young people. "I brought them into my room, took out the trays containing my most precious finds, pointed out the clam-like fractures on the face and edges, explained the methods used to produce the finished piece…and, I hope, sent my visitors away with awakened imaginations." (Fig. E, p xii)

He would be happy that young people are now learning from his collection and writing theses on his artefacts.

Critical Reception and Publishing History

Someone Before Us received more attention in the press than any of GFC's previous books, but they were mostly puffs based on a couple of pre-publication interviews. In one he said offhandedly, "I refuse to grow old," and that became the peg on which the folksier notices were hung. Most of the rest took their cue from a long piece by Ted Jarrett, a Woodstock journalist, emphasising GFC's age (eighty-four), his beautiful house and antiques, the diversity of his writing—and, when they got to the book itself, his amusing stories and lifelong advocacy of First Nations rights.

---

5   http://www.unb.ca/fredericton/arts/departments/anthropology/laboratories/gfcartifact.htm l#gfc

These were among the few perceptive comments:

> The seriousness of this fine book's themes does not prevent its being written in the same lucid and incisive style, enlivened by the same wealth of anecdote, as Dr. Clarke's novels and stories of New Brunswick life.

> He has brought the excitement of a detective story to the unravelling of clues discovered in prehistoric campsites…

> Dr Clarke takes the reader from the beginnings of pre-history to the social conditions facing the Maliseet in New Brunswick today—sometimes in the space of one page. Such is his depth of knowledge, the sense of involvement, the conviction and the excitement that one is swept up, intrigued and committed in the space of that page. It is a remarkable process. He enjoys life immensely, and the reader is handed great dollops of this enjoyment.

> Dr David Sanger, head of Eastern Canada section of archaeology division, National Museum of Canada, was most appreciative of the publication. "A gifted author with a remarkable talent for description, Dr. Clarke has brought to those who have read 'Someone Before Us,'" he said, "an eloquent and vibrant picture of the aboriginal inhabitants of the province. This book, and the man who created it, will mean more to the people of Canada than thousands of dry, technical manuscript pages."

The Text

Someone Before Us went through three editions in GFC's lifetime, in 1968, 1970 and 1974. (It has had none since, till this new edition.) Text and illustrations were identical in all three, except for one change, which greatly pleased GFC. In 1968 the dust-jacket illustration was a curiously unpleasant drawing of Adney's *Noel Bear Smoking Meat*. For the next two editions he was able to use a reasonably good colour photograph of the painting.

I have worked from the first edition, silently correcting a few typos.

GFC's footnotes are marked with stars and daggers. I have silently amplified or corrected a few.

My footnotes are marked with numbers. They give dates, sources for quotations that GFC left unattributed, and definitions of terms that may be obscure to non-archaeologists. A few add expert information from David Black.

GFC was habitually vague about dates, His habit of saying, "five (or ten, or forty) years ago," meaning, more or less, "about that long ago, give or take a few years," makes it hard to guess what year he is referring to. The problem is compounded because he wrote parts of *Someone Before Us* over such a long period of time and, when incorporating them into his final text, often forgot to change, say, "five years" to "ten (or forty)." Where I can, I have pointed out his dating errors in footnotes, in case the dates of excavation are useful to students.

The word "Indians"; the new subtitle

GFC lived before the term "First Nations" was in common use. He called First Nations peoples Indians, and it was what they then called themselves. I have not changed his usage. I have also kept his spellings of the names of First Nations peoples, such as Maliseet and Micmac.

I have, however, changed the subtitle. It was: "Our Maritime Indians" in the first three editions. But "Maritime" is too broad. GFC says little about the other Maritime Provinces, and hardly more about the north, west and south of his own. "Our" is also problematic. He used it polemically: he never missed a chance to insist that First Nations should be included as equals in political and social life. But today it has paternalistic overtones.

The new subtitle is David Black's inspiration. "Buried History in Central New Brunswick" beautifully describes the book's main themes: the pre-history of the area as revealed in stone artefacts, and the history of European impact on the First Nations of New Brunswick.

The Illustrations

The first editions of *Someone Before Us* had forty-three monochrome photographs. Thanks chiefly to David Black and the Department of Anthropology at UNB, this new edition has sixty-one photographs, fifty-three of them newly photographed or derived from high-quality originals. Twenty-two are in colour. They are all better, some dramatically better, than the plates in the first editions.

Only eight plates have no surviving original. I have scanned them (with an inevitable loss in quality) from the plates in the first edition. (Figures 11 and 47 are pre-digital snapshots of snapshots and even lower in quality.)

The George Frederick Clarke Project

Chapel Street Editions has undertaken a grand publishing project called the George Frederick Clarke Project. It will publish all of GFC's books over the next few years, at the rate of four a year. I am editing the series.

Three books launched the Project, in September 2015:

- my biography of GFC: *The Last Romantic: George Frederick Clarke, Master Storyteller of New Brunswick*
- GFC's first fishing memoir: *Six Salmon Rivers—and Another*
- the first collection of all his surviving short stories: *The Ghost of Nackawick Portage: the Collected Short Stories of George Frederick Clarke*

This fall of 2016 sees the publication of:

- GFC's second fishing memoir: *The Song of the Reel*
- his two books for young children, complete in one volume: *Jimmy-Why and Noël Polchies: their Adventures in the Great Woods*

and this book:

- *Someone Before Us*, the story of his archaeological finds and adventures

The next two book in the project will be *David Cameron's Adventures*, an exciting novel for young adults, and its sequel, *Return to Acadia*.

Mary Bernard
Cambridge, England
September 2016

Editor's Acknowledgments

My thanks are due first and foremost to David Black, professor of anthropology in the Department of Anthropology at the University of New Brunswick. Not only was he instrumental in arranging the donation of GFC's artefacts and related documents to UNB (where they now constitute the George Frederick Clarke Artifact Collection); he is also a major contributor to this new edition of *Someone Before Us*. He had new photographs taken of many of the Figures in the first edition and had scans made of the surviving large-format negatives and plates. He has answered dozens of questions; some of his answers went straight into the footnotes. He has provided technical captions to the illustrations; and he has written a fair and generous Afterword, which describes GFC's debt to nineteenth-century and early twentieth-century anthropology, and examines his archaeological ideas in the light of modern professional archaeology. Finally, he gave the book its wonderfully fitting new subtitle.

I would also like to thank the UNB Department of Anthropology for its cooperation in re-photographing so many of the plates in the new edition, and for making available to me its collection of GFC print and manuscript materials. Elise Rowsome of The Canadian Museum of History kindly provided me with the dimensions of the birchbark canoes once owned by GFC and now in the Museum.

My brother, Ian Bernard, and my cousin Stephen Homer have answered all sorts of questions, and David Myles has answered more than you can shake a stick at.

I want to thank Brenda and Frank Creighton for allowing me to photograph Tappan Adney's painting of Noel Bear. I arrived on their doorstep a stranger, and they were immediately generous with their time and their trust. The painting was under glass, and when they saw that I was having a hard time avoiding reflections, they took it out of its frame and let me prop it on the edge of their verandah to get the best light. It was a lovely afternoon.

I want to thank Michael Saunders for permission to use his photographs; and Rob Blanchard, at UNB, for providing excellent photographs of GFC's artefacts. Technical photography at that level is a great deal harder than most people guess.

Someone Before Us is part of the George Frederick Clarke Project. My deep thanks to Keith, Brendan and Ellen Helmuth of Chapel Street Editions, publishers of the Project, who make each volume just as good as it can be.

The web has been more help in editing this book than I can easily sum up. I'm not an archaeologist; I've been online every day checking stuff. I've cited a few sites in my footnotes, but I trawled hundreds more in my search for explanations and definitions—above all Wikipedia, that great and by now almost unimaginably complex testimony to people's desire to share their knowledge for the common good.

I well remember the labour of digging up information before the internet existed. It has a dark side, but the bright side says something surprising about human nature. There are thousands upon thousands of people who want to help others by putting their expert information online in long, helpful, often anonymous, articles, and who participate in forums where they patiently (for the most part) answer questions from the simplest to the most complicated. Before the web existed, if you had asked me whether such a thing was possible, I'd have said: no, if they're experts, they'll want to charge. But they mostly don't. It's an extraordinary, ongoing, mass act of generosity; it's something new under the sun.

Mary Bernard
Cambridge, England
September 2016

SOMEONE BEFORE US
BURIED HISTORY IN CENTRAL NEW BRUNSWICK

PREFACE

More than forty years ago, a famous New Brunswick guide named David Ogilvy, and a companion, were hunting moose far in the wilderness bordering the province of Quebec. They had followed a big bull for several miles and finally coming to a small lake, with a barren at its lower end covered with cat-spruce, scraggy birch, tamarack and the usual Labrador shrub, they found that the antlered monarch had fled along the muddy foreshore which bounded the southern border of the lake. The hunters proceeded warily, sometimes clambering over blow-downs from the bank above. Long since the fallen trees had been shorn of limbs, the barkless trunks grey from exposure to wind, sun and waves. Suddenly David Ogilvy, who was in the lead, saw a small triangular-shaped object lying in one of the hoof marks made by the moose in the soft, upturned black soil. He bent, picked up the object, and held it, wonderingly, in the palm of his open hand. It was a beautiful translucent white quartz arrowhead—a perfect example of aboriginal craftsmanship. How many undated centuries it had lain embedded in the soil on the shore of this lonely lake, no man could say... David Ogilvy turned to his companion, who was now beside him, and holding his extended palm upward, said in low, awed tones: *"Some one has been here before us!"**

---

* From *TOO SMALL A WORLD*, by the author of the following pages.

xix

Acknowledgements

To K. C. Homer, historian, free-lance script writer for the CBC, for his kindness in reading the manuscript and correcting grammatical errors and punctuation. My sincere thanks to Mr Ian Montagnes who arranged with the Royal Ontario Museum for me to use the painting by Arthur Heming used in the poem *The Birch-Bark Canoe.* To Mr John Stevens, of Glen Margaret, Halifax County for his sketches (after E. T. Adney) illustrating the steps in the construction of a birch-bark canoe. To John McKinlay (Harvey Studio, Woodstock) for photographing the original painting of a Maliseet Indian, by E. T. Adney. The original painting is now owned by Miss Isobel Mair of Guelph, Ontario. To my daughter Jane, and my granddaughter, Mary Bernard, for their patience in going over and correcting the author's and other errors in this work.

CHAPTER 1
INTRODUCTION

An arrow killed Thorvald Erikson, second son of Erik the Red, founder of Greenland.

It is now almost generally conceded by historians that about the year 1000 A.D., Leif Erikson, eldest son of Erik the Red, sailed to the mainland of North America and discovered a region he called Vinland. Many writers maintain that it was Nova Scotia, others Newfoundland rather than, as others say, the New England coast, or even more southerly parts of the continent.

Two years later Leif's younger brother Thorvald, with a crew of thirty in his galley, made a summer voyage to Vinland in order to make further explorations of the country, and the winter following occupied the sheds that Leif had built. When summer came they continued their explorations; sometimes along the coast, at others entering upon the land. One day they "saw upon the sand three skin boats (canoes) and three men under each. Then divided they their people, and caught them all except one, who got away with his boat. They killed the other eight, and then went back to the ship."

A little further on in the Saga we read: "Then rushed out from the frith an innumerable number of skin boats and made towards them. Thorvald said unto them: 'We will put out the battle skreens and defend ourselves as best we can, but fight little against them.' So they did, and the skraelings shot at them for a little and then ran away, each as fast as he could. Then asked Thorvald his men if they had taken any wounds; they answered no one was wounded. 'I have gotten a wound under the arm,' said he, 'for an arrow fled between the edge of the ship and the shield in under my arm, and here is the arrow, and it will prove a mortal wound to me.'"

And before he died Thorvald told his men: "Get ready instantly to depart, but first you shall bear me to that Cape...there shall ye bury me, and set crosses at my head and feet, and call the place Crossanes forever in all time to come."

The foregoing is the first reference I can find to skin canoes (doubtless birch-bark), and the use of the arrow in North America. Whether it was of stone, bone, or native copper, doesn't matter.

*   *   *

I was eighteen. With a man more than three times my age I was hunting ducks at Maquapit and French Lakes. We were tented beside the thoroughfare connecting these two bodies of water. One day, shortly after the noon hour, I left my companion napping

1

in the tent, and walked along the wide sandy beach flanking French Lake. I had not gone far when I decided to clean my shot gun. I did this, then idly began making little circles in the sand with the cleaning rod. Suddenly I disturbed and turned over to my view a small white object, and picked it up. Although never before had I seen a stone arrowhead, some inherited instinct told me what it was. I was as much surprised as was Robinson Crusoe when first he saw human footprints in the sandy shore of his desert island, and, like Crusoe, before he rescued his man Friday from the cannibals, I was quite alone. And out of the past I conjured a picture of an Indian stealthily paddling his birch-bark canoe towards a moose, or perhaps a flock of ducks, or a beaver near where I now stood; and finally, within shooting distance, picking up his bow, and selecting a shaft headed with the milky quartz[6] arrowhead I now held in my hand, loosing it towards his hoped-for prey.

Wind and waves had covered it with sand. How many undated centuries it had reposed there until I turned it up with my cleaning rod, no man could tell. But that day an archaeologist was born; and, although the following year[7] I discovered the precise area where of old stood the most important village of the St John River Indians, several more years were to elapse before I actively began searching for other prehistoric campsites.

But my interest in Indians stems much farther back than an avid reading of Cooper's *Leather-stocking* tales. For when I was a very small child my mother, born in 1855 (whose girlhood and early womanhood were spent on the Main Southwest Miramichi River), used to tell me about Micmac Indians who each summer camped near the brook that flowed through her father's farm. Here they made many baskets, both of ash splints and sweet grass; others of bark decorated with dyed porcupine quills (Fig. 1 a, p 54), and small purses covered both back and front with hundreds of varicoloured beads, similar to one given her grandmother by the wife of an old chief prior to the great fire of 1825. My sister has this little purse.

One of my earliest recollections is the vivid word-picture my mother re-created for me of the Indians, in their birch-bark canoes at night, with flambeaux of oily birch bark lighting up the bosom of the water as they moved back and forth spearing salmon between the Grey and the White Rapids.

Then, too, perhaps I subconsciously inherited an interest in Indians from an early ancestor who, in February 1644, with a force of 130 Dutch and English colonists, broke the power of Algonkian tribes under their renowned chief Mamaronock; and earlier, in 1637, with Captain Mason, commanded a force of English colonists which attacked and destroyed the palisaded fort of the powerful Pequot Indians at Mistik, on the Connecticut river, with a loss to the Indians of more than six hundred souls. In his book, published in England 1638, he tells that, on his return to Boston, he brought with him several well-woven rugs and delightful baskets.

---

6 "A hard white or colorless mineral consisting of silicon dioxide, found widely in igneous, metamorphic, and sedimentary rocks, and often coloured by impurities."— www. thefreedictionary.com.

7 About 1903-1905.

So, with such an heritage, it is not to be marvelled at, that with hunting and fishing, our northeastern Indians should be for me of abiding interest. But, although familiar with our colonial history and its Indian wars, and how he was often as sinned against as sinning, my sympathy for him has broadened with the years.

Twenty-five years ago I briefly visited the site of my grandmother's home, and that of the Micmac camp ground at White Rapids. Here I found flint flakes[8] where their remote ancestors had chipped their arrowheads and other weapons of war and chase. And a relative, Howard Curtis, gave me a fine stone gouge (Fig. 2 a, p 55) and another object perhaps used in skinning animals, both of which he had ploughed up on the high upland of his farm half a mile from the river. For several years he had used the flat smooth inner side of the handle of the gouge on which to sharpen his razor and butcher knives. The bit of the gouge is very narrow (about an inch and a quarter; the overall length eleven inches.) The other object seems to have been covered with a reddish substance: perhaps oxide of iron.

⋆　　⋆　　⋆

A hundred years ago only a few enthusiastic students in North America had given themselves fully, or even in their spare time, to the task of unearthing and studying the buried records of our prehistoric past. On the other hand, ever since the country was first settled by white Europeans, and found to be widely populated, historians have advanced theories as to the country or countries from which the Indians originated, by what routes and at what period they arrived here. But today, in several of the seats of learning, regular courses are given in the science of anthropology and its kindred branches. These include Ethnology: the study of the relations to one another of races and groups of peoples. Linguistics: the study of languages. Palaeontology: the study of ancient writings and inscriptions.[9] And finally Archaeology: the study of primitive stone and other implements made by man.

This last definition should be widely amplified. David T. Smith, in his essay *An Archaeologist's Memories,* Blackwoods Magazine, Feb. 1934, quotes Dr Anderson's definition of archaeology as "science which deduces a knowledge of past times from a study of their existing remains." And Smith makes this comment: "The term belongs to all history and has far too long been annexed by those who study only ancient remains."

Thus "existing remains" (included in Dr Anderson's definition) covers not only the

---

8　"Flint is a hard, sedimentary cryptocrystalline form (with a crystalline structure so fine that no distinct particles are recognizable under a microscope) of the mineral quartz, categorized as a variety of chert. It was a primary material for stone age tools and weapons."—Wikipedia. "In archaeology, a flake is a "portion of rock removed from an objective piece by percussion or pressure." [Andrefsky, W. (2005) Lithics: Macroscopic Approaches to Analysis.] The worker chooses a stone to make into a a tool, then uses a hard object (e.g. an antler tine) to direct a sharp blow to the surface, often on the edge of the piece. The process continues as the flintknapper detaches the desired number of flakes from the core, which is marked with the negative scars of these removals."—abbreviated from Wikipedia.

9　GFC meant "palaeography". Palaeontology is "the branch of science concerned with fossil animals and plants."—www.thefreedictionary.com

3

study of stone and bone implements left on their campsites and villages by the diverse northeastern tribes we call Indians. The term covers a wide range of subjects of more or less varied interest: antique furniture, iron-work, silver; and, of paramount importance, old books, legal documents and manuscripts. In brief, anything written or created by man which reveals greater knowledge of the material culture, customs and history of those who have lived before us. And these, as Mr Smith implies, need not necessarily be of a remote past, but of our own colonial period, and even more recent times.

I make no apology for being an amateur. The doing of anything for the pure love of it which adds to our knowledge and does no harm to any one, has its own reward. Especially is this true in that branch of archaeology which deals with the stone age. It takes me out of doors beside brooks and rivers along intervale lands and terraces where primitive man had his temporary wigwam or more permanent palisaded village. It trains the eye, makes for good health and an appreciation of all phases of nature. When I am tired of walking or digging, I sit and watch the river rippling over the shallows and around the heads of the islands. I am interested in everything: in the little spotted sandpiper running along the beach, stopping often to bob and bow; in the kingfisher as it plummets—a symphony of blue and white—into the pellucid depth of the pool in which its sharp eyes have detected some small form of fish life. I am interested in the wild flowers: the blood-root, arbutus, violet, the linnaea, the wild rose—all the galaxy of beauty that blooms from early spring until late autumn.

As the motto of the Flyfishers Club, England, "It is not all of fishing to fish," sums up my ideal of angling, so (for me at least) it is not all of digging to dig for Indian relics.

The search for prehistoric campsites presents much the same sort of challenge as that confronting the detective assigned to unravel some complicated infraction of the law. There are the same false leads, disappointments and thrilling successes.

I remember my eldest daughter who, some forty years ago, her hair flying in the wind, came bounding over a ploughed field towards me, holding a hand high above her head while she cried exultantly: "I've found one! I've found one!" It was a beautiful red jasper arrowhead.[10] (Archimedes was not more excited when he sprang from his bath crying "Eureka! Eureka!") For her the chase had been won, and new horizons opened up. Thenceforth prehistoric man and his artifacts assumed a new and profound significance.

Many times I've been asked how I manage to find Indian artifacts. A quite natural question. Henry David Thoreau, the famous author of *Walden,* and *The Maine Woods,* was once asked the same question by his friend Emerson, as they were walking over a newly ploughed and harrowed field near their home in Concord. Thoreau replied: "By looking for them," and bending, picked up a stone spearhead.

On three different occasions I had much the same experience. The late Tappan Adney and I were walking along the beach above Upper Woodstock; he was slightly ahead of me and almost stepped on a beautifully-chipped stone knife. I picked it up, called to him to stop, and showed him my find. A few days later we were in the same locality and

---

10   Jasper is "a high-quality chert or agate often used as raw material for the manufacture of stone tools. It is…opaque, fine-grained or dense, usually brick red to brownish red."— www.archaeologywordsmith.com.

the previous incident was repeated. He was surprised, more than a trifle chagrined, and asked me if I had had the knife in my pocket.

The pieces had been washed out of the high bank by the spring freshet. I dug here a few days later and discovered a quite important campsite, of which more in time.

Once, in late autumn, I was walking with one of my Indian friends across a newly cropped oat field to reach the river St John. Noel was in advance of me, and stepped over a fine spearhead lying in the stubble. I picked it up and with a laugh chided him on his poor eye-sight. *I* had been *looking* for it, as I had been looking for the pieces Adney had almost stepped on. I had developed an archaeological eye.

But the answer given by Thoreau to his friend Emerson and the personal experiences I have just related are only fractional answers to the question how do I find Indian relics. Certainly by looking for them, but it also calls into action other facilities than mere keenness of vision. It is a knowledge acquired by long and intensive detective work.

Metaphorically speaking, I put my feet into the moccasins of a native American, try to think as he did. So I have made reconnaissances by walking over ploughed fields both in the autumn and the early spring after the frost has left the ground and the rains washed the brown soil. In these walks I have covered hundreds of miles along the St John and Tobique rivers.

The burned and cracked beach stones on the top-soil tell me that here the Indian made his camp-fire; the flakes of chert, quartz, argillite,[11] that here he chipped his weapons of war and chase in the form of arrowheads, spearheads, knives and scrapers. Occasionally I find a whole or broken artifact and get a thrill out of it; but it is *excavating* a campsite that gives me the greatest pleasure and satisfaction. The number, the variety of implements, and the depths at which they occur tell a more complete story.

The sherds[12] tell me that he manufactured crude pottery vessels, both large and small. The gouge, that he made wooden bowls; the diversified forms of scrapers, that he used them in dressing hides and pelts, fashioning the woodwork for his canoe, paddles, salmon spear. The chisel, adze[13] and wedge also formed part of his armamentarium in his canoe building. The stone maul was used both as a war club and for pounding stakes. The grooved stone axe he used to aid him in felling trees after he had first girdled them with fire. Some of his finer polished specimens of the grooved variety, as well as those ungrooved, were doubtless used in his wars. The plummet-shaped[14] objects and the perforated stone tablets were probably ceremonial pieces.

---

11 Chert is "an extremely dense type of quartz, including jasper and flint, having a dull, opaque luster and made up of microscopic crystals."—www.yourdictionary.com. Argillite is "metamorphic rock, intermediate between shale and slate, that does not possess true slaty cleavage."—www.yourdictionary.com.

12 A sherd is "a historic or prehistoric fragment of pottery."—Wikipedia.

13 A "tool similar to an axe, with a blade set at right angles to the shaft and curving inwards towards it, used for cutting or slicing away the surface of wood."—OED.

14 A plummet (also called a plumb bob) is a piece of lead or other heavy material attached to a line, used for determining perpendicularity. Archaeologists use them when excavating and mapping sites. David Black suggests that they may have named the plummet-shaped objects they found by analogy with the plummets they themselves used.

But often, without any visual evidence of burned stones, chippings and other objects, I have stood on a terrace from which I could get a good view both up and down. Here, I told myself, I would camp *if I were an Indian.* For the river was his highway; he could see his friends coming or going, or the approach of an enemy.

I have found most campsites handy to good salmon pools, and at the beginning and end of rapids; at the beginning and end of portages from one waterway to another. At all such places I have dug and seldom failed to find important artifacts. And I am swept back face-to-face with our own prehistoric ancestors who in summer went practically naked, and in winter wore rude coverings of fur-bearing animals. The arrowheads remind me that the ancient Scots and Britons and Welsh used such objects in war and chase; that our more recent forebears used the bow and arrow at Hastings, Crecy, Poitiers and Agincourt, and during the whole reign of the First Elizabeth. I find that Thomas Mayneman, of Greenwich, bequeathed in his will, dated 1562, several objects to my remote ancestor. What is of particular interest at the present moment is the following: "I geve unto him (Thomas Underhill) my seeve and my buckler a bowe and a sheaf of arrows; a black byle, a javelings IJ shawling bowes and a quiver with arrowes..."

I find among old writings of long-dead historians who came to the new world, that the superstitions of the people we mistakenly call Indians, were much the same as those of the peoples of the British Isles two thousand years ago—some of which persist to the present day. I find that the earthen pots of the Indian, his knives, scrapers, arrowheads, spearheads and stone adzes were similar in shape to those in the British Isles, France, Germany, Spain, Hungary, Japan, China and Siberia. In short, over all the known world thousands of years before Babylon, Nineveh and Nimrud had risen above the sands of Mesopotamia.

And when, after laborious work, I have unearthed even one treasure, I experience the same sort of thrill as when I hook a lordly salmon and, taking the line over its shoulder, it darts like a rocket down the pool!

Fundamentally the archaeologist is a romantic. If he weren't he wouldn't be an archaeologist.

Scores of times, during the last forty years, children and even grownups have come to my door and asked me if the stone object they held out to me was an arrowhead, spearhead, axe or some other specimen of Indian craftsmanship. On only a few occasions (two or three at most) was the "treasure" a genuine artifact. But if not, it was always painful for me to tell them the truth, especially when the bearer was a child. He or she had been *so sure.* But I always brought them into my room, and opening the drawers of my cabinet, took out the trays containing some of my most precious finds, pointed out the clam-like fractures on the face and edges, and explained the methods used to produce the finished piece. And told them how stone tomahawks, adzes and gouges were made; and, I hope, sent my visitors away with awakened imaginations, and less disappointed than when I had told them that what they had brought me had never been worked by man.

On many occasions I have taken one or more youngsters with me on my digs, and after a little tutoring they have become quite expert. My twelve-year-old grandson has developed an archaeological eye, handles a spade and trowel with meticulous care, and already has made some important finds. This also applies to Garfield Saunders, a couple of years older than Stephen (Fig. 3, p 56). Both would prefer a dig to a big turkey dinner. For they are taking part in an adventure into the past, and now know, when they find stone artifacts, that they are face to face with their own remote ancestors.

Each year the more richly endowed museums send out parties of field workers, comprising students under one or more graduate archaeologists, to open up old villages and campsites both near and far. The result is a vast accumulation of stone and other artifacts in the various museums. These, and the often quite important private collections of amateurs to which we have access, are interesting and informative, but in themselves give only a limited knowledge of primitive man's way of life. For to get an approximately complete picture of the native American at the time of the entrance of the early white explorers and colonists on the scene, we must have recourse to the narratives they left us, and to those later books written by careful observers before the tribal customs had been changed or radically modified by contact with Europeans. We have the Norse Sagas, Cartier, Verrazzano, Lescarbot, Champlain, Biard, Bradford, Pring, Rossier, Denys, Gyles, the Jesuit Relations, and a host of others.

History, then, helps partially to fill up the gap created by the fact that the North American Indian left no written records. But the anthropologist has not been content only with histories to help him (and rightly so); he supplements these by venturing into many byways: linguistics, tribal divisions, the similarity of the many types of artifacts among remote tribes; the migrations of diverse tribes, the age of the Indian's artifacts, the route or routes by which he came to America, his mortuary customs, myths, songs, dress and other matters. Most of the published works (and they are legion) have appeared in scientific journals; many "embalmed" in Latinized terms which, even though the lay reader had access to them, he would understand as little as he would Hindi. But occasionally, from books such as *The Indians of Canada* by Diamond Jenness, and *Antiquities of the New England Indians*, by Charles C. Willoughby, (both written in less scientific terms) and from articles appearing in magazines and the daily press, we have become increasingly aware of our prehistoric past. True, we have no monuments as in Egypt, Mesopotamia, Yucatan and Mexico, yet what we have is interesting and vastly informative.

But few subjects, if any, have been more productive of diverse theories than anthropology and its branches. These have made for confusion in the minds of the student and the general reader (who has been prepared to accept as true *all* the conclusions arrived at by some well-known scientific observer just because he has become famous as an expert in his special field of research.)

Quite the contrary. For even the best known scientists often differ on some of the simplest matters, and in the light of further investigations have often had to revise their previous deductions. In other words science is not static. It is a succession of blunders and changing theories tending towards greater truth and more knowledge. As the *Talmud* so wisely puts it, "the rivalry of scholars advances science."

Those critics who are generous, while reserving the right to differ with this or that deductive theory, leaven their criticisms with the recognition that even the most honest worker may make errors in his analysis. It is only with "snap judgment" and the grossly sensational that we are impatient.

"To be entirely just in our estimate of other ages is not difficult—it is impossible. Even what is passing in our own presence, we see but through a glass darkly. The mind, as well as the eye, must add something of its own, before an image, even of the clearest object, can be painted upon it. And in historical enquiries, the most instructed thinkers have but a limited advantage over the most illiterate. Those who know the most, approach least to agreement. The most careful investigations are diverging roads—the further men travel upon them, the greater the interval by which they are divided."[15]

If the foregoing be true of historical investigations, how much more does it apply to the writer on archaeological matters. For while the writer of history has access to actual or supposed events in the life of nations in historic times, the archaeologist, on the other hand, who excavates some prehistoric village or campsite, is in contact with a people who, as we have already said, left no written records.

Let me repeat: stone implements and other objects tell a story; but it is a limited one. Without history we would be very much in the dark. But even history, supplementing as it does archaeological findings, doesn't tell the whole story. Much of man's past is hidden and may never be known. And here the archaeologist may be allowed a restricted latitude of conjecture. In other words he may theorize; but mere theories must not be announced as actual facts. For a theory is not a fact until it is proven to be such. And it is this disposition of many present-day students (as it was in the past) to fill in chasms in their information and announce their conjectures as indubitable fact, a practice with which the present writer takes issue. For "when philosophy reconstructs, it does nothing but project its own ideas; when it throws off tradition it cannot work without a theory, and what is a theory but an imperfect generalization caught up by a predisposition."[16] Or to put it otherwise: men start out with an already-formed theory, and attempt to forge a chain of evidence to prove their case with links of supposed facts which are capable of a dozen contradictory interpretations.

David T. Smith wrote the following: "One of the principal lessons which my connection with archaeological matters has taught me was, not to take for granted as true everything I read, but to do my own thinking." This I made my shibboleth many years ago.

I have seen many singular and contradictory theories regarding the antiquity of prehistoric man and his material culture in North America, and dates have been soberly set down with a dogmatism that is astonishing and often ridiculous. Accidental associations of human artifacts with extinct species of fauna have been assigned to a very archaic past, without considering the possibility that the now extinct animals may have, and probably did, survive until comparatively recent times. Or that geological changes occasioned by floods with subsequent deposits of sand, mud and gravel, may in a few days or weeks have covered the sites where prehistoric man had camped; or that certain

---

15   James A. Froude, "The Dissolution of the Monasteries," essay, 1857.

16   Froude, "The Lives of the Saints," essay, 1852.

types of arrowheads, knives and scrapers found in the St Lawrence River basin were in all probability manufactured by New Brunswick or Nova Scotia Indians.

Hardly a week passes but we read in the newspapers of some prehistoric finds to which remote dates have been categorically assigned quite as though they were pieces of hall-marked silver!

Many of these finds have been made by students of anthropology, who, as a necessary prelude to a university degree, must write a thesis. The result is that they often make wild and unfounded statements that have no basis in fact. (But these are not the only culprits); I could, were I so disposed, cite several that have recently come under my personal notice. Only last summer a two-year student looked at some of my stone artifacts, and with an assumption of omniscience that startled me said: "Four thousand years old."!

In my edition of the *Encyclopaedia Britannica* is the following: "The stone age of Britain or Denmark is analogous to that of the Polynesian islands. Nor could the most experienced archaeologist undertake in every case to discriminate between the flint arrowhead dug up from some primitive barrow of undated centuries before the Christian era, and the corresponding weapon brought by some traveller from Tierra del Fuego, or regions beyond the Rocky Mountains." And again: "The student of archaeology will act wisely in pushing forward his researches, and comparing all available data, without hastily pronouncing any absolute verdict on the question."[17]

17   Wilson, Daniel, *Anthropology and Archaeology*, 1885: 39-40.

CHAPTER 2
WHERE DID THEY COME FROM

It's doubtful if historians will ever cease advancing theories as to the remote origins of the people now known as Indians—a name given the inhabitants by the early voyagers who when they reached this continent, imagined it was an eastern extension of India.

It has been categorically stated that they were descendants of the Ten Lost Tribes of Israel; of the Egyptians, Polynesians, Japanese, Chinese, Greeks, Romans, Irish, Welsh, Phoenicians and Scythians. And the proponent of each theory has attempted to prove his case with often fanciful, sometimes ludicrous and, occasionally, reasonable arguments. Now that the moon and Venus have been reached, we may expect some archaeological data "proving" that the Americans received their population from one or both of these celestial bodies!

Daniel Neal, A.M., writing two and a half centuries ago, says: "They who think America was peopled from Europe, Asia, or Africa, differ among themselves as to time, place and manner in which it was done. The learned Hornius, who has taken a great deal of pains in his enquiry, concluded that America received its inhabitants at different times from these three nations: the Phoenicians, the Scythians and the Chinese."

*   *   *

When the early French and English explorers first came to North America, they found different tribes of people inhabiting the seaboard adjacent to all the important rivers. In later years, it was found that the whole country was populated from Newfoundland to the Pacific, and from the far south to and including the Arctic regions. It was found, too, that the majority had Mongoloid physical characteristics, and resembled each other, save for such natural differences as would result from previous intermingling of diverse racial stocks. "Yet other tribes, among them the Iroquois, if clad in European garments, might readily have passed for Europeans but for the slight coppery tinge in their skins." Thus, just as the English race is the result of admixture of several diverse peoples for as far back as we can trace, so, it would seem, the Indians of North America are admixtures of several racial stocks which had their build-up in north and east Asia. In other words, there is the same variability, or lack of homogeneity, in the physical characteristics of our North American Indian, that is so apparent in the people of the British Isles, Europe, and among the whites now living on this continent. The Eskimo seems an exception. Although descended from an Asiatic people, it would seem that he broke off from the parent stock before miscegenation or intermarrying with other stocks had changed the original type. Thus the Eskimo type is quite constant; and the language of the widely dispersed groups of these people which extend from the Atlantic coast to the Pacific, is readily understood by all. Whether the Eskimo arrived in America before or after the people we call Indian is a big question and, it seems to me, is unanswerable.

At what period in the world's prehistory the first migration of man to North America took place, is shrouded in the mists of time (although attempts have been made to date what is undatable). But some authorities claim it was before the extinction of the huge mastodon, the Columbian elephant, camel, sabre-toothed tiger and the great cave bear. Some writers also insist that they must of necessity have entered the continent when Siberia and Alaska were connected by a land or ice bridge where Bering's Strait is now. But although such may have been the case, neither a land nor ice-bridge was necessary. They could, and possibly did, cross open water by boats or canoes. According to the late Edwin Tappan Adney—our greatest authority on the canoe—the birch canoe was made by the natives of the Amur river.[18] And if it should be argued that crossing Bering's Strait (which is only thirty-six miles wide at its narrowest point) would be an impossible feat, we must remember that in 1607 some four hundred Micmac warriors embarked at Port Royal, in Acadia, in birchbark canoes, crossed the turbulent Bay of Fundy to Grand Manan, and from thence proceeded along the coast to Massachusetts Bay to make war on the Armouchiquois[19] who, in 1605, had killed a Micmac chief named Penoniac. (In all a distance of 160 leagues.)[20] And in 1713, in the dead of winter, Madame Louise de Freneuse, with her son and an Indian paddler, set out in a bark canoe from the mouth of the St John River, and crossed the Bay of Fundy to Port Royal—a distance of forty miles.

What I wish to emphasize, is that it *was* possible for prehistoric man to cross Bering's Strait in either boat or canoe. He *may* have entered the continent by land or ice bridge; but I like to think he came by open water.

Thus we can imagine some prehistoric prototype of Erik the Red setting forth from Siberia in a dugout or birchbark canoe, crossing Bering's Strait to Alaska, where fish, game and furbearing creatures abounded, then returning to his people to tell them of his great discovery. Then the exodus. A romantic but not impossible picture. Without doubt there were several successive migrations; how many we cannot know; nor how long they remained on the northwest continent of America before the necessity of finding new hunting grounds, or just the inherited spirit of their ancestors, impelled them to move on. Such has been the history of mankind throughout all ages and all climes. But I firmly believe that the ancestors of our Algonkian peoples (to which the Micmac and Maliseet belong) were among the first to reach America, and the first to begin the long trek across the vast continent.

We can imagine them following the waterways, footing it along valleys and over mountain ranges. We can imagine their amazement as they reached the foothills and, Balboa-like, shading their eyes with cupped hand on brow, gazed on the broad prairies that stretched for endless leagues towards the eastland and the risen sun.

---

18   It forms the border between the Russian Far East and Northeastern China.—Wikipedia.

19   The Armouchiquois lived along the New England coast south of Saco River, Maine.

20   770 km.

Some of them moved into and occupied Manitoba, others the vast territory that stretched from Lake Winnipeg southwards to the Great Lakes, and still farther south to Pamlico Sound. Others occupied the region about Hudson Bay and eastwards to Labrador. Other restless spirits occupied the St Lawrence River valley to the mouth of that mighty river, the Gaspé Peninsula, Bay Chaleur and the Maritime Provinces.

All this must have consumed a very long time—perhaps untold centuries. So long that innumerable generations had passed away. There must have been many stops, many break-ups, new tribal units and new dialects formed, but still retaining their original root words; and those who spoke them knew not the remote origins of their forebears.

Thus it was, that when the Irish Celts or Scots left Ireland, invaded the west coast of Caledonia and formed the kingdom of the Dalriad Scots, and a century or so later the great missionary Columba visited the Pictish king, he had to have an interpreter, so greatly had the Celtic tongue changed.

Of this we are assured: the natives seen by the early French and English navigators on the discovery of Acadia, whose ancient boundaries the French claimed included all the present Nova Scotia and its Islands, New Brunswick and the Gaspé Peninsula were the same people who now abide here, and tribal units of the great Algonkian people who have inhabited Canada from Lake Winnipeg to the Atlantic for as far back as we can trace. Some authorities claim that they were of partly white descent, and 17th-century navigators commented on their light tawny skins. But I find a much earlier and fascinating reference to northeastern Indians in Fabian's chronicle, as recounted by Hakluyt in his *English Voyages*: "In the 14th year of Henry VII, there was brought unto him three wild men taken in New found Island by Cabot. They were cloathed in the skins of beasts, and spoke such speech as no man could understand them, and in their demeanour were like brute beasts, whom the king kept for a time after, of which, about two years ago, I saw the men apparelled after the manner of Englishmen in Westminster Palace, which I could not distinguish from Englishmen till I learned what they were. As for speech, I heard none of them utter one word."

Less than one hundred words; yet what a vista they opened up: three wild men stolen from their homes and families in far-off America—which was then, and for many years following, a wonder world. A world, in which, it was said, dwelt men with their heads growing out of their chests; of unipeds, or one-legged men able to run with incredible swiftness. A world in which, we read, "If an Indian had been seen wearing a headpiece of copper which bowed easily, this flexibility proved it to be tarnished gold."[21] Then, too, from a report in the English State papers, American women were spoken of as "wearing great plates of gold covering their whole bodies like armor." That "in every village pearls could be found; in some houses a peck and there were banqueting houses made of crystal, with pillars of massive silver and some of gold. Pieces of gold as big as a man's fist were to be picked up at the heads of rivers." Even Frobisher, of Welsh ancestry, who had penetrated the northwest coast of America to the latitude of 74 degrees, in an effort to find a passage to Cathay, found black earth which he believed to be gold ore; and, on

---

21   This and the next two quotations are from Edward Eggleston, *The Beginners of a Nation*, London, 1897.

a third voyage, in which thirteen ships took part, brought back to London full cargoes of the worthless stuff. And so it went, and it was a long time before it was realized that the wealth of North America lay in the fur trade.

*   *   *

People we know today as Micmac and Maliseet were living on the St Lawrence near Quebec and at Tadoussac a long, long time before Cartier came up that enchanting river. Why, you ask, do I speak so confidently? Because *Kebec*—as the French pronounce it—is the Micmac name for a strait: a narrow or constricted body of water connecting two larger bodies of water. *Kepec*, the Maliseet term—means the same. There is a strait at Quebec. Donnacona, whom Cartier met in 1535, is a Maliseet surname according to Peter Paul (Fig. 4, p 15),[22] meaning one who rules over many.

At what period some Maliseet broke off from their Quebec kindred and found their way to the valley of the St John, is unknown, although as in so many similar migrations, efforts have been made to date it. The same holds true of the people we call Micmac, which name is said by some writers to mean "Allies". In all probability the word is from *Megawe*; *Megwaak—Mik-mak* meaning "red". An ally, in Micmac, is *Widoogwembmk*; *Mowomajik*. The Micmac, at the coming of the white man, occupied part of the Gaspé Peninsula, all of Bay Chaleur, the eastern coast and its river, and the present Nova Scotia and its islands.

There is a tradition (but tradition is not always a safe foundation on which to base facts) that the Micmac were earlier arrivals and occupied the valley of the river St John, and that the Maliseet came at a later date and drove them out. This is extremely doubtful. "If there actually was any division of the country, it is more probable that it was by peaceful mutual agreement, since the two tribes were never engaged in war within historic times, and the entire lack of enmity between them indicates that mutual friendship was of long prehistoric duration."[23]

There is also a tradition that when the Micmac came to Acadia they found a people occupying the land (whom several writers have tried to identify as the Red Indians of Newfoundland of early historic times), and that they made war on them and drove them out of the country. Ganong says that "if any earlier race than the Micmac and Maliseet ever occupied the province, every trace of it has vanished." Perhaps it would be better to say that if any earlier people were here, archaeologists have not been able, up to the present, to positively classify their remains as belonging to any other people than those we now know as Maliseet and Micmac.

---

22   Peter Lewis Paul (1902-1989), LLD 1970, Order of Canada 1987. Wikipedia calls him an ethnohistorian, but that is too narrow. "He has contributed greatly to the study of the ethnology and linguistics of the North American Indian, promoting consistency and uniformity in the way Indian sounds are written. It is due to his efforts as a linguist, historian and restorer of Indian artifacts that much of the Malecite history and language have survived."—non-sourced statement (probably from his investiture in the Order of Canada) in his entry on http://www.findagrave.com. There is a chapter about Peter Paul in *The Last Romantic*, see footnote 2, p. viii.

23   Source not found.

On the other hand, I have been told on more than one occasion (both by Maliseet and Micmac Indians) that the two tribes were originally one people, and that at some remote date there was a division among them; several families remaining on the St John River where their original dialect greatly changed. I do know that there are a multiplicity of like idioms, that their names for many of the fauna and, with some slight variations, many of the place names are similar. There also seems to be indubitable evidence that all the tribes from Nova Scotia to the Kennebec river in Maine were originally one people. We positively do know that there was a division of the Maliseet of the St John in prehistoric times; some remaining here, others removing to the mouth of the St Croix river, which vents into Passamaquoddy Bay. Hence they are known as Passamaquoddy. A second exodus of a few families from the St John to the same place occurred during the latter part of the 18th century, due to their displeasure over the sale of some Indian lands to English settlers. All Indians at Passamaquoddy speak Maliseet—their mother tongue.

4 Peter Paul, canoe trip on Eel River Lake, July 1978

CHAPTER 3
THE ST JOHN RIVER AND MEDOCTEC

In 1693 La Mothe-Cadillac made a canoe voyage of one hundred leagues[24] up the St John River, and was so charmed with its manifold attractions that, after describing its islands, intervales and various species of trees, added: "It must be conceded that it is the most navigable, the most favoured, and the most beautiful river in all Acadia." Since his day hundreds of thousands of tourists have been quite as enthusiastic about it as was the renowned soldier, founder of Detroit, and governor of Louisiana.

But neither Cadillac, nor any other writer since his time, nor any of the various artists who have attempted to portray it, have been able to do it full justice. For neither words nor artists' brush can convey to the mind the haunting spiritual significance of its waters, nor of the innumerable islands and intervales; nor the gently sloping uplands which, fold on fold to the horizon's rim, embosom this other Eden we call the St John River and its valley.

Rising in northern Maine, and separated from the Penobscot by the famous Northeast Carry, this mighty river, four hundred and fifty miles in length, and the largest body of water between the St Lawrence and the Mississippi, swings in a wide half circle for its first 145 miles entirely in Maine territory. Then it reaches New Brunswick, and for another 75 miles forms the international boundary nearly to Grand Falls. The remainder of its course is wholly in New Brunswick. Finally, having received innumerable tributaries (some of which head almost to the St Lawrence) and drained an area of 26,000 square miles, this extraordinary river tumultuously plunges twice each day between high perpendicular palisades of rock, and twice each day is forced backward by the high tides of Fundy.

There is an old legend, that when the French first came to the river, one end of an enormous pine tree, shorn of limbs, was wedged in some deep crevice of the rocky bottom. When the tide was at ebb, several feet of the trunk were visible above the raging torrent and bobbed back and forth like some animated denizen of the waters. And the superstitious Indians shot arrows into it, either in attempts to kill it, or as gifts to propitiate its fancied wrath.

It is my opinion that the Maliseet migration to the St John River valley consisted originally of only a small number—perhaps a few families, and that this took place not earlier than two thousand years before the coming of the French and English to our shores; possibly much less. For although I have discovered and excavated dozens of

---

24   480 km.

prehistoric campsites, neither the number of whole and broken artifacts, nor the flakes struck off in their manufacture, nor the depths at which they occurred, would indicate a very long period of occupation by primitive man. Indeed it is very doubtful if at any time the population numbered more than six or seven hundred souls. Perhaps one of the reasons was a low birth rate induced by unsanitary living conditions, the fact that the mothers nursed their children for two or three years, during which they avoided their husbands, and occasional plagues that swept the country.

But we have other than archaeological evidence that the Indian population on the St John river was small. During Governor Villebon's *regime* (1691-1698) at Fort Nashwaak, at the mouth of the river of the same name, the maximum number of warriors he was able to recruit from these warlike people seldom exceeded one hundred. Forty years later, Captain John Gyles (of whom more later) estimated the number of males—he means men of fighting age—as one hundred. Half a century later the Anglican missionary, Frederick Dibblee, listed some 337 people: men, women and children who attended his mission school at Medoctec, and received seed-corn, blankets, hoes, gun flints, powder, and lead for bullets.

The Indians named their river *Wul-ahs-tukw,* which means pleasant beautiful flowing river (or water). They called themselves, and were known by their kindred on the Penobscot and Kennebec rivers, as *Wul-ahs-tuk-wiuk*; or as we would say today: people of the *Wul-ahs-tukw* or St John River. A Penobscot Indian, asked if he could speak Maliseet, replied: "No. But I can sing it." We also have the word in different forms, such as *Malicite, Merechite, Amaliseet* and *Milicete.* Perhaps *Maliseet* is the form more in general use today. But in whatever form, it is said by tradition to have been applied to the St John River Indians by the Micmac, from *Mal-i-se-jik,* a word in their dialect used derisively to denote poor or broken talkers, or "he speaks badly".

But the Micmac have another nickname for the Maliseet: *Kuk-bus,* plural *Kuk-bus-soukie—muskrats.* Very probably also used in a derisive sense because they ate muskrats. The Maliseet retaliated by calling the Micmac *Porcupine people* because they were fond of eating this creature.

But however much the Micmac ridiculed the Maliseet, and called them poor talkers, it is a fact that the Maliseet dialect is much more euphonious than that of their detractors.

Rand, in speaking of the Micmac, says: "There is some diversity of pronunciation it is true in the language as spoken in different places. It extends merely to the use and pronunciation of a few words. The Indians of Cape Breton Island amuse themselves occasionally at the expense of the Nova Scotia (Micmac), and are themselves laughed about in turn by the latter party for their improper and uncouth utterances. And the Indians on Prince Edward Island, and at Miramichi, are as susceptible to the ludicrous as their brethren, and as conscious of their superiority."

*　　*　　*

The St John River Indians, like most other tribes, were a migratory people, and although they grew corn at Medoctec and other places, roamed vast distances in search of game, fish and fur bearing creatures, camping wherever fancy or necessity dictated.

Thus one finds evidences of temporary campsites along practically the whole length of the river, and at suitable places along its numerous tributaries which the Maliseet Indian explored and gave names to in his descriptive and euphonious tongue. And, although a wanderer, he did have permanent villages where he fortified himself and abode part of the year. The most important of these (both in prehistoric times, and for one hundred and fifty years following the coming of the French to Acadia) was at Medoctec, eight miles below the site of the present town of Woodstock. At its greatest width the intervale extends westward from the river about sixty rods, then slopes gently downwards to a lower intervale twenty rods wide to the base of a wooded hill which ascends abruptly some seventy feet to the upland.

But contrary to generally accepted belief, the prehistoric palisaded fort *was not* in the immediate vicinity of the high wooden cross which today marks the site of the Maliseet chapel built in 1717, and the small tree-enclosed cemetery. It was almost three quarters of a mile distant, near the extreme lower end of the mile-long intervale. The Reverend W. O. Raymond, our most noted historian of the St John River, evidently didn't know this. For he speaks of the old Maliseet palisaded fort and village as being in the immediate vicinity of the chapel and cemetery, and makes no mention of any other. But sixty years ago I discovered archaeological evidence to prove my point—that the prehistoric fort was at the place I have stated above. However, we do find a few flint flakes near the upper or northern end of the intervale. Then, near the site on which the chapel was built, we find scores of European artifacts (mostly stems and bowls of clay pipes, and some other objects to be described later)—but no flint implements. Then, below the cemetery a few rods, are two or three superficial rows of chippings. As we go southwards these increase in numbers until, near and at the extreme lower end of the intervale, literally thousands of chippings, many whole and broken artifacts, pottery sherds, fire and food pits, burned beach stones, provide indubitable evidence that this was the site of the prehistoric fort and village.

Although many stone artifacts have been picked up from the surface, and visiting archaeologists twice had the ground ploughed and took away about one hundred pieces, this area deserves much more intensive excavating than I have been able to devote to it.

I dug here more than forty years ago, found many pottery sherds, part of the bowl of a stone pipe, a large stone knife (Fig. 5, p 57), arrowheads, knives and a fine spearhead (Fig. 6 c, p 58). Since then I have found several European objects: a hasp for a chest (Fig. 7 d, p 20), clay pipes, bits of copper, two arrow or drill points—one seemingly of copper pewter, and a cylindrical bead of copper. Contiguous to a small brook and ravine I found three very small knives of crude manufacture. Below these was a line of ash that finally curved downwards to a fire-pit about three feet in diameter and the same in depth. Above the pit was a Queen Anne table knife (Fig. 7 e, p 20). At the bottom of the pit were several pieces of European china-ware; among them the greater portion of a dainty sauce boat. Perhaps all these European-made objects had been looted by Medoctec Indians during one or more of their many deadly forays against the farmsteads and villages of New England during the Indian wars of the eighteenth century.

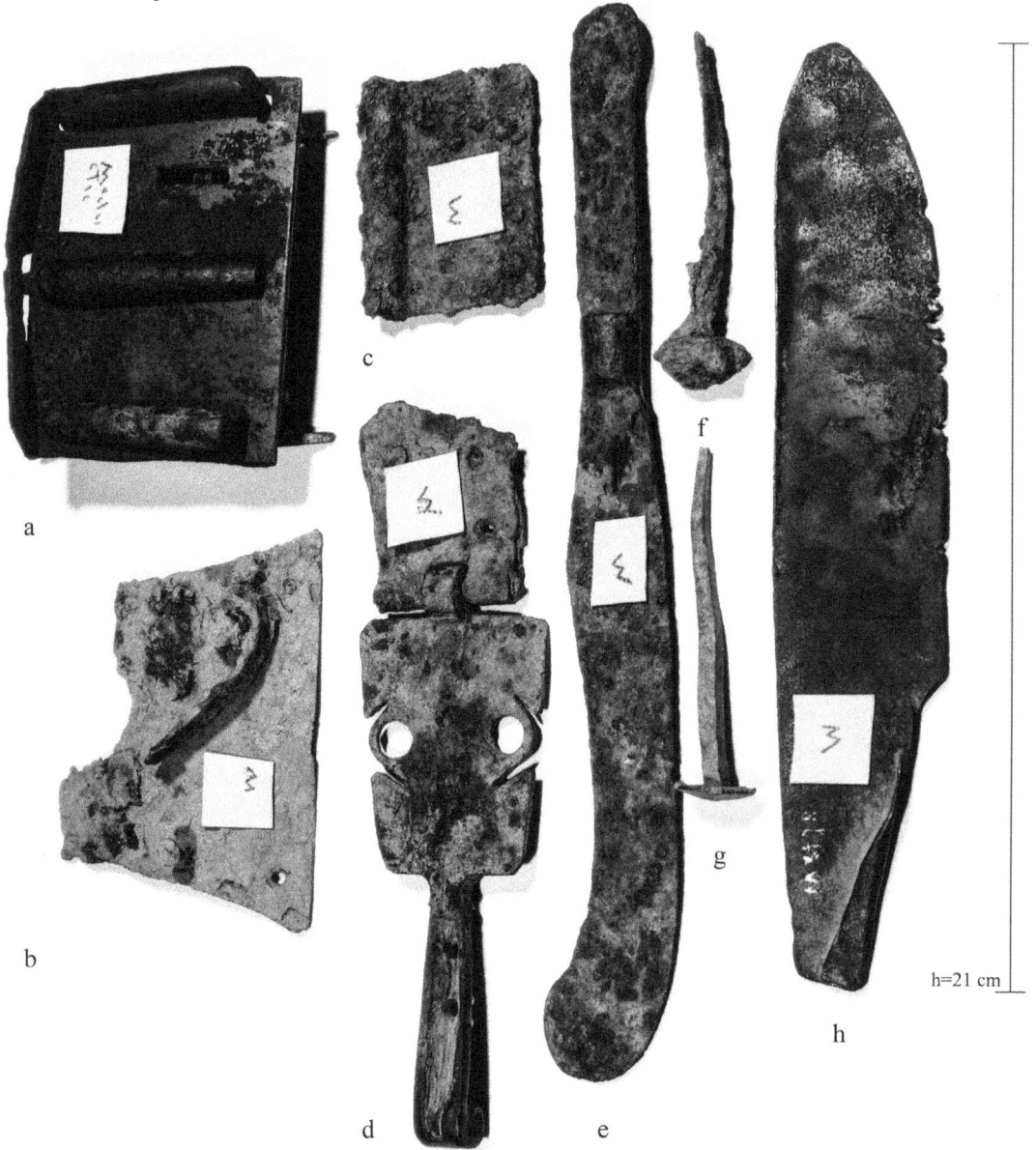

7 Post-European, 18th century objects, Medoctec flat, St John River, May 1964

But why were the stone knives in soil at a much higher level above the fire-hole which contained the European objects? The answer is that, following the coming of English settlers after the end of the American Revolutionary War, the plough had filled in the fire-hole. Then, at some subsequent period, a high spring freshet had carried huge cakes of ice to the area and forced the top soil containing the stone knives over the already filled in fire pit. I actually saw similar effects caused by ice at this very spot several years ago.

Recently I received a copy of *Anthropologica*—a publication of the research centre for American anthropology, University of Ottawa, from which I have extracted the following: "I know of no sites containing pottery which have been excavated containing any traces of European artifacts, and hence there is no evidence that they were inhabited after the first European contact. It would certainly be unlikely that any site which was inhabited before the coming of Europeans would cease to be inhabited just after that event." Quite so. I accept the above last sentence as logical. In the previous sentence the author, Mr Mechling, states that he knows of no sites containing pottery (Indian ware) which have been excavated containing *any evidence of European artifacts.*" (The italics are mine). As the reader will have observed, just such evidence exists at the lower end of Medoctec intervale!

SITE OPPOSITE EEL RIVER

Three miles below Medoctec is another long intervale opposite the confluence of the Eel River with the St John. It is about half a mile in length and extends backwards about fifty rods from the river to the beginning of the upland. For a part of its length there are three distinct terraces, and at intervals, from east to west, it is cut by two deep ravines which convey small rivulets to the river.

From archaeological evidence this intervale was a campsite of St John River Indians over a long period of time. Indeed its occupancy may very well have exceeded in duration that of Medoctec. For on practically every yard of the three terraces one finds flint flakes and the fire-stones where wigwams once stood. Here I have not only found arrowheads, slate[25] knives and chert spearheads but a very fine gouge, an adze, and pendants, or as the latter are often called, plummets. My son-in-law picked up one of these three years ago. At Medoctec plummets, gouges and adzes are absent, or, if there, I have not been fortunate to recover any. It may be that visiting archaeologists at various times carried them away. (Editor's note: one of the Eel River adzes is shown in Figs. 32, p 219 and 33 a, p 220.)

This campsite (opposite Eel River), perhaps I should designate it village site, deserves intensive digging operations, for it is rich in prehistoric implements. If I had twenty summers to dig and as many helpers at my disposal, I couldn't thoroughly excavate this important place. A year from now will be too late. The reason will soon be explained to the reader.

Several years ago, on the 10th of May, I took with me my Indian friend Noel Moulton (Fig. 8, p 59), and worked several hours at this site. We had just dug a small trench on the first terrace from the river, and uncovered a deep deposit of ash, firestones, flint chippings and two broken arrowheads, when the owner of the intervale appeared. He said he didn't want us to do any more work; gave as his reason the possibility of a June freshet which might enlarge the hole. I explained that we intended to fill in the trench when we were through work, but be still refused to allow us to continue our digging. Then I asked him if I could do a little digging on the third terrace, which was high above any conceivable rise of water. He grudgingly said yes, then departed to his home a short distance away.

Noel and I boiled the kettle, made tea, ate our lunch, then went to the place and sunk a trench about eight feet in length. Soon, at a depth of ten inches, we found a long gouge, and a little later another gouge; a long slate knife (Fig. 9 b, p 60) and a few other slate

---

25 "A fine-grained gray, green, or bluish metamorphic rock easily split into smooth, flat pieces."—archaeology.wikia.com/wiki/Slate.

objects. The longest gouge is twelve inches, a raised spine running down the back, and is almost wholly patinated[26] a dark red which might be oxide of iron (Fig. 2 c, p 55). If found in Maine this piece, because of its peculiar patination, would be assigned to a so-called *Red Paint Culture,* of which more in its proper place.

Presently I looked up and saw the owner of the field approaching (I hurriedly hid the objects we had found.) When he arrived he sat down and said: "If you find any money, or gold, it's mine."

I assured him we weren't hunting for gold; but he wasn't convinced. For two or three hours he sat there and watched our every movement. Finally he got up, and said he was going to the house, then added: "Come in before you leave for home." (I had parked my car in his dooryard).

I was reminded of Henry VII's bargain with John Cabot, before giving the Venetian navigator a charter to set out or his famous voyage to the New World, that he, Henry, was to have one-fifth of any gold, diamonds and other things of worth which the Cabots might discover. And of his strict orders to them not to put in at any foreign port on their voyage, but to come direct to Bristol and pay him his share of the profits. Of course there were none. But the parsimonious Henry did open his purse, and presented John Cabot with £10 for having discovered a continent!

To be short, when Noel and I returned to the car, the farmer was seated in a chair in front of the kitchen window. He hastened out. To allay any suspicion that we had found gold or money on his place, I showed him the stone objects we had. He glanced at them carelessly, gave us a long, suspicious look and, without searching our pockets, allowed us to depart.

A couple of weeks later, when I again visited the place, the intervale had been ploughed, harrowed and sowed with oats and grass, and has not since been ploughed. But next summer I hope to complete my digging of this particular area. But Noel will not be with me. Last year he went to join his Indian forefathers and the grandmother who, at the age of 112 years (when he was a small boy) told him old legends of his Passamaquoddy Indian ancestors; and prophesied that he—Noel—had not been born to be drowned, although he would be in danger scores of times while shooting Big Black rapids on the St John waters, the Tobique Narrows, the Kennebec and the Miramichi.

In fancy I can see him, standing upright in his canoe, as, one with all its motions, his dark eyes shining with the excitement of conflict with elemental forces his ancestors had dared for untold centuries, he steered it down the boiling narrow waters of Big Lewey, and the more dangerous descent of Burnt Hill rapids.

No. Noel was not born to be drowned, but, even had his old grandmother not assured him of this fact, I don't think he would ever have been afraid of "White Waters."

I recollect the many times we dug out prehistoric campsites, when, working at one end of the trench, he had straightened his body, and, one hand cupped over the palm of the other, he approached me with slow inturning footsteps to where I was. Then, his eyes a-twinkle, he said: "Guess?"

---

26   Patination is "the altered surface and coloring of an artifact made by natural weathering or exposure to soil acids."—http://www.archaeologywordsmith.com.

I knew it was something more precious than arrowhead or knife, but, not to rob him of the joy of surprising me, I said: "An arrowhead, Noel?" Then he would remove his upper hand from the concealed object, and hold out to me a superb spearhead.

I remember numerous occasions, at the end of the day when it was time to eat, and I said I'd get the water to "boil" the kettle, or wood for the fire, he would say: "No. You sit down, smoke your pipe. I'll get the water, wood, fry bacon, eggs, make tea." And he had got a log or block of wood, set it at the base of the tree, and again would say, in his firm, gentle voice: "You sit down, rest, smoke your pipe. Supper it not be long."

Some day, in another world, I know I shall again meet Noel, and he will say: "*Wul-e-gis-kit*—Fine day, Doc."

Eight or ten years ago I was driving home from Fredericton, and coming opposite Phillips Intervale saw that the extreme northern end (where I had never discovered any signs of Indian occupation) had recently been ploughed. It was only a small area, but I stopped to inspect it, and among turned-up ashes and firestones found the big object depicted on Figure 10, p 61. As the reader can readily see, it is an irregular-shaped beach or field stone, with a deep notch struck off on either edge, but not grooved across the face. Whether it was axe or hoe or plough I cannot answer. But its primitive form, and its weight make it a most interesting relic of the past. It weighs four pounds.

The name Eel, as applied to the tributary opposite Phillips Intervale, has no reference to the snake-like fish *Anguilla vulgaris*. It is that of a Major Eel who, more than a century ago, owned a grant of land which bordered a portion of the stream. The Indian name is *Med-a-wam-ke-tuk*. French maps bear the name River Medoctec.

Eel River, to give it its present name, heads from a series of lakes respectively named First, Second, and Third Eel River Lakes. Its upper reaches are bordered by swampy glades; in other places it assumes lake-like expansions. It has always been the habitat of numerous wild-fowl, beaver and other fur-bearing creatures, and, until recent years, that monarch of the forest, moose, in abundance.

The last twelve miles, until it vents into the St John, the Eel is a turbulent stream broken by rough rapids, falls and large boulders, which make navigation extremely hazardous for even the most expert canoeman. To get around these obstructions, the Indian, at some remote period, paced out with splendid sense of direction a five-mile path or portage from Medoctec Village to the Eel River above the Falls. Here they put in their canoes. The route then led up the Eel River to the First Lake, then a three-mile portage to North Lake, and paddled down this into Grand or Chep-ut-net-i-cook Lake. They could continue down this to the St Croix, which in turn supplied communication with the Passamaquoddy Indians; and also, by the Schoodic lakes, reach the Machias River and thence to the coast. But, if they desired to reach the Penobscot, they took out their canoes at a place called Davenport's Cove on Grand Lake, carried to the Baskahegan, paddled down this to the Mattawamkeg, and thence to the Penobscot fort and village. From this a short portage led to an eastern branch of the Kennebec River on which, at Neuwidgewaak, was a palisaded fort of the Kennebec Indians.

This system of waterways and relatively short portages, had been used from time immemorial both from and to the St John River, but the Penobscot and Kennebec route was to become of vital importance in those stirring years when French and English struggled for mastery in the New World: a period when the Indian village, fort and portage at Medoctec, became famous in the annals of both peoples.

The first historical reference I can find to the portage and its connecting waterways (although he fails to mention them by name), is contained in his Relation of 1653, to the Propaganda at Paris, by Father Ignatius, a Capuchin priest. After speaking of portages leading to the St John River from the north, he says: "In the district of Pentagoet" (Penobscot, where there was a mission as early as 1642) "half way up the River St John, there is a certain path that leads by forests and lakes to that region."

No other place on the St John answers to this description.

The reader will soon understand why I have been at such pains to describe this system of waterways and portages leading to and from Medoctec.

A famous historian once wrote that the meaning of the name Medoctec was unknown. Then, several years later, my Indian friend Noel was in my office, and we were measuring a piece of moulding I needed to make repairs to an antique bureau-desk. When we got to the end, Noel said: "*Medoctec.*"

I was startled, wondered if I had heard right, and asked: "What did you say, Noel?" His answer was slow, deliberate: "*Medoctec*...it mean the end." Then he picked up a lead pencil from the bench, and running a forefinger from one end to the other, drawled: "End of any thing it mean *Medoctec.*" He paused, gave a low chuckle, and continued: "Tobique Valley Railroad it go from Perth to Plaster Rock, then no more. All right, we say *Medoctec,* because it the end."

I was delighted. The meaning of the place-name of the ancient Maliseet village of Medoctec, that for so long had puzzled historians, was now partially explained. I say partially. For was it named such because the portage ended here, or because the fort and village were at the lower end of the intervale we commonly call Medoctec Flat? I don't know, nor does anyone else. But a week or so following Noel's visit to my office, I was talking to the editor of one of our provincial daily newspapers, and during our conversation I told him of my discovery, and added: "I can imagine, many centuries past, a party of Indians carrying canoes over the five-mile portage to the St John River, and, when they set them down, exclaiming Medoctec—the end of our journey. The end of our portage, or trail."

A short time later I read an article by the famous historian (who had previously said the meaning of the name Medoctec was unknown), in which he now stated, without giving the source of his information, that "the name Medoctec means the end of the trail." As I have already said, that is one possible explanation. But the place-name Medoctec is capable of other applications than the end of the trail: the end of anything; although we can logically assume that it either referred to the end of the trail, or specifically to their village at the lower end of the Intervale, and was finally applied to the whole area of which the village was a part. At any rate, if I hadn't picked up an antique bureau-desk lacking a piece of moulding, and if Noel, by chance, hadn't come into my office in time to assist me in measuring it, it is possible that future historians would continue to refer to the meaning of the place-name Medoctec as "unknown".

Be that as it may, Medoctec was the principal palisaded village of the St John River Indians for untold centuries before the coming of the white man, and for a long time after.

Here the medicine man, with his simple herbs, howlings and incantations, treated the ills of the community from whom he exacted tribute often out of all proportion to the cures he effected. Here too, was the sweat lodge. This was an enclosure of birch or spruce bark capable of holding a dozen individuals. First a circle of beach stones was laid on the ground in the centre of the lodge, and a fire of wood kept burning until they were almost red hot. Then, those whose turn it was to take the "bath" (for it was a communal custom) entered the lodge and seated themselves in a circle about the hot stones, upon which, from time to time, water was poured and clouds of steam arose. Naturally the occupants sweated copiously. They endured this for perhaps an hour then, if the season was winter, they dashed outside into a snow drift, or, if summer, into the river, then emerged and dried themselves. "By this means they purged themselves of all ill-humours."

Here they chipped their arrowheads, spearheads, knives and scrapers from flinty chert, jasper and various kinds of quartzite,[27] doubtless fashioned stone axes, chisels, gouges and adzes, made their toboggans, snowshoes, birch-bark boxes (Fig. 1 b, p 54), baskets both big and small, wooden bowls and birch-bark pails to hold water.

The alluvial soil produced most excellent corn and pumpkins; springs of pure cold water gushed from the hillside. The river teemed with salmon, sturgeon, trout, shad, gaspereau and other fish. The forest, both near and far, abounded in game and fur-bearing creatures. Birchbark was handily available for their canoes, pails and drinking vessels. There were deposits of bluish-grey clay, a short distance below the village, which they shaped into pots both big and small, and decorated them with various designs before baking them. Firewood was plentiful in all directions. The women did most of the work, including filling in the webbing of snowshoes, helped sew bark on canoes, made moccasins, leggings and cloaks of moosehide.

During summer months the men went practically naked save for a breech-clout[28] fastened both before and behind the belt of rawhide above the hips. In winter they wore a cloak of moosehide, otter or beaver skins. These were thrown over one shoulder, leaving the right arm free and fastened down the middle by latches of rawhide. They wore moccasins and encased their legs in leggings made from the skins taken from the legs and shanks of moose. The garb of the women in summer consisted of a breech-clout and a short kirtle[29] of tanned moose or caribou hide. In the winter, besides these, they wore a cloak of skins fastened at one side by latches. Infants were swaddled in cradle-boards (Fig. 11, p 26); dried moss used as diapers.

---

27 "A granular metamorphic rock consisting essentially of quartz in interlocking grains."—http://www.thefreedictionary.com/quartzite.

28 "A strip of material (bark, cloth, leather) passed between the thighs and secured by a belt."—Wikipedia.

29 "A tunic or coat, originally a garment reaching to the knees or lower, sometimes forming the only body-garment."—OED.

11 First Nations family (probably Maliseet) with baby in cradleboard
late 19th or early 20th century

Apart from the fact that the lower end of the intervale at Medoctec must occasionally have been imperilled during exceptionally high freshets (I once saw a huge cake of ice up on the bank), it was an ideal place for habitation.

*   *   *

Untold centuries passed away; the seasons came and went: spring, summer, autumn and winter, when many of the inhabitants of Medoctec broke up into small parties of eight or ten and departed on their winter hunt, not to return until the ice broke up in the river. Then came the planting of corn, and after this short trips to spear salmon and dig for roots along the intervales and islands.

Then on June 24, 1604, a little vessel of eight tons, with a motley crew of French gentlemen, soldiers of the Swiss nation, and workmen, entered a fine harbour at the head of the Bay of Fundy, rediscovered the noble river of the Maliseets, which they named St John.

It's amazing how historical errors persist from one generation to another. Historian after historian, as well as news writers repeat the same thing without taking the trouble to learn the facts. (I wish *I* were wholly exempt from the foregoing criticism.)

One of the most persistent fallacies we hear repeated—especially in the Maritime Provinces—is that Samuel Champlain discovered the St John River. I don't want to appear to take away from or disparage the achievements of that magnificent man. He stands on a pedestal too high for my poor pen to belittle. There have been many attempts at debunking national heroes just for the lust of pelf, or because of a perverted sense of personal frustration by the authors. I am only interested in the truth, and it's high time that some matters should be tidied up.

Champlain didn't discover the river St John. He makes no such claim in his published *Voyages.* He gives a fairly accurate plan of St John harbour, which, he says, "lay at the mouth of the largest and deepest river we had yet seen, which we *named* the River Saint Jean because it was on this saint's day that we arrived there." (The italics are mine.)

Mark Lescarbot in his Nova Francia (Paris 1609—17th century English translation by P.E.) makes the matter quite clear.

The facts are these: On the 8th December, 1603, the king of France gave the Sieur de Monts a patent which begins with this preamble: "Henry, by the grace of God, king of France and Navarre: to our dear and well beloved Lord of Monts, one of the ordinarie Gentlemen of Our Chamber, greeting... Have expressely appointed you and stablished you, and by these presents, signed with our own hands, doe commit, ordaine, make, constitute and stablish you our Lieutenant General for to represent our Person, in Countries, territories, coasts and confines of La Cadia, to begin from the 40th degree to the 46th, And in the same distance, or any part of it, as farre as may bee done, to establish, extend and make knowne the might of our Name... Might and authorite... Given at Fountain-Bleu, the eighth day of December in the yere of our Lord 1603, and of our Reigne the fifteenth." Signed "Henry."

No mention is made of Champlain in the long document. He was invited by De Monts to accompany the voyage, which he did in the capacity of King's Geographer.

The rule in recounting discoveries of new lands has always been to credit them to the leader of the expedition.

Of course Champlain was one of the company, as were Pontgrave, the Baron de Poutrincourt, Champdoré, Dorville and several other gentlemen, besides sailors and workmen of various trades. So it may truthfully be said that they were co-discoverers. But, to make the claim as has been done by countless writers, that Champlain discovered the River St John, is equal to giving the whole credit to one of the workmen who helped prepare the metal for casting Benvenuto Cellini's famous bronze masterpiece *Perseus,* rather than to Cellini whose genius conceived it! Or, to make another comparison: that one of the sailors on the little *Matthew* discovered the Island of Newfoundland and the mainland of North America, rather than Cabot.

Champlain doesn't even say that he ascended the river, nor does Mark Lescarbot pen such an event. But in 1608 De Monts' secretary went up it several leagues. However, Champlain, with other gentlemen, viewed the Reversing Falls, and in his map indicates the portage used by the Indians to get around the Falls, and the three islands above, in midstream.

Nor was the habitation built later at Port Royal, Champlain's, as has so often been asserted. It belonged to De Monts and, three years later, when his monopoly of the fur trade was revoked, to the Baron de Poutrincourt, who earlier had been given Port Royal by De Monts who had the right to do so under the terms of his charter. This grant was later ratified by the king.

Now despite the foregoing, there is no doubt that certain people will continue to say that Champlain *discovered* the St John River. Why?

Even our beloved historian, the Reverend W. O. Raymond in *The River St John*, published in 1905, of which a new edition, edited by Dr J. C. Webster, C.M.G. came out in 1943, made an error that should be corrected. As the reader has already seen, De Monts, Poutrincourt, Champlain and others came to Acadia in the early summer of 1604. On June 24 they discovered and named the River St John. Raymond says: "Lescarbot, the historian, who accompanied De Monts, says they visited the cabin of Chkoudun, with whom they bartered for furs." As a matter of fact Lescarbot didn't come to Acadia until the spring of 1606, and the visit to Chkoudun's cabin *didn't take place until August of the following year.* In the meantime De Monts had returned to France. A full account of Lescarbot's visit to Chkoudun will later be told in his own words.

*   *   *

In 1607 Virginia was settled by Englishmen. In 1608 Quebec was founded by Samuel Champlain, representing the Sieur De Monts. In 1620 the Pilgrims landed at Plymouth Rock, and ten years later the Puritans arrived at Massachusetts Bay.

The English population grew rapidly. By 1685 it numbered 150,000 souls. That of New France—which included Acadia—12,149. Of this number only five or six families lived on the St John River.

The Indians of the Gaspé Peninsula, Acadia—which included the present Nova Scotia and its islands, New Brunswick, and the State of Maine as far south as the Kennebec River—early came under the influence of the French clergy. But for three quarters of a century the St John River Indians were only sporadically served by priests. Then an event occurred after which they were seldom without a missionary.

In early May, 1686, two or three canoes, paddled by Indians, left Quebec and threaded a labyrinth of waters through an almost trackless wilderness to the St John River. In one of the canoes was Bishop Saint Vallier, bound on a pastoral visit to the few missions in Acadia north of the Penobscot; the most notable being at Port Royal—the oldest permanent settlement north of St Augustin in Florida.

The first part of the route was one not often used by the Indians. In many places snow yet lingered in the woods, and sometimes the streams were so obstructed by fallen trees that they had to be cut away or portaged around. It was a trying ordeal for the Bishop and his party until they reached the swollen waters of the St John. Here they made rapid progress. and coming to Medoctec were joyously greeted by the inhabitants. The Bishop set up a little lectern, intoned the Mass, and told his hearers that he had come to tell them that he was going to establish a mission for them. He slept that night at Medoctec, and next day proceeded down river. In his book, published at Paris 1688, he describes Medoctec as "the first fort in Acadia." This fort as I have said was at the lower end of the intervale, and not to be confused with the later fort about three-quarters of a mile distant.

Not long after the Bishop's visit, Father Simon, a Recollet of the Franciscan Order, arrived at Medoctec, and began his mission to instruct his flock in the elements of the Christian religion. Father Simon was a good man: kindly, charitable and humane, and did what he could to wean them from their savage nature and cruelty to their captives taken in war. But, while attending to their spiritual needs, he was also solicitous to promote French interests and ascendancy in Acadia. More than once he accompanied the warriors on their expeditions against the New England settlements, and it is said of him that on one occasion he stood in a church doorway and refused to allow his Indians to burn it.

Although his ministry included the whole river, he spent the greater part of his time at Medoctec. We have no record whether he had the Indians make him a bark lodge in which to hold mass and instruct them in religious matters. The Recollets, unlike the Jesuits, were not their own annalists, and most of their missionary efforts were never recorded.

CHAPTER 4
MEDOCTEC CONTINUED

For forty years—save for playing a minor role during the last year of the Indian war of 1676 headed by Philip, chief of the Wampanoags, and twelve years later in an attack on Dover, during which several English were killed—the St John River Indians, and their allies the Penobscot and Kennebec had remained at peace with the English colonists. But in the latter quarter of the 17th century an event occurred that was to play an important part in the relations of the eastern Indians and the New England colonists. The young Baron Saint Castin, an officer in the Carigan Salières regiment that had been disbanded at Quebec following the French-Iroquoian Indian war, decided to come to Acadia. He settled at the mouth of the Penobscot River, raised a palisaded fort and truck house, engaged in the fur trade, and in the years that followed amassed a considerable fortune. He married Matilda, a daughter of the Penobscot chief Madocawando, indubitably the most renowned warrior of his time in all Acadia. The union gave St Castin enormous influence over all the Indians from the Kennebec to Cape Sable: an influence that, in later years, extended to his half-breed sons.

Charles II had given his brother, The Duke of York, large territories in America, which embraced St Castin's fort, so in 1688 Sir Edmund Andros, governor of New England, embarked in the frigate *Rose,* sailed to Penobscot, and during St Castin's absence looted his house and fort. He told an Indian chief to tell St Castin that, if he would come under obedience to the English king, his goods would be restored. Of course the haughty and spirited Frenchman repudiated the offer.

There seems little doubt that St Castin got into communication with his Indian kindred and induced them to make war on the English. At any rate, to redress old wrongs and at the same time avenge the insult to their great white chief, they started hostilities in the early summer of 1689. Among other places, they attacked the palisaded fort at Pemaquid, on the New England coast between the Penobscot and the Kennebec rivers, killed several of the garrison, reduced the fort to ashes, and among others captured John Gyles, a lad twelve years of age. He was brought by his Indian master to Medoctec where he remained six years, then was sold to a Frenchman who lived at the mouth of the Jemsec on the St John River.

The destruction of Pemaquid and other places during this year synchronized with the beginning of hostilities between England and France, known as King William's War.

31

It lasted ten years, drenched the country with blood, and resulted in the destruction of hundreds of farmsteads, hamlets and towns almost to the environs of Boston.

Thus the St John River Indians, their allies the Micmac, Penobscot and Kennebec, were caught up in the intrigues and successive wars which, with but brief intermissions, only ended at the fall of Quebec and the Treaty of Paris, 1763.

For three years John Gyles faithfully served his French master, then, at the end of the war, he was given his freedom and returned to New England. In 1736 he published his memoirs and gives a graphic account of his capture, and of his long journey through the wilderness to Medoctec: "We arrived at a long carrying place to Medoctec fort... My Indian master went before me and left me with an old Indian and three squaws. The old man said (which was all the English he could speak), 'By an' by come to a great town and fort.' So I comforted myself in thinking how finely I should be refreshed when I came to the great town.

"After some miles travel we came in sight of a large cornfield and soon after of the fort, to my great surprise; for two or three squaws met us, took off my pack, and led me to a large hut or wigwam where thirty or forty Indians were dancing and yelling round five or six poor captives... I was whirled among them and we looked at each with a sorrowful countenance."

Having told of his great fear that he was going to be killed, he goes on: "A grave Indian took me by the hand and led me out...he carried me to a French hut about a mile from the Indian fort. The Frenchman was not at home, but his wife, who was a squaw, had some conversation with my Indian friend... We tarried there about two hours, then returned to the Indian village, where they gave me some victuals."

This statement by Gyles, that he was taken about a mile from the fort to the Frenchman's house, gives confirmation (if any were needed) to my archaeological evidence that the old prehistoric fort and village were at the lower end of Medoctec intervale. And several years ago I discovered an old stone cellar about a mile up the intervale. The distance from the fort and cemetery, depicted by Raymond, is approximately only five hundred yards, or one-third of a mile.

Gyles pays high tribute to Father Simon. He says: "The priest of this river was of the order of St Francis, a gentleman of a humane, generous disposition. In his sermons he most severely reprehended the Indians for their barbarities to captives. He would often tell them that excepting their errors in religion the English were a lot better than themselves."

During Gyles' captivity at Medoctec, René Damours, Sieur de Clignancourt, who with his brothers owned most of the land bordering the river from its mouth to the Grand Falls, came to Medoctec two or three times each year and traded with the Indians for their furs, giving in exchange brandy which debauched them and caused them to fight with each other for days on end.

Medoctec and its portage famous? Yes, to the historian, and all those for whom the past has any charm, and the imagination to sense their importance in those stirring times when France and England struggled for mastery in the new world. During the years of which we write, they became of increasing strategic importance. Medoctec was the rendezvous for the Micmac as far distant as Cape Sable, and for those of northern

Acadia, who with their St John River kindred joined in the dog feast, danced and chanted their war songs then, their faces and bodies daubed with red paint, they shouldered their canoes and sped over the portage to finally join their other kindred on the Penobscot and the Kennebec.

*   *   *

Versailles, and especially the governors of Quebec, while concerned for the conversion of the eastern Indians, were also fully alive to the fact that it was a potent factor in preserving their loyalty. This especially applied to the St John River Indians whose palisaded fort guarded the eastern end of the now famous portage leading into New England. Not only was it the most direct, it was the shortest route by which the Penobscot and Kennebec could reach the St John, which France was determined to hold. For this river was also the most important gateway from Acadia to Quebec. Thus, with the Indians and the few French soldiers at Fort Nashwaak, under the fiery Villebon, in control of the river, they would serve as a buffer against the encroachments of the English against the seat of French power in Quebec. At the same time it was by way of the river St John that Quebec maintained her communications with Isle Royal and Isle St Jean (Cape Breton and Prince Edward islands), also with old France during the season when the St Lawrence navigation was impossible. In brief the possession of this route was "indispensably necessary to France."[30]

Over this famous portage and its connecting links came Thury the Jesuit, priest to the Penobscot, to confer with Villebon at Fort Nashwaak, fifty miles down river from Medoctec. Again he passed up the river to Quebec to report to Count Frontenac and receive instructions; then back to Medoctec and over the trail to reach his charges at Penobscot and transmit messages to Father Bigot, priest to the Kennebec.

Nothing happened during the secret conclaves of his flock that he didn't know the following day or even sooner. From Bigot, priest of the more distant Kennebec, came couriers to warn him of any disaffection among *his* charges. For the English were holding out inducements to both tribes to discontinue the war that was creating untold havoc in lives and property.

He sent messengers by swift couriers to Manidoubtik, chief of the Medoctec Indians— who never once wavered in their loyalty to the French—and he in turn relayed the intelligence to Villebon.

In May, 1692, while the snow was not yet out of the woods, Villebon sent de la Broquerie, his own brothers Portneuf, des Isles, and twenty Canadian soldiers by way of Medoctec, to join the Kennebec and Penobscot, with others to advance into the enemy's country. On the 25th, Micmacs arrived from Cape Breton and la Have and Cape Sable; a week later others came from Minas and Beaubassin, with their missionary Baudoin. On the 18th, twenty-five Medoctec Indians came to tell him they were going fifty strong. He gave them all presents and sent them on their deadly mission.

---

30   W. O. Raymond, *Glimpses of the Past: History of the River St John, A.D. 1604-1784*, 1905, quoting Jean-Louis Le Loutre's report to Father L'Isle-Dieu...concerning the Acadians and their lands, 1754.

And the women, children and old men of Medoctec saw them shoulder their canoes and on moccasined feet start over the portage on the long route to the Penobscot and Kennebec to join with their allies in that quarter.

On April 27, 1692, one hundred Kennebec warriors came over the portage to Medoctec, from thence proceeded to Fort Nashwaak where they received a warm welcome from Villebon. Speeches were made, Villebon's brother, Portneuf, sang a war song in their language. A barrel of wine was broached and emptied in fifteen minutes. The following day they all entered their canoes and departed upriver to Medoctec, then over the portage and its connecting links to their fort and village at Neu-wig-e-waak.

In May, 1694, another large body of Indians from the Penobscot reached Medoctec and proceeded down river to confer with Villebon. On this occasion Villebon adopted Taxous (one of the most renowned warriors and orators of the northeast) as his brother, and gave him his best suit of clothes.

Again, in June 1695, more than two hundred Kennebec and Penobscot warriors, accompanied by Thury, their priest and interpreter, arrived at Medoctec on their way to confer with Villebon and, for they felt they were being cheated by the French fur traders, demanded a suitable tariff before going on with the war. At Medoctec they were joined by Father Simon and several of the Indians there, who had filtered back to their ancient village, following the subsidence of a plague that had swept away many of their kindred the year before. With them was Madocawando, St Castin's father-in-law who after the death of Manidoubtik, who had died of the plague, had come to Villebon and applied, with the consent of the Medoctec Indians, to settle on the river and become their chief.

Perhaps never before had so many warriors assembled at Medoctec at one time. The chiefs alone numbered thirteen. The river was black with their canoes as they paddled towards Nashwaak on this most momentous conference with their great white "Father," second only in importance to the redoubtable Count Frontenac—the man who later reduced their hated enemies the Iroquoian confederacy.

King William's war ended in 1697, but Villebon didn't get the news until the following spring. In the meantime, in the dead of winter, a large number of Indians had travelled all the way to Ipswich (now Andover in Massachusetts) and killed Captain Chubb, former commander at the *new fort at Pemaquid,* in revenge for the slaying for some of their kindred who had come to him under a flag of truce.

Father Simon died in 1701. The previous year Villebon had recorded in his journal that the priest was sick at Jemsec. Whether he died there or at his beloved Medoctec is not known. For twelve years he had been a faithful servant of his order, his heart always on the side of mercy.

"Father Aubrey, of the Society of Jesus, was the next priest at Medoctec. His mission lasted seven years, when he was removed to the Abenaki mission at St Francis. Here he laboured for forty-six years and died at the age of eighty-two." We further learn from Raymond that "Chateaubriand drew from his character and career materials for one of his characters in his well known romance *Atala.*"

*   *   *

It was now that Father Jean Baptiste Loyard, S. J., came to Medoctec. He was zealous for the welfare of his flock by whom he was loved and esteemed; and it was during his ministry that the first church on the St John River was erected at Medoctec. He caused it to be built about three quarters of a mile north of the prehistoric Indian fort and village, at the spot correctly indicated by Raymond in his ground plan of a portion of the intervale. The reason for the priest's selection of this area was undoubtedly its higher elevation. Doubtless he employed two or three more of the Acadians who lived on the lower river, for the Indians had no knowledge of carpentry (although it is very probable that he employed them in cutting logs from the western border of the intervale). After the church was finished they removed from their old palisaded village at the lower end of the intervale to be nearer the priest.

A gift of 1,200 livres was donated by Louis XV, towards the expenses of building the church, to which the Indians contributed beaver pelts worth a considerable sum. The king also sent a small bell which doubtless was brought up the river in a canoe poled by Indians. The chapel was raised in 1717 and finished in 1720. "It is mentioned", says Raymond, "by one of the Jesuit fathers as 'a beautiful church (*belle église*) suitably adorned and furnished abundantly with holy vessels and ornaments of sufficient richness.'"

For twenty-four years—with but two or three brief intervals which necessitated his absence, Father Loyard was a loyal minister of Christ to his people. "His last journey to Quebec was to seek medical treatment; but soon after he had recovered from the exhaustion of his long and arduous journey, he begged to be allowed to return to his people. Here, while attending the sick, he contracted the illness that resulted in his death. He was interred in the shadow of the little chapel he had laboured so assiduously to build, mourned alike by the Indians and the few Acadian settlers on the lower river."

Raymond says that from official correspondence by Vaudreuil, governor of French Canada, we gather that he was considered by both the French at Quebec and Versailles as their political agent. (So were clerics of all nations employed politically.) But, while there is no shadow of doubt that the building of the church at Medoctec helped cement the ties of loyalty between the Indians and the French, I do not for one instant believe that Jean Loyard primarily considered it otherwise than raised to the glory of God and a permanent solace to his flock.

The next priest at Medoctec was Pierre Danielou, followed by the aged Loverjeat. At the same time as the latter's ministry at Medoctec, Father Germain—the most active of the partisans of New France in this part of Acadia—had a mission at Ek-pa-hawk, a few miles above the present city of Fredericton.

The church at Medoctec stood for about fifty years, or until 1767, then we are told by Raymond, the missionary Bailly recorded in his register that "the Indians having abandoned Medoctec, and the church having been put to the most profane uses," he had caused it to be dismantled, and the bell, the furnishings and holy ornaments transferred to Ek-pa-hawk, opposite Savage Island. Here, I was told by Peter Paul, it remained until, the chapel, having fallen into decay, the bell was again transferred to a new church erected at Middle Kingsclear. There it continued to peal out its summons until 1904, when fire destroyed the church and melted the bell, when it was made into miniature bells and sold as souvenirs to help defray the expense of repairing the present striking edifice.

But the Medoctec Indians didn't abandon for long their ancient village site and its cornfields. Many of them returned and remained for another three or four decades.

In July 1777 Medoctec and its famous portage again became the scene of great activity. Following the outbreak of the American Revolutionary War, a Colonel John Allen, formerly a British subject at Halifax, Nova Scotia, defected to the Americans. He immediately began raising trouble on the St John River, and so well succeeded in attracting the Indians to Congress that a strong force of English proceeded up the river to Ek-pa-hawk, where Allen and a large number of Indians were congregated. Learning of the pursuit, Allen and his Indian friends fled up the river to Medoctec and persuaded the Indians there to accompany him to Machias. The exodus began July 13. Four hundred and sixty Indians: men, women and children. The sick and aged were carried pick-a-back over the portage to the Eel River above the Falls. The journey occupied three weeks during which they had to make temporary camps, and hunt and fish to keep from starving.

But once at Machias they became homesick for their river, its islands and intervales, and before the war's end most of them had drifted back home and taken the oath of allegiance to King George.

* * *

In 1787 Frederick Dibblee, loyalist refugee to New Brunswick, was appointed agent for the Society for the Propagation of the Gospel to native Indians of New England and adjacent parts, to build a school for Medoctec Indians. Besides teaching them he distributed seed-corn, hoes, gun-flints, powder, lead, blankets and other necessaries. He lists 98 men, 74 women and 165 children who frequented Medoctec at different times.

After the coming of the members of the disbanded Loyalist regiments to the river, Medoctec was granted to three members of DeLancey's First battalion. Evidently they were afraid to assert their rights under the Crown for they made no effort to till the soil. At length, in the early years of the 19th century, commissioners came up the river from Fredericton, and, landing, were met by the Indians in full war regalia. The leader of the commission asked the chief by what right he and his people held this land. At which the chief drew himself to his full height, and pointed with a regal gesture to the graveyard said: "There lie the bones of our grandfathers; there lie the bones of our fathers. There lie the bones of our children." (Raymond—*The St John River.*)

To which eloquent words the commissioner could make no suitable reply, and he and his companions departed with more haste than dignity.

But as time went on, the continued encroachments of the white man, with his insensitive and cynical disregard of the rights of the original owners of the land, forced a gradual migration of most of the Medoctec Indians to mouth of Tobique and to Kingsclear. Finally, shortly after 1841, those few remaining removed to a few acres below Woodstock, provided for them by Government.

*   *   *

In the year 1890 Mr A. R. Hay, then owner of a portion of the intervale, "picked up a stone tablet near the northwest corner of the little Indian cemetery. It is of black slate, in length fourteen inches by seven in width, and about an inch in thickness. It was found quite near the surface, just as it might have fallen amid the ruins of an old building, covered merely by fallen leaves. The inscription is in excellent state of preservation and without abbreviation reads:

Deo Optimo Maximo
In honorem Divi Joannis Baptiste
Hoc Templum posuerunt Anno Domini
MDCCXVII
Malecitae
Missionis Procurator Joanne Loyard Societatis Jesu
Sacerdote.

"The translation reads: To God, most excellent, most high, in honor of Saint John Baptist, the Maliseets erected this church A.D. 1717, while Jean Loyard, a priest of the Society of Jesus, was procurator (or superintendent) of the mission."

In the lower left hand corner the name Danielou, Loyard's successor, faintly scratched, is, says Raymond, "evidently of later date; but its presence there is of historical interest."

Since 1923, when a high freshet, carrying massive cakes of ice, gouged away a considerable portion of the plateau opposite the old church, I have known that this cemetery contained only a small number of interments. For, visiting the scene soon after the freshet had subsided, I observed skeletal remains strewn along the beach, others protruding from the sloping bank. But I didn't know, until recently, how small a portion of the area described as a cemetery by Raymond, and depicted on his ground plan, was actually used for burials.

12 Iron bolt, probably from chapel, built 1717, at Medoctec, St John River

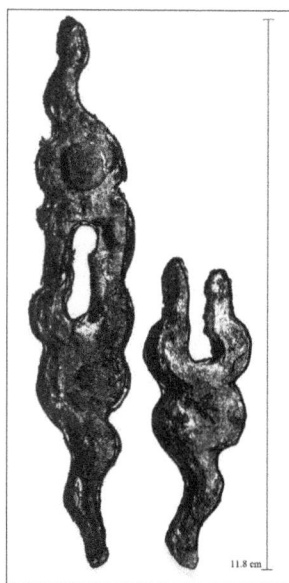

13 Iron key escutcheons, probably from a cabinet formerly in priest's house, contiguous to chapel built in 1717, destroyed latter part of 18th century, found May 12, 1964

Three years ago my friend and archaeological helper John McClement was digging along the northern perimeter of the tree-enclosed cemetery, marked on its western border by a tall wooden cross, and discovered scores of old hand-forged nails and spikes, and a so-called butterfly hinge. The deposit led inwards. A year later we followed this deposit southwards about ten feet; there were no skeletal remains, but we uncovered more nails, spikes, a beautifully made iron bolt, and the much decomposed remains of an ancient lock. The bolt, depicted on Figure 12, p 37, is similar to those made in Quebec during the late 17th and early 18th centuries. We also found several butt-end hinges (Fig. 7 c, p 20), a whole iron key escutcheon and half of another (Fig. 13, p 38). These last had evidently been on a cabinet or small chest, the wood of which had rotted away. Then, a year ago,[31] digging slightly eastwards from our previous finds, we uncovered the base of what seems to have been a huge stone fireplace. (See Fig. 14, p 63 and Fig. 15, p 63.) The past had again been unrolled to or perhaps before the year 1717, when Jean Loyard, of the Society of Jesus, had erected the frame of the Maliseet Indian chapel.

I feel confident we could have found more objects had we been allowed to continue digging; but we were stopped by the New Brunswick Electric Power Commission, who had already hired archaeologists to dig out the area at the suggestion of the New Brunswick Museum.

The day following discovery of the fireplace, some one communicated with the Power Commission, and the manager sent up one of his men, who purchased from the owner of the land the sole right to do any further excavating.

Why the sudden interest of the New Brunswick Electric Power Commission in archaeology? The answer is that the NBEPC was building a huge dam at a place called Mactaquac, fourteen miles above Fredericton, to generate electric power. The dam has created a huge pond sixty miles in length, and in places more than a hundred feet deep. It has destroyed all the islands and intervales, the trees along the shores, and displaced some two thousand people. It has destroyed old buildings—some of which have withstood the ravages of time for more than one hundred and fifty years; gracious examples of colonial architecture when men built not only for utility but with an eye to beauty. Houses with H and HL hinges and other hardware of a bygone age. Houses wherein are many fireplaces with wide mantels that would make antiquarians gasp with astonishment that such furnishings exist this far up the river. And beautiful churches wherein men and women and children have worshipped throughout the years. And the cemeteries where under the sod lie the remains of the first pioneers whose lives were spent tilling

---

31   It was in fact in the same year, 1964, as the discovery of the bolt and escutcheons.

the fecund soil granted them and their heirs and assigns for ever by a grateful king. It covers dozens of ancient campsites where under the soil lie buried innumerable stone objects made by the native Americans we call Indians.

But this destruction, we are told, is progress. In such so-called progress the 14th, 15th, 16th and seventeenth century Roman nobles destroyed or removed from their original historic settings many of the monuments of ancient Rome.

A stagnant pond—sixty miles in length has replaced the waters wont to ripple over the bars and around the heads of the islands. The singing waters which, ever since the retreat of the glaciers, have washed the reflected stars and constellations as they moved across the bowl of the sky.

Man is the great destroyer, the insatiable predator, but with all his science he cannot create one blade of grass, nor the smallest flower, nor a tree, nor a bird, nor a waterfowl. True, he may reach the moon and the stars, but it's possible he may destroy them and this world, as we know it, as was suggested by the great scientist Einstein soon after man had perfected the atomic bomb!

*　　*　　*

A few days after John McClement, Stephen Homer and I had uncovered the old fireplace, we were told by Mr R. Tweeddale of the N.B.E.P.C., through the *Atlantic Advocate,* that a team of "experts" was now excavating under the old Medoctec fort, that the objects under the ground had lain there for centuries, and no one had done anything about them; we were told that the New Brunswick Electric Power Commission was acting as a catalyst, the artifacts found would be tabulated and be preserved for future generations to see and study. All this in spite of the fact that it was well known I had excavated the most important collection of Maliseet artifacts in existence.

Who were the experts? The only member of the team who could properly be described as an expert was Mr Caywood, from Arizona, loaned to the Power Commission by Stuart Udall, Secretary of the Interior, Washington, D.C. His field was not pre-history. A few days after he came, he admitted to me that he was not a stone-age archaeologist. He thought he had been hired to dig out an old French fort. He had two students with him: Mark Dornstreitch, taking ethnology at New York University; and George Long, a two-year archaeology student from Virginia. The other eight workers were boys without any previous archaeological experience. As Mark Dornstreitch said to me: "Political archaeology is the worst kind of archaeology."

They were told that any artifacts would be below the twelve inch level, so the team dug down to that depth, threw the soil into wheel barrows and dumped it over the river bank. Thus many European clay pipes and we don't know what else were lost. The "dig" covered almost three months. It disclosed several deposits of beach stones around which fires had been built, signifying wigwam sites. Several post holes were discovered, pipe stems and bowls, some portions of what had evidently been copper kettles, two or three musket frizzens,[32] the same number of broken iron tomahawks and some other objects. But all combined to prove (if any proof were needed) that the palisaded fort was slightly north of the cemetery. I do not believe that the palisades had enclosed the cemetery and the chapel. Mr Caywood's boys soon developed a *digging* technique that won my hearty approval.

The Rev. W. O. Raymond, in his booklet "Old Medoctec Fort and the Indian Chapel" (1897) has this: "The late Wilmot Hay says that when his father purchased the property, there was an embankment four or five feet high running at an angle from the northwest corner of the old graveyard towards the river bank. This was levelled by the aid of a team of horses and a scraper, but with difficulty, as the Indians had employed stones as well as earth in its construction."

Another team, from Toronto made a reconnaissance of the terrain between Mactaquac and Medoctec. I believe they reported that they had discovered no prehistoric campsite between Mactaquac and Pokiok. I could have told them there was one at Mactaquac, and fully a dozen between that place and Pokiok.

I must be fair to this Toronto crew. The chap in charge came to me and asked if I would show him where the old campsites were. I said gladly, on three conditions: first, that I must be paid a suitable salary while I was working; second, that any stone objects recovered must be divided between the York-Sunbury Museum, Fredericton, and the Woodstock Historical Society; third, that my services would be without prejudice to my determination to fight the Mactaquac project. No further attempt was made to enlist my help. The summer's work of the two teams must have cost the province a good deal of money.

In the summer of 1967 two separate parties, each headed by a young woman from Ottawa, excavated in the vicinity of the old graveyard in the hope of discovering some evidence that the Indian chapel stood on the site indicated by the plan in W. O. Raymond's book, but without success. Perhaps this was inevitable. Some years ago I discovered several large boulders, flat on one surface, over the river bank. My theory is that these had formed the foundation, or supports, for the sills of the chapel, and there was no other foundation. The sills would decay, and little or no vestige of them remain after two hundred years.

But, although successive teams of archaeologists found no remains of the church, the numerous large, hand-wrought iron nails, the base of the stone fireplace, the iron bolt with the fleur-de-lys terminals, the key escutcheon with sea-horse terminals, the butterfly hinge, the butt-end hinges, the antique lock, and the tablet, picked up by Mr A. R. Hay in 1894, with its Latin inscription, would seem to this writer ample evidence that this was the site of the chapel erected in 1717; and that no further evidence is needed.

*   *   *

Was the old fireplace that John McClement, Stephen Homer and I discovered two years ago built by Father Loyard at the same time as the Maliseet chapel? No one will

---

32 A frizzen is "an L-shaped piece of steel hinged at the rear used in flintlock firearms."— Wikipedia.

ever know. But I like to think that the good Father Simon reared it, stone by stone, with his own hands, to give him warmth and comfort in a little cabin apart from the clamour and filth of the Indian village at the lower end of the intervale. It is quite possible; and that Father Aubrey also used it during the seven years he was at Medoctec; and that their successors also got comfort from it.

In fancy I can see the good Simon seated winter nights before a fire of logs and reading his breviary before retiring to his rude couch. I vision the intervale covered four or five feet deep with snow. I hear the north wind keening and howling from the polar regions, the cracking of trees split open with frost, and occasionally, from the ice-bound river, the whistling of imprisoned air rush—back and forth with the speed of a torpedo.

And when day dawns, I can see the aged priest rise from his couch, and put more logs on the coals in his fireplace, then prepare his simple meal.

I see him, in his hooded cassock, go outside his little cabin, put on his snowshoes, then stride off over the drifted snow to give comfort to the sick and the aged in this remote wilderness so far removed from the France he was never to see again.

*　　*　　*

In fancy I can see him, copper kettle in hand, trudging across the intervale to the base of the hillside where even as today an unfailing spring of pure, ice-cold water bubbled from the unseen depths. And I can imagine him perhaps recalling to mind *The Canticle of the Sun,* written by the founder of his order more than four hundred and sixty years before.

> O Most High, Almighty, good Lord God, to thee belong praise, glory, honour, and all blessing.
> Praised be my Lord God, with all his creatures, and especially our brother the sun, who brings us the light: fair is he, and he shines with a very great splendour. O Lord, he signifies to us thee!
> Praised be my Lord for our sister the moon, and for the stars, the which he has set clear and lovely in heaven.
> Praised be my Lord for our brother the wind, and for air and clouds, calms and for all weather, by which thou upholdest life in all creatures.
> Praised be my Lord for our sister water, who is very serviceable to us, and humble and precious and clean.
> Praised be my Lord for our brother fire, through whom thou givest us light in the darkness; and he is bright and pleasant, and very mighty and strong.
> Praised be my Lord for our mother the earth, the which doth sustain us and keep us, and bringeth forth diverse fruits, and flowers of many colours, and grass.
> Praised be my Lord for all those who pardon one another for love's sake, and who endure weakness and tribulation; blessed are they who *peacefully shall endure,* for thou, O MOST HIGH wilt give them a crown.

Why, you may ask, be concerned about the destruction of any of these places—least of all Medoctec? The old Maliseet chapel is no more. Stockade and wigwam and warrior are one with the age-old dust, and their descendants scattered. I answer: because it is history. Medoctec, as I have endeavoured to show it in the preceding pages is eloquent with memories of the history of the river in all its varied happenings. To me—as are all places where men have lived and died—it is a haunting place. The Indian was often cruel to his captives; he was also often kind, and there is no historical record that he ever violated the chastity of any of his white female captives. He often tortured his male captives. Alas! so did our own ancestors—using the thumbscrew and the rack, and the fires at Smithfield. And we tortured Quakers and so-called witches. We had our St Bartholomew's Eve and, in more recent days, Belsen and Nagasaki and Hiroshima. And only a few days ago on television I witnessed the slaughter of baby seals, and the skinning of them while still alive, so that society women might have seal jackets to wear (even in summer) at their never-ending social functions. And I thought how the "despised" Indian regarded the wild animals as his brothers, and begged their pardon when it was necessary to kill them for food and clothing. And, as I write this, I see the newspaper picture of a poor horse left by so-called civilised men in a wilderness hovel to die of starvation!

And reflecting on all these, I wonder which was more the savage: the white man, or his untutored prototype we call the Indian!

*   *   *

Today Medoctec Intervale is flooded but its image remains in my mind: its peaceful atmosphere, its apparent remoteness from civilisation. All the warring elements, both past and present, are momentarily forgotten. The intervale drowses in the afternoon heat. The stately elm trees thrust a canopy of greenery into the opalescent sky. A nectar-laden bumble bee lumbers past to plunder yet another wild flower. High over the river an osprey circles and banks as it searches the pellucid depth below for some form of fish life. The grasses and the ripening grain bend in rippling waves before a gentle wind. A thrush looses a few notes of flawless melody. A little cricket, in mourning cloak of black, climbs with sprawling legs over a fallen leaf at our feet.

No other place I know was so pregnant with mysterious enchantment. It was as though we were living in an age when last the glaciers retreated and birds and trees and grass and flowers and animals lived before ever man had discovered the valley and the river and called them beautiful and good.

CHAPTER 5
HISTORICAL COBWEBS

It is now necessary to sweep aside a few historical cobwebs that occur in *Indians of Quebec and the Maritime Provinces,* a recent publication of The Indian Affairs Branch, Department of Citizenship and Immigration.[33]

On page 29, the text says: An Indian chapel was erected at Medoctec in New Brunswick in 1717. As a royal gift, it received a small bell, now hanging in the belfry of the Indian church at Kingsclear."

Correction: As I've already said: The church at Kingsclear was destroyed by fire in 1904, the bell melted. Later it was cast into small or miniature bells and sold as souvenirs to help defray the cost of the present church. Until two years ago, when fire destroyed his house on the Reserve below Woodstock, Peter Paul had one of these souvenir bells.

On page 9, the text reads: "Many *Coureurs de Bois,* who had come from Quebec under French auspices, lived with them." (The Indians at Medoctec.)

Correction and comment: There is no historical record of more than *one* Frenchman living permanently at Medoctec. He was there in 1689 and had married a squaw. The St John River, from above Fredericton to the Grand Falls, had been granted to René Damours, Sieur de Clignancourt who came to Medoctec at certain periods of the year and traded with the Indians for their furs. Neither the St John River Indians nor Clignancourt would be likely to tolerate *Coureurs de bois* infringing on their rights. As I have said previously, it is very likely that when Father Loyard built the chapel, he had the assistance of two or three of the French settlers living below Fredericton.

On page 8 the text reads: "In 1610 Poutrincourt received the grant of the seigniory of Port Royal, but in 1613 Captain Samuel Argall looted and burned the settlement. Following this setback Poutrincourt returned to France." In *Building the Canadian Nation,* George W. Brown, Professor of History at the University of Toronto, says on page 75: "In 1613, however, Port Royal was attacked and destroyed by a raiding party from Virginia, and Poutrincourt had to return disappointed to France. Soon his son, Jean, was back, and so the French hung on."

Correction and comment: Poutrincourt was in France, and his son Jean (Biencourt) in charge at Port Royal when it was destroyed by Argall. Poutrincourt returned to Port Royal in 1614 to find the place in ruins, his son and a few other French wandering in

---

33   Published in 1967.

the woods with the Indians. Poutrincourt soon returned to France and during the civil war incited by the Queen Mother, Marie de Medicis, was killed at Méry-sur-Seine, while attempting to take that place for the young king, Louis XIII. Both Professor Brown and the author of *Indians of Quebec and the Maritime Provinces* have given a wholly wrong picture of the events discussed above.

Page 8, paragraph (a). The text says "In 1687 Minneval of France was appointed governor of Acadia." Paragraph 5: "Governor Minneval's brother, Villebon, came to Acadia to take command of the French forces."

Correction: Menneval, not Minneval. He was *not* Villebon's brother. Louis des Friches, Sieur de Menneval, was descended from Artus des Friches, Baron de Brasseuse of the district of Oise, by a marriage with Catherine Doria, of a well known family of Genoa.

Joseph Robineau de Villebon was born at Quebec Aug. 22, 1655, the second son of René Robineau, Surveyor-General of New France, and Marie le Neuf, a daughter of M. de Potherie, governor of Three Rivers. There were seven sons: René, Joseph, Francis, Jacques, Daniel, Michael and Pierre (Webster: Acadia in the 17th Century).

*   *   *

If some of the earlier historians made errors in writing about the Indian, they were largely due to the narrators' ignorance of the language of the people they met; that the chronicler was often dependent on the use of sign-language, or that he was speaking through an interpreter whose knowledge of French or English was meagre. Or that the Frenchman's or Englishman's question conveyed to the Indian a quite different thought or picture to that which was intended, and his replies were in keeping with his conception of what was required of him. For as Rand wrote in 1849, "The Indian thinks in his own tongue, and speaks in ours, following the natural order of his own arrangement."

Thus several of the early books differ in the names of the Indian tribes living in the same territory as today. Names by which the Indians were not known among themselves, nor by their neighbours. This too was inevitable. For few if any languages are more difficult to pronounce and transcribe than those of the native Americans.

We owe a deep debt of gratitude to Marc Lescarbot. For this lovable lawyer, poet, philosopher and historiographer, who came to Port Royal in 1606, has left us the first published account of the aboriginal inhabitants in those parts of Acadia we now know as New Brunswick and Nova Scotia.

In the summer of 1607, the charter which De Monts had received from Henry, king of France, was revoked, and the heartbreaking news was brought to Port Royal by a young man named Chevalier. But the Baron de Poutrincourt, in charge at Port Royal, was loath to depart until the grains he had planted had sufficiently matured to reap; for these fruits of the soil he wanted to take to France and show the king. In the meantime, since Chevalier was anxious to secure some beaver skins, he sent him in the care of Lescarbot to the mouth of the St John River. But let Lescarbot tell about the visit in his own words—much more picturesque than any I can use.

"Because Chevalier was desirous to gather some beaver skins, he (Poutrincourt) sent him in a small bark to the river of St John, called by the savages Ouigoudi... I was of the said Chevalier's voyage; we crossed the French Bay (Fundy) to go to the said river, where as soon as we arrived, half a dozen salmon newly taken, were brought us; we sojourned there four days, during which we went into the cabin of Sagamos Chkoudun, where we saw some eighty or a hundred savages, all naked except their privy members, which were a-making *Tabagy* (that is to say a banqueting) with the meal the said Chevalier had trucked with them for their old skins full of lice (for they gave him nothing but that which they would cast away)... Being among these savages, the Sagamos Chkoudun would needs give us the pleasure, in seeing the order and gesture that they hold going to the wars, and made them all to pass before us.

"The town of *Ouigoudi* (so I call the dwelling of the said Chkoudun) was a great inclosure upon an hill, compassed about with high and small trees, tied one against another; and within many cabins, great and small, one of which was as great as a market hall, wherein many households retired themselves; and as for the same where they make their Tabagy, it was somewhat less. A good part of the said savages were of Gachepe (Gaspé), which is the beginning of the great river of Canada; and they tell us that they came from their dwelling thither in six days, which made me to marvel, seeing the distance that there is by sea, but they shorten very much their ways, and make great voyages by the means of lakes and rivers, at the end of which being come, in carrying their canoes three or four leagues,[34] they get to other rivers that have a contrary course. All these savages come thither to go to the wars with Membertou against the Armouchiquois.

"After their feast they came forth some four score out of his (Chkoudun's) town, having laid down their mantles of fur, that is to say stark naked, bearing every one a shield which covered all their body over, after the fashion of the ancient Gaulois. Besides these shields they have had every one his wooden mace, their quivers on their backs, and their bow in hand; marching as it were in dancing wise. They go furiously, with great clamours and fearful howlings, to the end to astonish their enemies, and to give to themselves mutual assurances."

The foregoing is especially valuable in that Lescarbot tells us that they used shields in their wars. But he was incorrect in saying that the name of the Indian village was *Ouigoudi,* and that the river bore the same name. For the name *Ouigoudi,* or more properly Ouigoudic (or Wigodic) is the Maliseet name for a campsite. And the St John River, as I have shown previously in this, is *Wul-ahs-tuk.*

Once my Indian friend and I were going on a dig up the Tobique River valley; and when we had arrived above the Narrows he said: "Will we put up the tent at our Wigodic?" I asked him what he meant, and he said: "*Wigoudic* means my campsite. Where we tent last time."

Both Haliburton and Hannay repeated Lescarbot's error, which fact might not be necessary to mention were it not that all three might still be quoted in this particular. On a "New Map" of Nova Scotia, 1829, the river is still called St John, and in italics

---

34   15-20 km.

Ouangoudy a different spelling but meaning Wigoudic. Other historians, however, including Raymond and Ganong have corrected the error.

Thus, the fact that the natives seen by Lescarbot used the word *Wigoudic* to describe their campsite, is positive proof that they were the same people we know as Maliseet or St John River Indians, and not Micmac.

Yet Chamberlain says that "when the French first came to Acadia they found the Micmac just where they are today, with the exception of one campsite at the mouth of the St John River, which was abandoned by the Micmac some time before the advent of the Loyalists."

Ganong, in *Historic Sites in New Brunswick,* says: "There is some reason for supposing that at the time of Champlain's visit in 1604, the Micmac occupied the mouth of the St John, but if so, they must soon have abandoned it, as its later history is connected altogether with the Maliseet."

There is an apparent error in both of the foregoing statements. First: Chamberlain's; Ganong answers this conclusively and I agree with him. But Ganong's supposition that at the coming of the French in 1604, the Micmac occupied the mouth of the river is evidently based on the fact that, as he says elsewhere, many of the place-names on the St John River are Micmac. Quite true. But they are also Maliseet. It is also true that in historic times (during the winter of 1611-12), the Jesuit missionary, Enémond Massé, stayed at the mouth of the river with Louis Membertou—son of the old Micmac sagum who had vast influence over all the Indians from Cape Sable to Gaspé. But this fact that the mouth of the river was Maliseet territory wouldn't preclude Louis Membertou camping there in the year above mentioned. For, the fishing and hunting grounds often overlapped; they were on the friendliest terms, and no doubt there was intermarriage between them then as today.

CHAPTER 6
A PINT OF RUM

From the hillside flanking the highway border of the Intervale came the roar of a man's voice ordering me to get the hell off his land. I glanced over the top of the trench I had dug and saw the owner of the voice; and although he was fully four hundred yards distant, he loomed huge, behemothian (if one can apply Job's reference to behemoth to a human being). He had a dog at his side.

Again came the roar: "I can hit a runnin' buck nine times outa ten. Git off my land." I clambered out of the trench and, spade in hand, walked towards him, and he towards me, increasing in size. The dog, a mean-looking cur, with bristling hair and deep-throated growls made short dashes towards me, then retreated to the safety of his master, only to repeat his threatenings.

Finally I paused, and, both hands clamped about the handle of my spade, the blade of which was sharp as that of a pole-axe, awaited Behemoth's nearer approach. Within six feet of me he stopped and said, in a voice like that which historians ascribe to James the First: "What are you digging on my land fer?"

I told him, and smiled, hoping to placate his wrath. Neither words nor smile had any effect. He was more than six feet tall. "Got a map with you?"

"A map?" I queried. "No. I don't need a map. I know this valley quite well."

"The other feller had a map, with an animal on it. An' he had a pointed iron rod. He was from Connecticut. Now how come a feller from Connecticut had a map of this place; knowed right where to come? Tell me that, will you?"

"Perhaps," I said, "he was hunting for the same things I'm interested in."

"Ya think so?" The pupils of his eyes were extraordinarily small, but as sharp as needles. He wiped his mouth with the back of a hairy hand, then added: "It's a golden calf, the same as you." His involved words amused me. I wanted to tell him I wasn't a golden calf. But of course I knew what he meant. Here was another like William Q., who believed in the golden calf legend.[35] I said "Was there actually a golden calf?"

"Ya—" he began. Then, for his angry voice had evidently encouraged his dog to begin hostilities, he gave the growling beast a kick, told him to "Lay down, you hellion." With this little interlude, he repeated: "Ya. Of course. An' that's what you was a-diggin' fer."

"You needn't have kicked the dog," I said.

---

35   This story is told in *Six Salmon Rivers* 4th ed., 2015, pp 95-96.

He scowled at me and said: "He'd eat you up if I said so."

I thought of the sharp blade of my spade. I wanted to tell him what it would do to the skull of his dog. But because I knew the intervale was rich in Indian artifacts, I was anxious to get on the good side of him—if that were possible. I said: "Please tell me more about the golden calf."

He gave a loud guffaw meant for laughter, then said: "Mean to say you don't know all about it?"

"I've heard several tales about it, but I'd like to hear *your* story," I said.

He appeared somewhat mollified. "Set down," he said, "an' I'll tell you." He lowered his ungainly body to the ground, and I sat down in front of him, Then he began his tale.

In essence it was the same as told me by William Q., but differed in some details as legends often do. In brief, it seems that, in the late seventeen-hundreds, the Indians of *Ek-pa-hawk,* above Fredericton, had a golden calf, the size of a yearling heifer. During the American Revolutionary War, a Colonel John Allen stirred up the St John River Indians to attempt to drive the few English settlers from the country. They failed in their object, and English soldiers came up the river to Ek-pa-hawk to make them sign a treaty of peace. The Indians had advance notice of their coming, and the majority of them were persuaded by Colonel Allen to leave their village and accompany him to Machias, on the Maine coast. One of the chiefs, and another Indian, had the golden calf in their canoe, but on the way up river to Medoctec and the portage that led into New England, this chief decided that their new "father," General George Washington, might seize the golden calf and melt it down into coin to pay his soldiers fighting King George. So he lagged behind the other canoes, and finally landed at this place, halfway between Ek-pa-hawk and Medoctec.

They buried the golden calf and then, said my informant: "Fell afightin'. The chief was killed and the other Indian buried him. Then he cut a piece of birchbark from a tree and made a map of this intervale where the golden calf was buried. Then, instead of following the other Indians to Machias, he went back to Ek-pahawk." Behemoth paused in his story, then said: "Well, fifty year ago, the feller that then owned this place ploughed up an Injin skeleton, near the gulch over there, next the river. His skull had a big gash in it, an' beside him was an iron tomahawk an' a scalpin' knife. So what? You know that as well as I do. But how'd the white feller from Connecticut, that was here fifteen years ago, git hold of that piece of birch bark with the map on it, an' a critter that looked like a calf?"

I shook my head. The finding of the skeleton, knife and tomahawk, had been told me some years before by a young minister who declared he had seen them, and the iron objects had been taken to Houlton, Maine. But what particularly interested me was the fact that the old custom of placing the owner's weapons with the dead had persisted as late as the latter part of the eighteenth century. Later I was to get further confirmation of this practice.

"You told the story well," I said.

He seemed pleased at the compliment. "I could tell you a helluva lot about deer huntin'," he said, paused a few moments, then: "You fill up that hole you dug, an' don't come back; it's my land."

"I thought it belonged to the lower farm," I said. "Used to, but it's mine now," he growled.

"I'm sorry," I said. "Naturally you resent any one taking liberties with your property. But, look here, I've not done any harm to the place, and I'd like awfully to do some more digging. I'll be willing to pay you something. Come down with me to the hole and I'll prove to you I'm not digging for any golden calf."

"Nothin' doin," he said. "Fill in the hole."

I rose to my feet. "All right," I said. "Good luck with your hunting in October." Since then I've heard another version of the golden calf legend from a small boy I met at Nackawick.

*   *   *

Two weeks later I was going down river on another dig beyond my stubborn and suspicious friend's farm. Coming opposite his place, I saw him standing in the open doorway of his barn. I stopped the car, got out, went to where he stood, and handed him an object wrapped in brown paper. "A little present for having dug on your intervale without asking your consent," I said.

He gazed at me a few moments as though stupefied. Then he slowly removed the wrapping paper, which he crumpled in his hand and dropped to the ground. Then, as he gazed awesomely on the label that proclaimed that he held in his hand a pint bottle of Bacardi rum, his great moon face became wreathed in a smile of heavenly bliss.

I turned, was almost to the car when his voice called to me to stop. I didn't heed him. I didn't want to take all my fences at one leap. I opened the door, slid into the seat, started the engine and was out of sight in no time.

A few days later after this episode I was nearing my bank, where I had some business to transact, when I saw him, like some huge monolith in human form, with his back resting against the side of the doorway as though he were a permanent fixture placed there to give it further support. I said: "Hullo—how are you today?" and made as though to pass him, when he grasped me by the arm and said: "Hey, doctor, just a minute. You got away from me too quick last time we met... Look here—" he pierced me with his gimlet eyes—"you come down an' dig up the whole flat any time you want. Only—if you find the golden calf, it's share an' share alike, eh?"

"Of course," I said.

*   *   *

On four or five occasions since then, he has come to me for advice on some of his personal problems; and I, who often lack the necessary wisdom to unravel my own, have had to assume the role of a minor Solomon to straighten his!

I've never asked him why he chose *me* rather than a lawyer, but can only assume that my method of getting on the good side of him gave him an exaggerated opinion of my ability to adjudicate almost any matter. Be that as it may, I would suggest that all archaeologists carry a flask of some brand of spirituous liquor when they go on a dig. I regret to say that it works more wonders than a smile and soft words.

PHOTOGRAPHS
PART 1

A GFC digging in the early 1930s

ARCHAEOLOGY
of Central New Brunswick

George Frederick Clarke

C Cover or title page of GFC's 1946 monograph

a. birch box decorated with porcupine quills, Woodstock Reserve, St John River

b. old decorated birch box, Indian Reserve, St John River

1 Birch-bark boxes

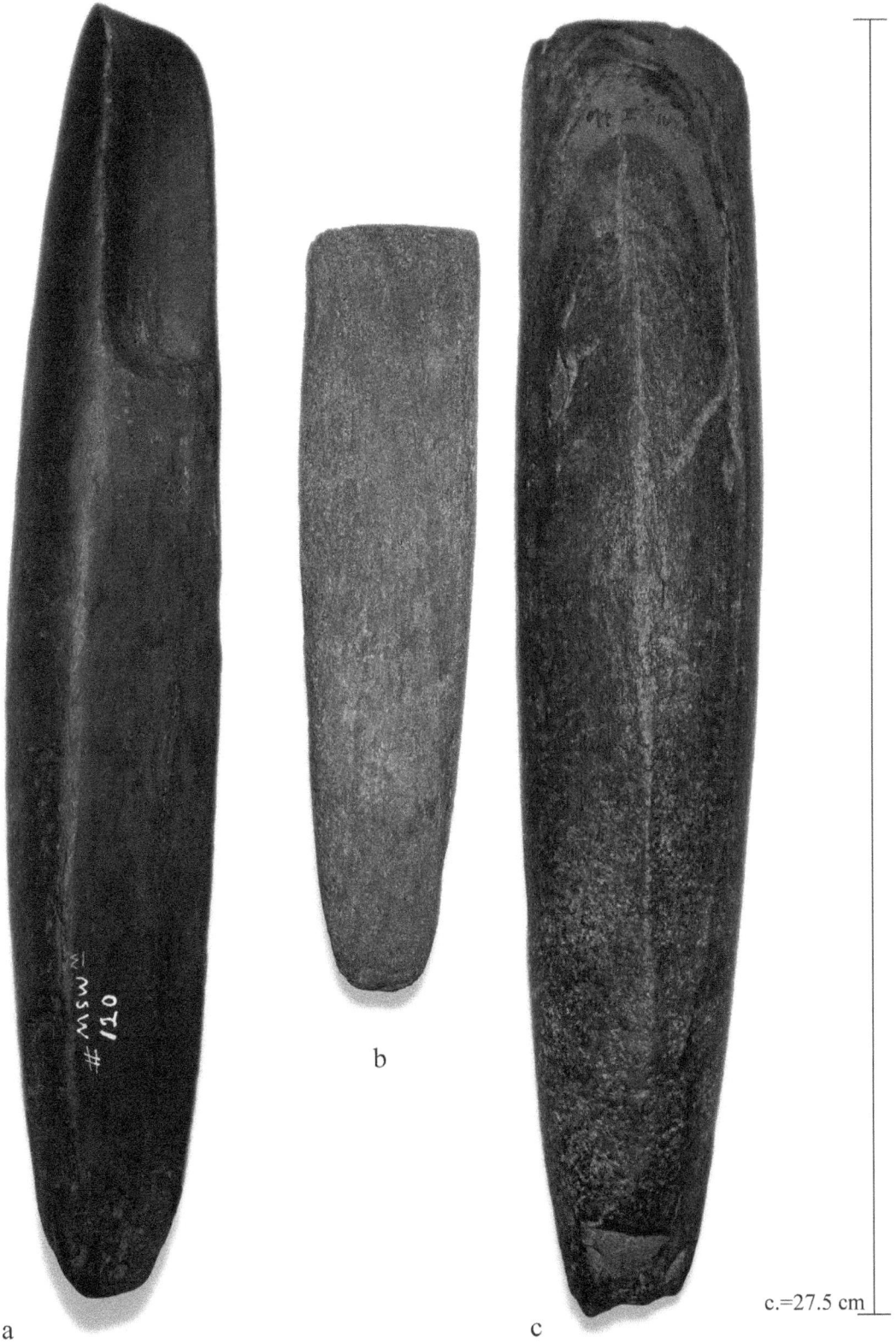

2 Gouges

a. Miramichi; b. Three Brooks site, Tobique River; c. from flat opposite Eel River, St John River

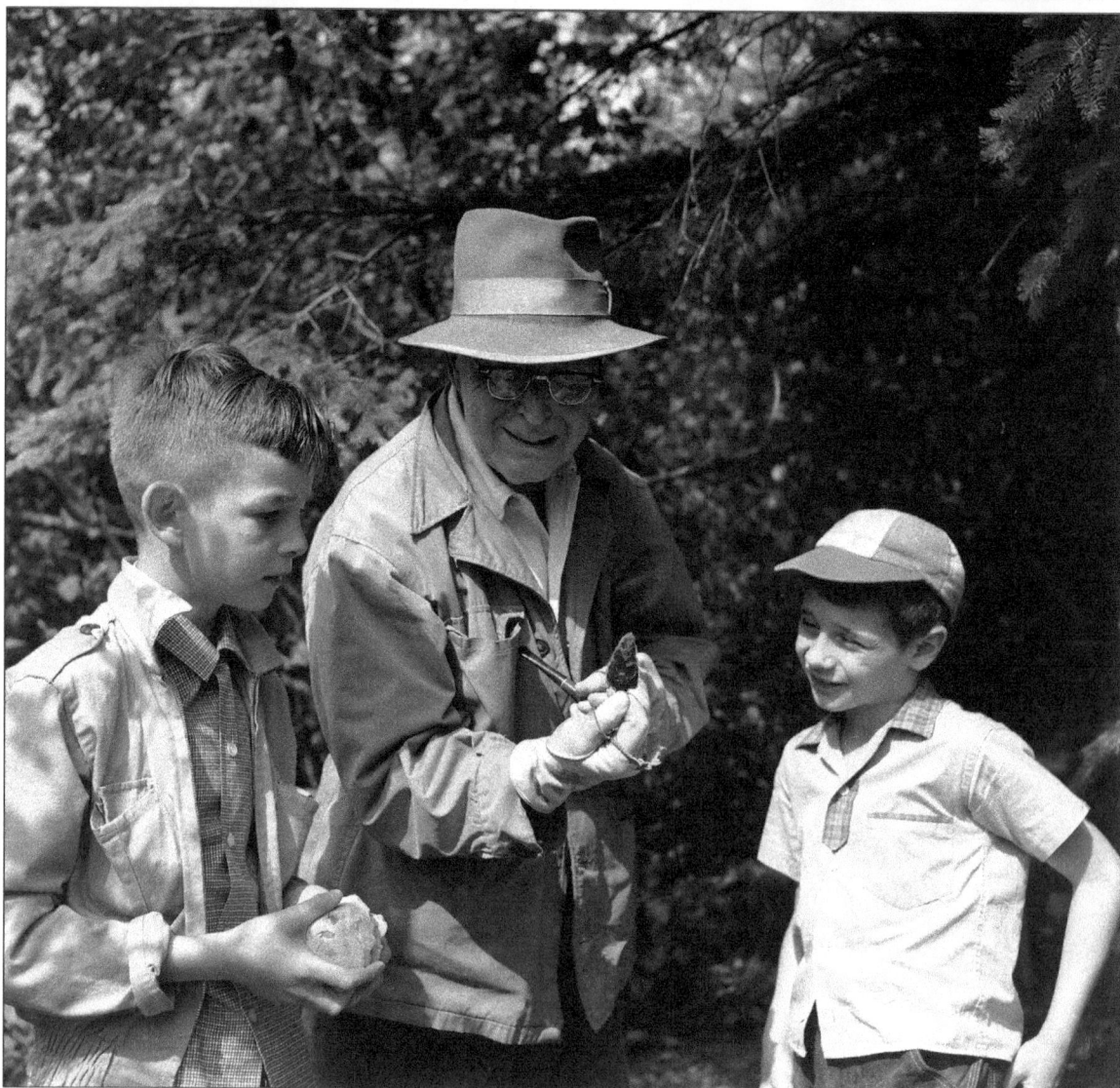

3 GFC, Stephen Homer and Garfield Saunders (left in bottom photograph) arrowheading, 1961 or 1962

5 Large knife of argillite, Medoctec, St John River

6 Scrapers, knives, spearheads

a. scraper, St John River; b. scraper from New Mexico; c. spearhead, St John River; d. milky-quartz knife, Forks Main S.W Miramichi River; e. chert knife from Lane's Creek site, St John River; f. triangular chert knife, Wapske, Tobique River; g. milky-quartz knife, Forks; spearhead, Medoctec, St John River

8 Noel Moulton, c. 1914

9 Knives and chisel
a. Slate knife, Grand or Chiputneticook Lake; b. slate knife, Phillips Flat, opposite Eel River;
Δ160c. chisel, Forks, Main S.W. Miramichi; d. knife, Bristol, St John River

24 cm

10 Big stone axe, Phillips Flat, St John River

14 Base of stone fireplace, probably in priest's house or in the old chapel itself;
(circa. 1717 or earlier), excavated 1964

15 GFC in the fireplace trench, Medoctec, 1964

a

b

c

d

e

f

g

h

i

j

k

l

m

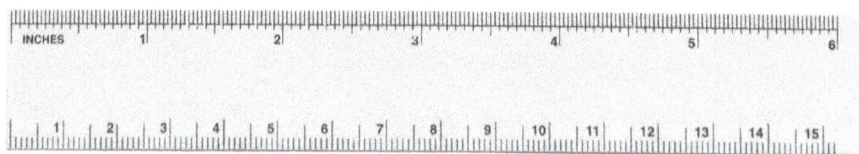

16 Series of scrapers, different sites

18 Knives
a. Chert knife, Tobique Narrows; b. unfinished knife or spearhead, Noddin's Flat, St John River;
c. large triangular shape knife, Bristol, St John River

19 Knives

a. Knife, St. John River (McGuire site); b. knife or spearhead of reddish jasper, with
white streaks, Grafton, St John River; c., d., e. and f. knives from Bristol, St John River

a   b   a=18.2 cm

20 Spearheads, Bristol, St John River

a

b

21 Adze and spearhead
a. adze of very heavy, dark stone, Nictau, Tobique River;   b. spearhead, Bristol site, St John River

15.2 cm

22 Large chert knife (could also be used as spearhead),
Bristol, St John River, actual size. GFC used this artefact on the
cover/title page of his 1946 monograph.

CHAPTER 7
MALISEET BUT NOT ETCHEMIN

For more than three hundred and sixty years historians have continued to perpetuate Champlain's error, that all the native tribes from the St John River to and including the Kennebec were *Etchemin*. Some writers have placed them no farther than the Penobscot; one as far as Boston. It is high time to straighten out the matter. The name is also rendered *Etechemin* and *Estechemin*. I shall, to make for less confusion, use the word *Etchemin*.

The tribal units which extended from Port Royal, (in that part of Acadia known today as Nova Scotia) to the Kennebec, are often referred to by Champlain and other historians. Included are the Souriquois (Micmac); the St Croix Indians, known as Passamaquoddies; the St John River Indians (Maliseet); the Penobscot Indians on the river of that name, and the Kennebec Indians on the river Kennebec.

Doctor W. F. Ganong, in his *Introduction to Chamberlain's Maliseet Vocabulary*, says: "The references to these Indians (mentioned above) in the works of the early explorers throw much light upon their customs. Champlain (*Voyages 1613-1632*) refers to them frequently, and groups all the Indians from the St John to the Penobscot as *Etchemin*. Lescarbot, *Histoire de la Nouvelle France*, devotes several chapters to them, and he likewise calls all the Indians from the St John to the Kennebec, *Etchemin*. Father Biard (*Relation of 1611*) describes them, as does De Laet in *Histoire de Nouveau Monde* (1640), both using the name *Etchemin* precisely as does Champlain. Denys: *Description Geographique and Histoire Naturelle* (1672) gives several chapters in his work to them, and applies the name *Etchemin* to all the Indians between the St John and Boston. But," goes on Ganong, "the first writer who actually lived among the Maliseet (of the St John River) was Villebon, governor of Acadia (1690-1700) and he applied the word Maliseet (*Malicitae*) precisely as his predecessors did the name *Etchemin*—to all the Indians from the St John to the Penobscot inclusive... The words *Etchemin* and Maliseet are therefore equivalent... The word *Etchemin* is by Maurault translated *men of the snow-shoe skin country;* but others find in it *good canoemen*." (W.F.G.)

There is considerable ambiguity in the foregoing paragraph, for not all of Villebon's predecessors confined the so-called *Etchemin* to the area "between the St John and the Penobscot inclusive". For Champlain, who voyaged along the coast of present day Maine, in 1605, and again in 1606, wrote: "So far as we could judge, there are few Indians on this river (Penobscot) and they also are called *Etchemin*." And again: "The tribe of Indians at Kennebec is called *Etchemin,* like those at Norumbega."—(Penobscot). It will have been seen that Lescarbot also extends the *Etchemin* to the Kennebec.

I have one other early writer: Charlevoix. "Formerly," he says, "all the Indians in the country from Port Royal, in Nova Scotia, to the Kennebecque (Kennebec) river, were known under the name Maliseet or *Etchemin.*" The late Fannie Eckstorm, in *Old John Neptune* (1945) remarks: "His, Charlevoix's use of the word Maliseet as even in his day the equivalent of *Etchiemin,* is important." And further on: "In old times Etchemin, who speak Maliseet, occupied the Maine coast from the Kennebec eastward, and also the Penobscot valley."[36]

Pierre François Xavier de Charlevoix (1682-1761) became a Jesuit priest, and from 1705 to 1709 taught at Quebec. After going back to France, he returned and wrote a history and description of New France—the result of his travels and observations in America.

Charlevoix, of course, had access to Champlain's and Lescarbot's writings and maps, and should have quoted them correctly, and not placed the so-called *Etchemin* at Port Royal. As for Maurault's translation of the word *Etchemin* as *men of the snow-shoe country,* and of others who found in it *good canoemen,* both are too ridiculous for comment!

We have seen, then, that some early historians have termed all those Indians *Etchemin* who lived on the St John, the St Croix, the Penobscot and the Kennebec; that others have placed these socalled *Etchemin* from the St John to the Penobscot inclusive; and yet others have given them a wider range; and a later writer, Mrs Eckstorm, places them from the Kennebec eastward. And other modern writers continue to soberly set down the name of all these people as *Etchemin.*

But in using the word *Etchemin* as a tribal name, all the writers are wrong. They may have been, and probably were, all Maliseet (from the St John to the Kennebec inclusive and spoke the same dialect), but not *Etchemin,* except that the word in its uncorrupted form collectively means human beings. Our Maliseet Indians have no knowledge or tradition of a people called *Etchemin.* To be short, the word is a corruption of the word *O-skitchin* or *Es-tig-in,* which simply means a *man* or *men* to distinguish them from other forms of animal life or objects, according to Rand.

Recently I read that the Micmac word *Ulnoo* or *Ulnu* means a Micmac Indian. It does. But more than that. "Although it is now the term for an Indian, its original meaning was the same as the Latin *homo,* and signified a man as distinguished from all other animals or objects."

Ganong: Monograph series (p. 164), says: "Of the origin of the word *Etchemin* used for the Maliseet by Champlain, it is, I believe, a form of the word *O-ski-tchin,* applied by the Maliseet to themselves, and constantly used by them in combination as *Ok-tchin-men-ek*—Indian Island." Peter Paul rendered it to me: *Skigin-owe-Munek.* Professor Ganong was nearest to the true meaning of but failed to grasp its whole signification:

---

36 Eckstorm, Fannie Hardy. *Old John Neptune and Other Maine Indian Shamans.* Portland, Maine: Southworth-Anthoensen Press, 1945. She was an ornithologist, folklorist and historian of the Penobscot Indians. Her letters include an amused and amusing account of meeting Tappan Adney in 1945.

that it not only means an Indian, but any human being as distinguished from other animals or objects.

When Champlain made his voyage along the coasts of what are now New Brunswick and Maine, he had as interpreter Chkoudun, chief of the St John River Indians, who had a few French words, and it seems probable that, when he asked who the St Croix, Penobscot, and Kennebec natives were, he was answered "*Es-tch-in*" (men), and that he corrupted it into *Etchemin*. It is significant that Chkoudun couldn't interpret the dialects of any of the other Indians beyond the Kennebec; and this very fact seems to confirm the statement of the early historians, that all the natives from the St John to the Kennebec were Maliseets and spoke the same language.

I have gone into this matter at some length in order to set right future historians. But this similarity of language is not so today, despite Raymond's assertion that the Indians who are now scattered over the St John River, the Penobscot and the Kennebec "readily understand one another's speech." For during historic times both the Penobscot and Kennebec tribes were augmented by several Mohegan or Mohican Indians from near New York; while in 1646, Father Gabriel Druilettes, of the Jesuit mission at Sillery, near Quebec, went to the Kennebec country, invited thither by converted St Francis Indians (made up of Montagnais and other converts *who had been* at Sillery). These facts alone would make for a mixed dialect among the Maine Indians. On the other hand the Maliseet of the St John River, their brethren the Passamaquoddy, as well as the Micmac, were more homogeneous than the Indians to the westward. As a result, their language has retained its more primitive form uncontaminated by borrowings from other tribes. As Powell says: "The author has everywhere been impressed with the fact that savage tongues are singularly persistent, and that a language dependent for its existence upon oral tradition is not easily modified. The same words in the same form are repeated from generation to generation, so that lexical and grammatical elements have a life that changes very slowly. This is especially true when the habitat of the tribe is unchanged."[37]

Moreover, I have been assured by several St John River Indians that they cannot understand the speech of the Penobscot, who, in early times, spoke the same dialect!

That Father Rasle, priest to the Kennebec in the mid-eighteenth century (as well as many other French writers), made errors in translating the Indian dialects is borne out by what Peter Paul recently told me about the priest's dictionary. Peter is a Maliseet of the Indian Reserve at Woodstock, and is at present assisting Professor Karl Teeter, of Harvard—a specialist in Indian dialects—to compile a work on the folklore and customs of the Maliseet.

Father Vetromile has said that Rasle compiled a "*perfect* dictionary of the eastern Indians," but Vetromile later made many errors in his own work on the Indian tongue, so that his estimate of Rasle dictionary should be taken with a grain of salt.

As three examples of Father Rasle's errors, I quote the following from my friend Peter Paul. First: Rasle asked an Indian the name of a cedar tree, apparently pointing to

---

37   Powell, J.W. *Indian Linguistic Families of America, north of Mexico. Seventh Annual Report of the Bureau of Ethnology.* Washington, D.C.: Government Printing Office, 1891, p. 141.

one. He was answered "*Sko-ksk-us.*" Rasle thought it was the name for any tree, and so wrote it down as such. Second: Rasle saw an Indian putting a cricket on his fish hook, and asked him its name. The Indian replied *Wag-an*, which means bait for fishing. The priest thought it was the *name* for the cricket, and so wrote it. Third: An Indian had his canoe laden, and was wading with it into deeper water before embarking. Rasle asked him what he was doing. The Indian, misunderstanding him, replied: *O-la-zoo-ga*, which means he was wading. So the good father set down in his dictionary, "he is moving his belongings." A case of each misunderstanding the other, but it shows how difficult it is to correctly translate the speech of an Indian who "thinks in his own tongue, and speaks in ours, following the natural order of his own arrangement."

Oh! by the way, historians have been much at odds about the name Norumbega, said to have been applied by some old Spanish navigator to a fabulous town at the mouth of the Penobscot. Now *Nol-um-bega* (there is no R in the dialects of the northeastern Indians, and the letter L takes the place of it) simply means water that is going *up* a river—as the tide. (Peter Paul.)

CHAPTER 8
THE RED PAINT PEOPLE

When I started this work, it was not my intention to write a text book. I don't like text books. I am wholly unorthodox. I follow no beaten path, but wander at will wherever fancy takes me. I tell my story just as I would if a visitor came to my room and asked me to tell him about the northeastern Indians. But, although I roam here and there, everything is relevant to the subject in hand, and to my desire to make my story interesting to the general reader. But, if he finds certain sections boring, let him skip them and go to another chapter. Perhaps *you* won't be interested about the Red Paint People in this….

*   *   *

It was a custom for certain northeastern Indians to use powdered oxide of iron (termed red paint) on their bodies during life, as well as in the interment of their deceased kindred. These people are by some writers said to have manufactured specialized types of stone artifacts not made by other native peoples. So much has been written about these *supposedly* ancient inhabitants of the Maritime provinces and New England, that the name Red Paint has, unfortunately, been incorporated into our archaeological and other literature, which fact, as the sequel will show, has led to a good deal of confusion, and a wholly erroneous impression by the laity unacquainted with archaeological and historical facts.

"The prehistoric inhabitants of the Maritime Provinces, New England, New Jersey, New York, a part of Pennslyvania, the northern part of Quebec, parts of Ontario and Newfoundland, have been classified by the late Dr Charles Willoughby into three groups: Pre-Algonkian, Old Algonkian, and Late Algonkian." The Old Algonkian are not placed in the Maritimes. For what reason I would give much to know.

Assuming that a Pre-Algonkian people once occupied the places mentioned, one naturally wonders who they were, where they came from, and what became of them.

The distinguishing traits by which they have been classified as different from other peoples are, (as has already been said the use of red ochre in life, in their interments, and the types of artifacts found in their graves. These artifacts include stone knives, slate spears, adzes, gouges, blades and points of "Labrador" quartzite,[38] plummets (so called), slate gorgets,[39] pendants, bar and bird amulets.

But as the sequel will amply show, neither the practice of using red ochre in life and in their interments, nor the manufacture of specialised types of stone implements, already noted as diagnostic traits of these "so-called" ancient peoples, were confined to an archaic past. On the contrary, we have abundant evidence that the artifacts under discussion were made and used until quite recent times: that is, up to the coming of Europeans to this continent. And the use of red paint was practised for a couple of centuries later. In other words, I must dissent from categorical statements that a different people from those we know as Algonkians occupied the parts of America under discussion if it be based upon the types of artifacts found here, and the use of red paint. Nor was the use of the pigment confined to this country. During Cro-Magnon times in Europe oxide of iron was common in their life, and in their burials. This persisted throughout untold centuries; and the latter custom would seem irrefragable proof that they firmly believed in and prepared their deceased kindred for a renewal of life. Daniel Neal relates that the practice of painting their bodies was a common custom among the Scythians of Cangigu, and we have Caesar's recording of the practice among the Picts of Caledonia and the people of South Britain. So did the natives of Czechoslovakia, Asia, and northern Siberia.

Although we definitely know that our Acadian Indians painted their faces and bodies in post-historic times, and no doubt commonly used red ochre in their interments, we have only a few recorded evidences of this latter custom in this part of the northeast.

The late Dr Wm. Wintemburg, F.R.S.C., gives a most interesting account of one of these red-paint burials. "This grave", he says, "was discovered in 1908 by Mr Alan Tozer and his son Alwin, while removing sand from the scarped bank at the east side of a laneway, running south from the highway at Sunny Corner to the north bank of the Northwest Miramichi River, North Esk Parish. It contained about twenty stone artifacts. Some time later the son found another but smaller lot of artifacts about twenty-five feet farther north. Associated with the artifacts in each case were a few small fragments of whitened bone. Both the artifacts and bone fragments are covered with powdered cuprite.[40] Particles and small lumps of the cuprite were found scattered through the

---

38 David Black comments: "It is now more commonly known as 'Ramah quartzite' or 'Ramah chert', because the only known sources are in the Ramah Bay area of northern Labrador. The stone is light grey in colour, semi-translucent, with distinctive blue-black banding. The texture is sugary, like a quartzite, hence 'Ramah quartzite'. Geologically, however, the stone is a visually distinctive chert that is geologically unusual because it formed during the Proterozoic eon. Apparently GFC did not believe that any of the stone tools he found were made from stone that came from Labrador, but modern research indicates that the stone from which six of his artefacts were made probably did come from there. GFC was sceptical for the right reasons...he was given conflicting opinions by professional archaeologists."—email, 4 May 2016.

39 A gorget is "a flat artifact made of stone or another material and worn as an ornament over the chest."—http://www.archaeologywordsmith.com.

40 An ore of copper.

sand at the spot where most of the artifacts were found. Along with these were several fragments of two thin slate plates, with flattened faces and ground blunt edges."

Dr Wintemburg goes on to say that probably these specimens were in process of manufacture, probably into gorgets. "Although," he adds, "gorgets are rarely found in New Brunswick." There was also an awl-like artifact of native copper, much corroded. "As far as I know," said Dr Wintemburg, "it is one of only two native copper artifacts from New Brunswick… The other artifact of copper is a tip fragment of what seems to have been an awl, about one inch long, apparently of native copper, in the collection of Mr William Kesson, (of North Devon, New Brunswick) found on the old campsite about one half-mile north of the artifacts above noted." I may say here that since Dr Wintemburg wrote the foregoing, I dug up from a two-foot depth, on the Main Southwest Miramichi River, an object of native copper that bears a striking resemblance to a rabbit, which I will describe more fully later.

Dr Wintemburg adds that: "the people who buried the partly incinerated bones and artifacts above described were probably not Micmac… No specimens covered with cuprite are known to have been found elsewhere in New Brunswick. The *nearest source of cuprite* is in Albert County, one hundred miles to the southeast, but it does not seem to occur in the powdered, or earthy form, seen on these specimens."

I do not know whether Dr Wintemburg based his qualified supposition that the people who buried the partly incinerated bones and artifacts *"were probably not Micmac"*, on the presence of the powdered cuprite, or on the types of artifacts. But if it be true that the knives were *not* of Micmac manufacture, then the people who made them were scattered along the St John River, the Tobique, the Main Southwest Miramichi; and the type was a general one. I have about one hundred specimens of these knives, whole or in part, and they were associated with other artifacts typical of Maliseet and Micmac manufacture. "These triangular-shape knives" says Dr Wintemburg, "are quite rare in the St Lawrence Basin. There are only a few from Ontario in the National Museum of Canada, and in the Royal Ontario Museum of Archaeology, Toronto. But the majority are much wider and considerably thicker. They do not seem to be common in the eastern United States." He quotes W. M. Beauchamp's *Aboriginal Chipped Stone Implements,* who illustrates one of a number of triangular points, and speaks of one hundred and fifty blades from a grave in Bellona, Seneca Lake, N.Y.

My Maliseet Indian friend, Noel Moulton, told me that while his father was digging a cellar for their home, near Maliseet, mouth of Tobique River, they discovered a skeleton encased in birch-bark, and covered with a finely powdered red substance, which had an odd smell. From his description I concluded it might be red ochre.

Willoughby* quotes J. P. Howley thus: "It appears to have been their (the Beothuk) universal custom to cover everything they possessed with this pigment (red ochre); not only their clothing, implements, ornaments, canoes, bows and arrows, drinking cups: even their bodies were so treated. Small packages of this material tied up in birch-bark, are found buried with their dead."

---

*   Dr Charles Willoughby: *Antiquities of New England Indians.*

And Richard Whitbourne, who made several voyages to Newfoundland prior to 1615, writing in 1618, says: "The natives of the country have a great store of red ochre, which they use to colour their bodies, bowes and arrows, and cannowes withal; which cannowes are built in shape like the wherries[41] on the river Thames, but they are much longer, made with the rinds of birch trees, which they sew very artificall and close together, and overlay every seame with turpentine."

This practice of placing red pigment in their graves prevailing among the Beothuk of Newfoundland, of prehistoric man in New England and New York states, Asia, England, in Upper Canada; at least in two authenticated cases in New Brunswick; and of prehistoric man in Europe, as cited by Osborn[42] and others, proves an affinity of mortuary customs that opens up a subject of intriguing interest.

In *A Relation of Plymouth** by Bradford, is an account of the opening of a grave by an exploring party of the early colonists, which I shall give in full, not only because of its quaint spelling and its fidelity to details, but, more important still, because the burial was post-European, and clearly proves the old custom of placing red ochre with the dead persisted from ancient times among the Indians of northeastern America:

"We found," says the old chronicler, "a place like a grave, but it was much bigger and larger than any wee had yet seene. It was also covered with boards, so as we mused what it should be, and resolved to dig it up, where we found first a mat, and under that a faire Bow, and then another mat, and under that a Board about three quarters long, finely carved and painted with three Tynes, or branches on the top, like a crown; also between the Mats we found Bowles, Trayes and Dishes, and such like trinkets; at length wee came to a faire new Mat, and under that two Bundles, the one bigger, the other lesse. We opened the greater and found in it a great quantitie of fine and perfect Red Powder, and in it the bones and skull of a man. The skull had fine yellow hair still on it, and some of the flesh unconsumed; there was bound up with it a Knife, a Packneedle, and two or three old Iron things. It was bound up in a Saylers Canvas Casacke, and a payre of Cloth Breeches; the Red Powder was a Kind of Embalment, and yielded a strong, but no offensive smell. It was as fine as any Flower (flour). We opened the lesse bundle likewise, and found the same Powder in it, and the bones and head of a little child; about the legges and other parts of it was Bound strings and Bracelets of fine White Beads. There was also by it a little Bowe, about three-quarters long." I know of no more moving account of a burial than that of this girl-child. It proves not only a deep love on the part of the parents but a firm belief in future life.

The first skeleton, the scalp still adhered to with fine yellow hair; the iron things, including a knife, packneedle, and sailors canvas cassock and cloth breeches, prove conclusively that the interred person had been a white man. The presence of the red ochre and the mats show that he had evidently been on friendly terms with the Indians,

41 A long light rowboat, pointed at both ends.

42 Osborn, Henry Fairfield. *Men of the Old Stone Age*. New York: Charles Scribner's Sons, 1915.

* *Purchas His Pilgrims Vol. XIX* p. 438. Bradford.

and that they had given him a burial according to the practice customary with their own kindred.

The point I wish to make is this, that neither red ochre, powdered cuprite, or stone artifacts in graves, can be positive factors in determining an antiquity such as is often claimed. In simple terms, it had been quite universal practice both in England, Asia, Europe and America for unknown ages, and continued in this country until and even following the coming of the white man.

As I have already stated: when the white man came to America he found numerous nations and tribes of people made in his own form, but of different colour and language. He chronicled quite accurately their myths, customs, religion, and material culture. Beyond this, everything written about them is compiled from tradition, similarities of language, myths, mortuary customs and their material culture. That we often go beyond the permissible in our conjectures to the sensational, is to be regretted.

It has been suggested that the pre-Algonkians made no pottery; both the grooved and the grooveless axe were unknown to them.* But *pottery has* been found in Maine at the bottom of shell heaps with types of artifacts classified as pre-Algonkian. Since the latter were not supposed to have made pottery the whole picture is confusing. Dr Wintemburg has drawn attention to the same ambiguous classification in Piers' comments regarding the Merigomish shell heaps of Nova Scotia, of which more later.

Now although one writer says the ungrooved hatchet is probably not pre-Algonkian, yet another depicts several as belonging to this "so-called" culture group!

Along the St John River, the Tobique and the Miramichi, I have found the grooved as well as the ungrooved axe, arrowheads of flint and quartz, pottery fragments, plummets (so-called) gouges, adzes, and, most important, several artifacts of so-called Labrador quartzite; the latter classified by *one authority* as pre-Algonkian, and by *another* as Red Paint culture. The two terms are synonymous.

The New Brunswick artifacts have been found, some on the surface, others excavated from campsites, and cannot positively be assigned to any people earlier than the prehistoric ancestors of the present-day Micmac and Maliseet. It is possible that earlier people lived here. On the other hand, the ancestors of the Micmac and Maliseet, found here on the arrival of the French, may stem from a quite archaic past, and the double-pointed blades, stemmed spear-heads, or poniards,[43] quite widely distributed along the St John and Tobique rivers have been left by them. But any attempt at classification into separate culture groups would seem to the present writer to be futile as well as deceptive.

Recently I read an article which referred to: "A people equipped with stone gouges, ground slate cutting tools, plummets, and bone harpoons, who in our postulated archaic

---

43 A poignard, or poniard, is a long, lightweight thrusting knife. The word has gradually evolved into a term for any small, slender dagger.—Wikipedia.

---

* Ritchie, "Archaeological manifestations and relative chronology in the Northeast," in: Frederick Johnson, *Man in Northeastern North America* (Papers of the Robert S. Peabody Foundation for Archaeology, Vol. 3), Robert S. Peabody Foundation for Archaeology, 1946.

time period worked their way southward from the Maritimes and the St Lawrence valley into New England, New York, and in diminishing numbers much farther south."*

Now this concept, at least to me, appears wholly untenable for the following reason: Although we find adzes and gouges in quite large numbers in Micmac territory of Nova Scotia, and along the coast of Northern New Brunswick, adzes, gouges, plummets, ground slate cutting tools, and bone harpoons are remarkably scarce in the valley of the St John, the Main Southwest Miramichi, and the Tobique. In all my excavations along the St John, I have only unearthed eight gouges, a dozen adzes, half a dozen ground slate cutting tools, four plummets, and know of but one bone harpoon—dug up by Mr Bert Shaw on his farm a few miles above my home town of Woodstock—and a bone spear I dug up a few years ago at the Big Clearwater site on the Main Southwest Miramichi River. Gouges are actually more plentiful on the river Tobique—a tributary of the St John River—but to date only half a dozen have been found on one of the most important campsites, Three Brooks; a gouge near the mouth of Tobique, and an adze at Nictau, sixty miles up the Tobique River from its source; while of three campsites I excavated on the Main Southwest Miramichi, I only found one gouge, one slate spear, two adzes, and one plummet.

If then, a people who used the implements cited by Mr Ritchie occupied the valley of the St John River, one would expect to discover more evidences of their distinguishing culture traits! The inference is, that the Indians of these specific areas used the artifacts in question only sparingly; or else, in their hypothetical migration to New England and adjacent parts, took the most of their tools, ornaments, and other implements with them.

Mr Wendell Hadlock, director of the Abbe Museum, Bar Harbor, Maine, sent me some pamphlets containing articles he had first published in *American Antiquity*, from which he kindly gave me the privilege of quoting anything I wished. Accordingly I quote two paragraphs: "At Indian Island, Maine, a lead shot of the size used in the early colonial period muskets, was found in a grave with five plummets, three translucent quartzite spear points, and three adzes. That this shot was buried with the other grave goods, or was on the body of the dead person was borne out by the fact that it was found completely covered with red ochre. A few feet from this find was another object made of iron, fashioned to the human likeness of a bearded human head, with a ring in the top, which might have been suspended from a cord. As in the case of the shot, this ornament was buried with other typical Red Paint artifacts, and completely covered with red ochre." At the conclusion of his monograph Mr Hadlock makes this significant observation:

"It may well be that many items thought to be of Red Paint origin are in reality examples of fine workmanship by eastern woodland Indians."

The present writer is most grateful to Mr Hadlock for his permission to use the foregoing excerpts, but cannot refrain from wondering why he differentiates between eastern woodland Indians and Red Paint!

Since writing the foregoing, I have read an article by Mr Frederick Johnston, Department of archaeology, Phillips Academy, Andover, Massachusetts, published in *American Antiquity* for October 1937, and delivered before the S.A.A., Washington, Dec.

---

* Willoughby, op. cit.

29th, 1938. I take the liberty of quoting the following paragraph, which seems to add particular emphasis to what I have been trying to say: "Previously I have attempted to show that we lack, almost completely, data from large and apparently significant areas in New England. It is true, also, that the excavation and research which has been done to date is very incomplete. I regret to say, in addition, that a number of inaccuracies and important omissions have produced results, particularly in the development of theories, which are extremely untrustworthy."

Swift would most certainly have applauded Mr Johnston's clarity of style.

Professor Arlo Bates is responsible for the name "Red Paint People," which is the group classed by the late Dr Willoughby as Pre-Algonkian. The late Warren K. Moorehead, in his report on the archaeology of Maine,[44] devoted much of the subject matter in his book to the culture of these supposedly Pre-Algonkians, which he, too, terms "The Red Paint People," due not only to the types of artifacts, but more specifically because red ochre was found in their graves, and patinated many of the objects. In a note Mr Moorehead said: "This is not the only feature however, which distinguishes them from the ordinary Indians of history and tradition. They also have their peculiar types of artifacts."

Both of the foregoing statements are incorrect. The presence of red ochre in the "graves" opened by Dr Moorehead (which contained no skeletal matter), *does not distinguish them as different from the ordinary Indians of history and tradition,* and many of the artifacts attributed to the deceased people *are widely distributed,* and have, moreover, been in use within the last three hundred years!

Dr Moorehead, on p. 150 of his *Archaeology of Maine,* refers to J. P. Howley's volume: *The Beothuk or Red Indians, the Aboriginal inhabitants of Newfoundland: and after stressing the dissimilarities between the Beothuk implements and those objects taken from Red Paint* graves, makes this astonishing observation: "And above all, the red Paint is missing from their burials." This despite Howley's statement that small packages of this material tied up in birch bark are found buried with their dead.

On the other hand, Dr Charles Willoughby is careful to say that "red ochre was in universal use by the Beothuk, found in most pre-Algonkian graves, in old Algonkian graves, and used also by the Algonkians in general."

Frederick Johnston, in his "Problems surrounding the classification of certain complexes in New England" says: "I explained at the meeting in Rochester last June that there is in existence no factual evidence supporting the several direct statements that these deposits (Red Paint) are very ancient. In fact the contents of some of the cemeteries suggest affiliations with cultures which are of no great antiquity... There is no dependable stratigraphic sequence of culture complexes which included the Red Paint types of artifacts, and so we are forced to depend upon the distribution of surface finds and the somewhat dubious association of these finds with types supposed to belong to other complexes. This procedure, unsatisfactory though it is, removes the aura of mystery and the curse of sentiment from the facts, so enabling us to see them clearly. We have come to a point where it is necessary to stop and attempt to introduce some order into this apparently chaotic condition."

---

44   Moorehead, Warren K., *Archaeology of Maine,* The Andover Press, 1922.

But if it be true that these actually *were* all graves discovered so plentifully in New England, one would naturally suppose them to be of much greater antiquity than the remains found in the Oftnet grotto, on the Oftnet, a small tributary of the Danube, northwest of Munich. For the Oftnet grotto contained thirty-three well-preserved skulls, belonging, according to Osborn, to the Azilion-Tardenosian times—about ten thousand years before our era. But we must remember that certain soils rapidly cause decomposition of skeletal matter, and as Dawson points out: "The decayed condition of burial mounds is well known to be a criterion of very uncertain value."[45]

To sum up: When one finds this red pigment associated with skeletal remains, as noted by Howley and Osborn, and as recorded by Wintemburg, the latter analysed and proved to be powdered cuprite; or the Emmerson and Sullivan cemeteries in Maine, the first of which contained 55.4 per cent and the latter 57.43 per cent of ferric oxide, as related in a paper by W. B. Smith, quoted in W. K. Moorehead's *Archaeology of Maine* p. 152, we know that it is so. On the other hand, we do not positively know that all these congeries of implements discovered during excavations, turned out by the plough, or picked up as "surface finds," were all actually mortuary offerings, without more positive evidence than has been produced up to the present time.

Even Dr Moorehead makes an astonishingly qualifying statement on p. 38 of his *Archaeology of Maine.* He says: "There were sixty or more deposits of ochre, *or of soil discoloured* red." (The italics are mine). Farther on in the same paragraph: "As was observed at Captain Hartford's, not a single trace of human skeleton was to be discovered in any of these graves."

A grave was accidentally discovered in July of 1947, by some workmen digging a cellar beneath the old court house below the village of Oromocto, on the St John River. Portions of a skeleton, presumably that of an Indian, an iron tomahawk, said to be of French make, some pieces of iron, shaped like chisels, and an unshaped bit of iron bar, were found with the bones. Above the interment, between six and eight inches, was a line of red about an inch deep. Some twelve feet or more distant another small deposit of reddish substance was found; but in this latter case no bones nor artifacts. The find created a good deal of interest, was chronicled in the St John *Telegraph Journal,* and some local archaeologists, with a knowledge of the so-called "Red Paint Culture" of Maine, adduced from the Oromocto find that it was evidence that the St John River Indians were descendants of the former people. As a matter of fact, I visited the scene at Oromocto, talked with the workman in charge, who found and reported the bones, and was told by him what I have related above, namely, the reddish substance was not in contact with the skeleton.

From the evidence then, it was a post-European burial. The reddish substance was six to eight inches above the bones. It is not positively known whether it was red ochre, or the residue left by a fire made over the grave with white pine wood.

Finally, to the present writer it would seem that the term "Red Paint People" as applied

---

45   Dawson, John William, *Fossil Men and Their Modern Representatives*, London: Hodder and Stoughton, 1888. Subsequent quotes from Dawson are probably also from this book.

to a so-called early group of Indians, and written about by so many archaeologists, is actually a misnomer, or at least misleading, since to the student, as well as to the average lay reader, its application suggests that the custom of using red pigment in interments was alone peculiar to this "so-called early people," when it is an established fact that it was a quite universal custom both in Europe, England, Asia and America. And the cognomen "Red Paint People" should either be deleted from our archaeological literature, or else applied to all peoples, as well in prehistoric as in certain historic periods.

"If then," as Dawson has pointed out, "we are to make any two-fold division of prehistoric man, it must be upon some other basis than the types of his artifacts." Let me amplify this: If we are to make any two-fold division of prehistoric man, it must be upon some other basis than this use of red paint!

As I have previously suggested, the diverse opinions regarding the antiquity of prehistoric man in America, as well as in Europe, and the many classifications and distinctions attended by trivial detail, or hair splitting, on the subject of his material culture—that is in most respects basically similar—makes for a resultant confusion in the mind of the student and the general reader that is most regrettable. There is nothing like good, wholesale argument on any subject; but the student in particular, all too frequently jumps to conclusions coloured by extravagant supposition, aggressive dogmatism, or just plain romance. Sometimes all three of these.

CHAPTER 9
ARTIFACTUAL CONFUSION

Few countries, if any, contain more evidences of prehistoric man's handiwork than does North America. We unconsciously walk or drive over them every day of the week. Not only rivers were his highway, but trails often paralleled their entire course. His portages led from lake to lake, over heights of land to other waters, wherever fancy or necessity guided his nomadic footsteps; and all these places he gave names in his descriptive and euphonious dialect. And this euphonious dialect is particularly noticeable in the Maliseet or St John River Indian. I maintain that it is the most musical of all Indian tongues.

The wind-blown sands of Saskatchewan have revealed countless arrowheads and other artifacts, left on innumerable campsites by prehistoric and even post-historic man as he followed the buffalo to their feeding grounds.

The St John River and its tributaries are a mine of different coloured stones, whose adaptability to take a conchoidal or clam-like[46] fracture he was quick to discover. He didn't have to barter for these stones as did many other tribes. He used the diverse materials he found at or near his camping place. He was pre-eminently a worker in stone, and, so far as I have been able to discover, seldom used bone for his artifacts.

*   *   *

I do not like gardening, but I like the fruits gardens produce. Some years ago, in mid-May, my wife suggested that I spade up and plant the usual variety of seeds in our small plot of earth we call our vegetable garden. I mildly protested, and she said: "If there were arrowheads in it, you'd make no objection." I admitted the truth of the gentle thrust, and did the necessary spading, raking. and seeding.

The following spring I repeated the chore, and picked up a stone arrowhead, two or three broken knives, and several flint flakes. I showed them to her and charged her with sowing them for the express purpose of exciting my interest in gardening. She resolutely denied the charge, and looked so innocent it was difficult not to believe her; but I recollected that all women are daughters of Eve, and that all men are gullible sons of Adam, so for the time I reserved any further comment regarding her innocence or guilt.

---

46 Conchoidal fracture "describes the way that brittle materials break or fracture when they do not follow any natural planes of separation. Conchoidal fractures often result in a curved breakage surface that resembles the rippling, gradual curves of a mussel shell."—Wikipedia.

Then two or three years later, our town council requested the privilege of building a road across the rear of our small estate.[47] Since the road would be fully two hundred yards distant, beyond a thick growth of trees, I gave them permission to do the work, and a bulldozer quickly made a highway over what had been wild land since the retreat of the glaciers. The following year, while walking over the road (which hadn't been hard surfaced), I picked up a knife of red jasper, and more than a handful of flint flakes.

So Indians had actually camped on our land, and I have absolved my good wife from my charge that she had "salted" our garden plot.

*   *   *

There are two schools of thought among American archaeologists; those who make the claim for independent invention of artifacts, and those who favour, with equal dogmatism, the transmission of culture traits from Europe, Asia or both. Years ago Lord Avebury[48] gave it as his opinion that the simple arts and sciences were evolved at different times, by different tribes and in different parts of the world.

To categorically state the contrary; that at some remote period man manufactured stone artifacts of war and chase, and for his domestic economy, and that this knowledge was then transmitted from one tribe to another over vast distances, is to assume that the inventive genius of early man stemmed from one central focus. Did it? We don't know. On the other hand, given certain mental capacities and necessities, it is only natural to suppose that widely separated peoples evolved the simple arts and sciences as suggested by Lord Avebury. As for the American scene, it is my personal belief that when the earliest Mongoloid immigrants entered America, as well as those who arrived later, they were acquainted with the manufacture of stone and bone implements, perhaps the art of weaving, the moulding of rude pottery vessels, the construction of the bark canoe, very probably the snowshoe, in some form; and that they continued to make the same types they had known in the Old World. But, as some of the people dispersed over the country and formed new units under conditions more favourable to material culture development, they gradually achieved a more varied lot of implements than those who continued a hunter-fisher-woodland life; although I believe they never surpassed, and perhaps never equalled, the finely chipped implements of those tribes who depended practically wholly on the chase.

This more diversified or richer culture was especially observed in the warmer areas, or where agriculture was more diligently practised, which fact made for a more settled sedentary communal existence, and "is one of the requirements of art in its broader

---

47   About 1945.

48   GFC mentions Avebury several times. The book he read is probably: Lubbock, John (Lord Avebury), *Pre-historic Times, as Illustrated by Ancient Remains*, London: Williams and Norgate, 1865. David Black comments: "This book was a standard text, published in seven editions between 1865 and 1913. It was reprinted frequently up to the 1960s. Lubbock introduced the terms 'Paleolithic' and 'Neolithic' into archaeology (he was named the first Lord Avebury in 1900 and that is the author attribution used in the 7th edition)."

sense."[49] But whatever their remoter origins, it's a fact that, for the most part, the diverse similar types of implements of bone and stone scattered over North America from Newfoundland to the Pacific are in the same degree, the same diverse similar types as found in Europe, Asia and the British Isles. Thus we cannot, in this cultural aspect at least, dogmatically assert, as was done a few years ago by an American writer, that the artifacts found on this continent "bear a distinctive American stamp which sets them off from the cultures of the Old World."[50] He should have said: *Several of the American artifacts have a distinctive stamp unknown in the cultures of the Old World.*[51]

Several years ago I had a visitor in the person of a Mr Tweeddale, a former New Brunswicker, but for fifty years living in British Columbia. He had visited the great Fraser midden, had done considerable archaeological work covering many years; and, making a comparative analysis of the flint implements in my collection, he said that every one of them might have been picked up in British Columbia, Alberta, or Saskatchewan.

As the diverse peoples of the Old World have enjoyed periods of peace, so have the Indians of North America. Thus trade between widely dispersed tribes was of common occurrence. There was a traffic in corn that extended from the Hurons to the Montagnais of the St Lawrence as far as Tadoussac. There was extensive traffic in finished flint objects such as arrowheads, spearheads and knives between those who lived near, and those more remote from, suitable rocks of chert, obsidian,[52] jasper, and the wide quartzite family. Marc Lescarbot tells us that in times of peace the Micmac of Nova Scotia trucked for wampum beads[53] with their more southerly neighbours, the Armouchiquois (eighty leagues[54] distant) on the coast of Massachusetts Bay. And Champlain, returning to France from his first voyage to the St Lawrence, tells of meeting a party of Indians, between Tadoussac and Gaspé, who were on their way to trade arrowheads and moose meat with the Indians of the interior for beavers and martens.

Thus, an archaeologist digging up stone implements at Tadoussac or other areas on or contiguous to the St Lawrence, might be tempted to say that they were made by these peoples, when actually they had been the product of natives hundreds of miles distant. The natural rocks of Connecticut are sandstone and slate, but artifacts of quartz, chert, and even of obsidian (whose source is two thousand miles distant) are there. Trade?—Of course! Therefore it is difficult, if not wholly impossible always to differentiate tribes of Indians by their archaeological remains, save, doubtless, the Iroquoian peoples—since throughout unnumbered centuries there was a continual fusion taking place in America

---

49   Source not found.

50   Source not found.

51   The sense is a trifle obscure here. GFC is criticising the American writer for making a statement about *all* North American artefacts instead of limiting himself to *several*.

52   "A naturally occurring volcanic glass… Obsidian is hard and brittle; it therefore fractures with very sharp edges, which were used in the past in cutting and piercing tools."—Wikipedia.

53   "Beads of polished shells strung in strands," used as currency by some Native American peoples.—www.thefreedictionary.com.

54   385 km.

as in Asia and Europe wrought by the intermixture of tribes by new immigrations, the absorption of weaker by more powerful units, and by confederation of several linguistic groups for the purpose of withstanding aggressive neighbours.

*   *   *

There persists the belief among some people that chipped artifacts, such as arrow points, knives and spearheads, were first heated in the fire, then cold water dropped on them which caused flakes to fall from the surface. Such, of course, is incorrect. The Indian chose suitable stones he knew from long experience had a fracture focus. Thus, with a hammer stone of another material, he struck the chosen flint rock a succession of blows which cracked and separated either thick or thin flakes. Then, still using percussion, he proceeded to roughly block them into a shape more conformable to the implement he wanted to fashion. Finally he placed a piece of rawhide on a block of wood for an anvil, and using a sharpened deer antler, or elongated stone picked up from the beach, he placed the smaller end against the side of the flint, and holding it at an angle of about forty degrees, struck the top sharp blows either with a beach stone or a block of wood. In this manner he successively struck off flakes, and the implement partook of the required shape he had in mind. This obtained, he did what is called secondary chipping along the edges of the piece, thus giving it a saw-like appearance, and made for a more effective cutting edge. I have several arrowheads and knives with this secondary flaking so minute that it could have been done only with the incisal or cutting edge of a bear, beaver, or some other animal tooth.

There was also another technique used to produce the finished artifact: The worker held the piece of flint stone in his left hand and pressed against the edge with an antler or stone flaker; this caused flakes to fall off, either large or small as required. Then the secondary flaking along the edge was, I believe, accomplished by using the incisal edge of an animal's tooth. I may say that by using the simple percussion method—that is holding the flint stone in my left hand, and striking the edge sharp, quick blows with a hammer stone, I was able to manufacture a reasonably good knife.

David T. Smith tells (but I had heard it before) of families of flint knappers in the eastern counties of England who made flints for flint-lock guns until the trade declined. Then they started making arrowheads and scrapers for farm hands to sell to budding archaeologists. But these were not the only gullible ones. A British museum was taken in for a long time, and had several of these arrowheads they had prized as beautiful specimens of prehistoric workmanship. Eventually the hoax was discovered and the objects discarded.

I know of a young school teacher (who spent his vacation at Washadamoak Lake) who made some of the most perfect arrowheads I have ever seen. We do not know how long prehistoric man lived in New Brunswick before the coming of the European white race. Nor do we know if there ever was an occupancy by an earlier people than the Micmac and Maliseet, nor how long the latter were here.

Mr H. T. Smith, *Ontario Anthropological Series* 119, p. 2, says that the archaeological specimens from Nova Scotia, or from the Maritimes in general, are not of great variety, nor of a very high order of technique and art, as compared with those from New York, Southern Ontario, Southern Manitoba, or Southern British Columbia. "This condition," he says, "suggests poorer people, sparser population, or a shorter period of occupation, if not all of these conditions."

Although I accept Mr Smith's statement regarding the limited variety of specimens in the Maritimes, as compared to a greater variety in the remote places he mentions, I must dissent from his inclusion of New Brunswick artifacts as inferior in technique to those from New York and the other regions he specifies. Evidently Mr Smith did not see, or was unaware of, the beautiful adze and gouge blades made by the Micmac of Chignecto, now in the Fort Beausejour museum. The specimens of chipped implements in the Provincial Museum at Saint John and many I have found, compare favourably with, and are often superior to, the same types in Harvard Museum, Chateau Ramezay, at Andover, Massachusetts, and from collections I have seen depicted as coming from Ontario, New York, Manitoba, and British Columbia. Perhaps Mr Smith saw only broken and inferior specimens found in shell heaps which were only resorted to at certain seasons of the year. I have seen photographs of stone implements recently found from interior campsites in Nova Scotia, and it would appear that there is the same diversity of type and workmanship as exists all over the country.

Piers, writing of archaeology in Nova Scotia, states that no palaeolithic or very old objects have been found there.

The term palaeolithic, as here used by Piers, is one that has led to much confusion, since it suggests inferior or very crude types of artifacts. I wonder—and doubtless the reader will wonder—if Piers meant the lower, middle, or upper palaeolithic stone culture. For it is the middle in which we get the very finest blades ever executed during the Solutrean period—approximately 25,000 years ago—and which have never been excelled.

I would suggest, without being dogmatic in the matter, that when prehistoric man first arrived in America, his best work had reached a stage when nothing better could be consummated. However, as I have said before, there were, and always have been poor or indifferent craftsmen, just as there are indifferent artists, carpenters and practitioners of other arts and crafts. On the other hand, ideal workmanship in the chipping industry was often conditioned by the type of stone the craftsman found to work. As Dawson says: "The Micmac resident in, or visiting, Prince Edward Island often had to use crude arrowheads made from quartzite pebbles of Triassic conglomerate, though in Nova Scotia they (the same people) employed beautiful weapons of agate[55] and jasper." I have ample evidence that the same differences exist in parts of New Brunswick.

And Dawson goes on: "American investigations show that the people who used the best stone implements for some purposes also used the rudest, and even naturally shaped stones for some purposes, so that out of any American village site one could pick up a collection of palaeolithic and neolithic implements." You see, even Dawson uses the term "palaeolithic" without making any distinction between the middle, upper, and lower

---

55   "A cryptocrystalline variety (with a crystalline structure so fine that no distinct particles are recognizable under a microscope) of silica, chiefly chalcedony, characterised by its fineness of grain and brightness of color."—Wikipedia.

Period during which he produced the very crudest of implements, and the middle and upper Solutrean, when he had perfected the chipping industry to the point when it was impossible to do any better.

Some years ago I saw depicted in an English magazine, a representative collection of stone implements in the British Museum. All but three in the twenty-one pieces have their counterparts in New Brunswick; and this is yet more evidence of how difficult it is to differentiate tribes by the types of artifacts found on their camp sites.

Doubtless claims and counterclaims regarding man's antiquity both in the New and the Old World will go on ad infinitum with the usual hair splitting. But should it happen, as happen it may, that the atomic bomb, or some later product of man's ingenuity, shall destroy most of the human race, and all the libraries and archives dealing with the past and the present, one can readily imagine future archaeologists combing over the rubble heaps along the Hudson, the Thames or our own St John River, and writing learned dissertations on the apparent number of centuries that elapsed between the manufacture of a recovered model T. Ford and a Rolls Royce engine!

I don't believe that the Indians in New Brunswick made dugout canoes as did the Indians of New England from beyond the Saco to Virginia. The stone gouge then, was most probably used here exclusively for the fashioning of wooden bowls and other utensils. Few of these wooden bowls have survived in New Brunswick, but they *were made here* as well as in New England. Willoughby mentions a wooden plate eleven inches in diameter which was obtained from the Passamaquoddy Indians (of the Maliseet tribe), and preserved, as those found among the Micmac, for use in the well-known Indian dice game.* I have seen one beautiful specimen on the Tobique Maliseet reserve, made from burly birch, and said by its then owner to have been handed down from generation to generation for more than three hundred years. There is another used for the Indian dice game at the reserve below Woodstock. This game is known by the St John and Tobique river Indians, as *al-tes-tug-inuk*, which will be described more fully later on. According to the late Rev. Silas T. Rand, the Micmac played the same game. It was called by them *Altestakum Omkwon*.† Sir Alexander MacKenzie, on his journey to the Arctic in 1793, said of the Indians he met: "Two young men being engaged in one of their games, a dispute ensued, which rose to such a height, that they drew their knives. The game which produced this state of bitter enmity is called that of the platter, from a principal article of it... The instruments of it consist of a platter, or dish, made of wood or bark, and six round or square but flat pieces of metal, wood, or stone, whose sides or surfaces are of different colours. They are put into the dish, and after being shaken for some time together, are thrown into the air and received again into the dish with considerable dexterity; when, by the numbers that are turned up of the same mark, or colour, the game is regulated. If there should be equal numbers, the throw is not reckoned: if two, or four, the platter changes hands."

---

* Sir Alexander MacKenzie *Journey across the N.W. Continent of America* p. 257.

† Rev. Silas Rand "Micmac Indian Legends."

This game, with but minor differences, is the same as that played by our prehistoric Maliseet and Micmac Indians, and is known to but a few of the older people of this day.

According to Bradford, Josselyn, Morton and others, as quoted by Willoughby, "the Indians of New England made many wooden bowls, trays, and drinking cups." Morton, in his *New England Cannan* says: "These are disposed by bartering one with the other, and are but in certain parts of the country made, where the several trades are appropriate to the inhabitants of those parts only."

Since these bowls, trays and drinking cups were of necessity made with gouges, adzes, and scrapers, they were contemporary. That is, both the wooden receptacles, and the tools used in their manufacture, can be positively dated as in use by the Indians as well before as following the arrival of the Plymouth Colonists in New England, and the French in Acadia and Quebec. Very probably their manufacture was the survival of a very old art.

Numerous types of scrapers, made from many different materials, are found in great numbers on all campsites. Some are large and long, many of medium size—no bigger than an inch at the widest part; yet others no longer than a thumb nail. (See Fig. 16, p 64.)

It has been claimed that the bow and arrow was not known to early man in America, and efforts have been made to date its discovery, or evolution. This postulates an antiquity for prehistoric peoples in America that has no basis for proof beyond the romantic wish to make it seem so. Man used the spear thrower in historic times on the west coast, and in quite recent times our own northeastern Indians used a type of stone thrower.

In *A Relation of Plymouth* (*Purchas, His Pilgrims*, p. 325) the Indian arrow shafts were some headed with brass, others with Hartes horne, and others with Eagles clawes.

It is interesting here to quote from Roger Ascham. Ascham was born in 1515 in Yorkshire, and in 1544 wrote his famous: *The Booke of the Schoole of Shootynge*. The quaint phraseology and spelling of many of the words is most revealing of the era in which he writes, as is the fact that he mentions several heads for tipping arrow shafts: "The men of Scythia," he says, "used heads of brasse. The men of Inde heads of yron. The Eithiopians used heads of a harde sharpe stone, as both Herodotus and Pollux do tel. The Germanes, as Cornelius Tacitus doeth saye, had theyr shaftes headed with bone, and many countreys both of olde tyme and nowe, use heades of horne."*

The skilled arrow-maker must have been a respected, busy and much consulted member of his tribe. One can imagine him exempt from all other labours, even the toils of the chase, bartering his beautiful productions for game, fish and corn. Moreover, I feel that the best examples of chipped artifacts were made by old men who had spent the greater part of their lives at the craft. Save for one arrow point and a knife made from sheet brass, and a bead presumably from pewter, most of my St John River finds have

---

* Tacitus: (about 54-117 A.D.) *Roman Histories and Victories.* One of his three principal works is an account of the German tribes along the Rhine. Herodotus: (Greek Historian 484?-425.) Travelled extensively in Egypt, Palestine and Asia Minora. Called the father of History.

been manufactured from bluish chert, chalcedony,[56] milky and translucent quartzite, crystal, red and black jasper, six artifacts of so called Labrador quartzite, a few pieces of slate, and in the case of some found at Shiktehawk, of a black, mottled flinty stone.

Stone knives are perhaps more plentiful than arrowheads on most campsites, though scrapers often outnumber both. The arrowheads used in the chase (several of which doubtless missed the mark) were not recovered, and it is likely that many of those remaining on campsites after the Indians acquired firearms, were used by boys for target practice.

Gyles, in referring to a winter hunt, wrote that the party of eight or ten Indians he accompanied had only two muskets on which to rely to keep them from starvation. Since he fails to mention bows and arrows it would seem that their use had been discontinued.

*   *   *

It has been stated by a recent writer that the snowshoe of the northeastern Indians was a late development in their economy; that formerly they subsisted by ice fishing, and that the moccasin, toboggan and bark canoe, bark baskets and several other objects of their material culture were evolved after they had learned how to make snowshoes.

The foregoing is almost too ridiculous for comment, and coincides with dozens of other such extravagant claims with which some writers on primitive culture and customs have thought necessary to burden us. I would ask the proponent of these fantastic ideas what the Indian would use on his feet if he didn't make moccasins in some form? He certainly wouldn't go barefoot in the dead of winter in a temperature that must often have dropped to 40° below zero, as it occasionally does even in the present era!

Are we supposed to believe that he only subsisted on fish? As for the birchbark canoe, it is my opinion that he knew how to construct them before ever he migrated from Siberia, although I don't insist that this is so. It is also conceivable that he had evolved some sort of snowshoe. He came from a Siberian climate that is very severe; a country of tundras—vast tracts extending inland from the Arctic coast and frozen for the most part of the year.

With the snow six or more feet deep (as I have seen it in our northern woods) how would the Indian gather firewood without some sort of snowshoe on his feet? A toboggan was necessary. Would our writer have us believe that the construction of the snowshoe was the *magic sesame* that opened the door of the Indian's intelligence, which revealed to him the other objects of his material culture, as our writer not only suggests, but dogmatically asserts? That before this snowshoe complex his intelligence was on a level with that of the Peking man!

Away with such nonsense. It is this sort of snap judgment; this assumption of omniscience, mentioned in the first chapter of this book, with which I am impatient.

---

56   "A cryptocrystalline form (with a crystalline structure so fine that no distinct particles are recognizable under a microscope) of silica, composed of very fine intergrowths of quartz and moganite… It has a waxy luster, and may be semitransparent or translucent… The most commonly seen colours are white to gray, grayish-blue or a shade of brown ranging from pale to nearly black."—Wikipedia.

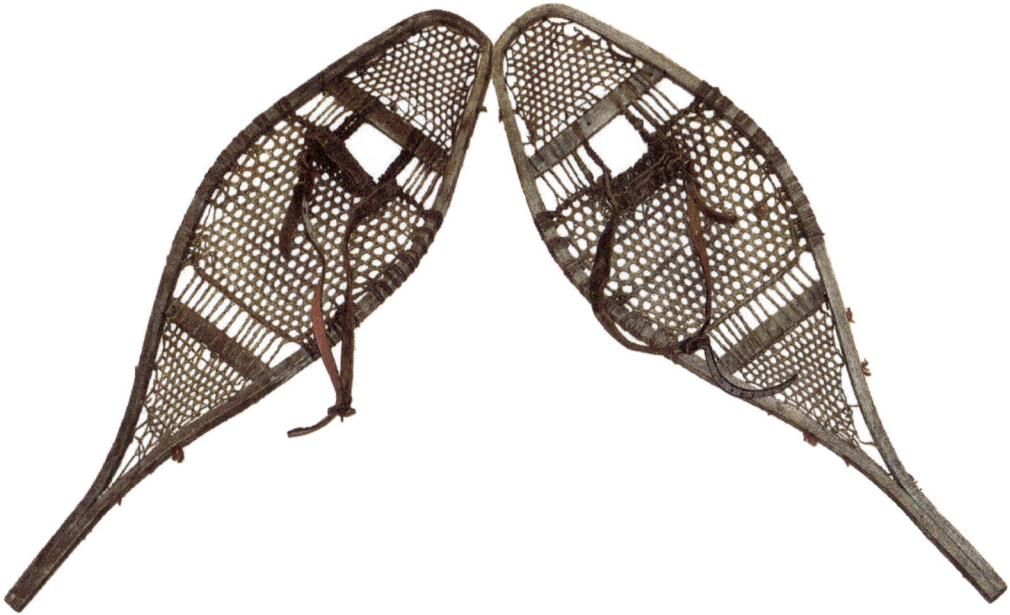

17 Child's snowshoes made by Noel Polchies c. 1925

*   *   *

I have a pair of Maliseet snowshoes (Fig. 17, p 93). The frames are filled in with strings of caribou hide. The mesh is very close together in contrast to that of the modern snowshoe which is almost as large as the gill nets used to catch gaspereaux. This latest snowshoe is yet another example, among many others, of imitating the Indian and falling short of his perfection. Oh, of course the modern snowshoe is pretty; it catches the eye, but it cannot compare in utility with its old-time Indian counterpart. For it will readily be seen that the Maliseet snowshoe, with its small mesh, would be more resistant to snow, and prevent the wearer sinking as deep as he would were he wearing its modern prototype.

Fifty or sixty years ago, caribou hide was still used and preferred because it was more resistant to snow-water than were moose and deer hides, thus less liable to "bag". When caribou became scarce and finally disappeared, the Indian was compelled to use moose, deer and calf skins for his webbing, but preferred horsehide when he could get it, since it more nearly possessed the qualities of caribou hide.

CHAPTER 10
THE SHIK-TA-HAWK SITE

It's odd how accidental meetings with people (or are they accidental? I am somewhat of a fatalist) often set in train a sequence of events that fit into a picture like the different coloured segments of a mosaic! A chance meeting with an art dealer; an introduction to a beautiful young lady in a railroad coach; a talk about fishing with a brother angler I had never before met, nor had I known of his existence; a book read by a native of South Africa. And—but, a book the size of this would hardly contain all the events that followed chance meetings with widely separated people during my long life of almost eighty-three years.

Thirty miles north of Woodstock, at the upper end of the village of Bristol, the Big and Little Shiktahawk streams vent into the St John River.

There is an old legend among the Maliseet that at this place two chiefs—one a Mohawk, the other a Maliseet—fought together all one afternoon, and that finally the Maliseet killed his opponent. Hence the name *Shiktahawk,* or more correctly *Sixtahaw,* which, translated into English, means "I killed him." If he had killed two, or more, it would have meant *Sixtahawk*: the letter K making the plural. However, the name has been corrupted to Shiktahawk and even, of late years, to Chick-a-dee-hawk.

Between the Big and Little Hawks (as they are often termed by local residents) and below the old Ferry road, are an upper and a lower flat or terrace flanking the St John River for about three or four hundred yards. The upper terrace is bounded on the east by the Canadian Pacific Railroad and the provincial highway. About three hundred feet westward, on the river side, this upper terrace ends, and the terrain slopes downward some twenty feet to the lower terrace. A couple of hundred yards beyond its northern or upper extremity, the ice-cold waters of the Big Shiktahawk meet the St John and form an excellent salmon pool, where hundreds of the silver beauties congregate during July, August, and early September. The Big Shiktahawk reaches backward to within a few miles of the South Branch of the Main Southwest Miramichi River. The present highway road leading from Bristol to Foreston and the aforementioned South Branch follows practically the same route as the ancient portage used by the Maliseet of the St John to reach the Miramichi waters.

It is reported that, during a fishing trip taken by Lieutenants Davenport and Rowan, of the 62nd Regiment stationed at Fredericton in 1859, a portage was made from near the mouth of the Shiktahawk to the South Branch of the Main Southwest Miramichi, and that Gabe Atwin, their Maliseet guide, carried his bark canoe on his shoulders the whole twelve miles, putting it down only twice while he took a brief rest.

Some few years ago I was told that in a field, half way to Foreston, is or was an enormous maple tree, and that the Indians, on their way over the portage, always stopped here, set down their canoes, and, while they rested in the shade of the wide-spreading foliage of the maple smoked their pipes, then, refreshed, took up their burdens and went on. I was told that finally the owner of the farm sold out and moved to another part of Canada, but that when he deeded the property, he inserted a provision that this ancient tree never was to be cut down. It must always remain as a resting place for both Indians and whites going over the portage. It's a pretty tale, and I hope true.

Because of the existence of this ancient portage, and on account of the rare salmon pool at its western extremity on the St John, I had long since decided that the terraces between the two "Hawks" would be a natural camping ground for the prehistoric Indians. But for years it had been in grass, and I hadn't had the courage to ask the owner if I could dig there. But on the 27th of May, 1932, I was going by motor to fish salmon on the upper Tobique River, and noticed that the upper terrace had recently been ploughed. Being with friends I couldn't then stop to inspect it.

On Sunday afternoon of June 4,[57] I went alone to the place. In the meantime it had been harrowed and rain had fallen. I began walking back and forth over the whole length of upper terrace, my head bent, my eyes fixed on the brown soil, and saw hundreds of big and small spalls of chert and cracked beach stones, sure evidence that men of the stone age had camped here over a long period of time.

Presently I was joined by four or five bare-legged youngsters. One of them, a lad of eight or nine with blue eyes, freckled face and carrot coloured hair asked me: "Did you lose something?"

I answered no, then told them that a long, long time ago Indians had camped here; that they had made arrowheads, spearheads, knives, axes and other things of stone, and I was searching for any they might have left or lost.

They were at once intensely interested. They fanned out on either side of me, and scurried back and forth like a flock of sheep, picking up rocks they brought to me and asked; "Is this an arrowhead?" "Is this a stone axe?" So it was difficult for me to concentrate my eyes on the ground. They chattered like magpies. I was alternately amused and annoyed at their intrusion, but not for worlds would I have sent them away.

One of them informed me that they had been on a trip to Houlton, Maine, and were returning to their homes in Caribou, Presque Isle, or Fort Fairfield, (I can't recall which) and had had car trouble. "Dirt or water in the carburetor," he added with a great show of indifference, "and the garage man—" he pointed diagonally across the railroad track and the highway road—"is takin' it apart to find the trouble."

They wanted to know my name, where I lived, my age, what I did for a living; if I was married; if I had any kids. Then they darted away and returned with more rocks— many of them chipped chert and quartz. I would gladly have parted with five dollars if each

---

57   June 4, 1932 was a Saturday, not Sunday.

of those eager eyed youngsters had found a finished specimen of Indian workmanship. But among all the scores of flakes covering the soil, not even my experienced eye was able to detect even one crude scraper.

Finally, approaching the extreme western border of this terrace, I saw that a portion of the lower terrace had been ploughed and harrowed. So down I went, followed by my companions, And, as before, we paced over the length and breadth of it. But there were only a few cracked beach stones and big spalls of flint at the base of the incline, which I thought might have been tumbled over the crest of the upper terrace by the harrow or plough. However, I persisted in my inspection of this terrain.

It wasn't long before I had evidence that the youngsters' enthusiasm in archaeology had begun to abate. Certainly there was now little to keep the spark burning. Several times they paused, gathered in a close circle apart from me, and began whispering together, occasionally stealing me furtive glances. Then one of them touched his forefinger to his brow; the others followed his example, nodded their heads, and again began whispering or talking in low tones I couldn't catch; but the import of their head-touching was as revealing as words.

Finally they again joined me, and the lad with the bright eyes and carrot-coloured hair (both of which fascinated me), said: "I—we—thought—" his mouth closed on the words with a click like the spring of a mouse trap. His face flushed to the roots of his carroty hair; even the freckles on his nose and cheeks seemed to expand and grow redder.

I laughed. "A little cracked?" I suggested. And on the instant regretted that I had put him on the spot.

His eyes reflected the embarrassment he couldn't conceal. He shifted his weight from one foot to the other, then, looking me straight in the eyes, he said: "Yes, sir; but don't blame the other kids. I thought of it first."

I could have hugged him for his candour. That wasn't the first time nor was it the last that people have thought me cracked. It's one of the penalties for being an archaeologist. Then I assured my youngsters it was quite true that Indians had camped at this place hundreds of years before white men had discovered New Brunswick and the St John River. And told them that if ever they should come to Woodstock, I'd enjoy having them come to my home, where I'd have great pleasure in showing them my collection of arrowheads and other stone objects the Indians had made.

They thanked me, and for a little while longer patiently followed me back and forth. Then one said that the carburetor should be fixed by now. I accompanied them up the incline to the upper terrace where they bade me goodbye, and off they ran, their legs twinkling over the brown soil.

For a few more minutes I concentrated on the upper terrace; but some inner voice urged me to inspect again the smaller ploughed area I had lately left. Had I not heeded that voice, it is extremely doubtful if ever I would have discovered what are probably the most important stone relics ever unearthed in this part of northeastern North America!

I had only taken two steps over the brow of the incline when I saw a long triangular blade lying on the brown earth, and picked it up. The piece is eight inches long, by two wide at the base, and heavily patinated a rich creamy colour. Evidently it had formerly belonged to the upper terrace, and been deposited by the plough or harrow at the spot I found it (Fig. 18 c, p 65).

Again on the lower terrace, I paced slowly back and forth for perhaps ten or fifteen minutes, and was about to leave the place, when to my surprise, my eyes caught the form of a large laurel-shape object lying almost at my feet (Fig. 19 f, p 66). It's a skinning knife of black, flinty rock with tiny flecks of grey. The piece is symmetrical and tapers to a point at both ends, with one end containing a small nub or peduncle like that of the fore-shortened stem of a leaf. I put it in my pocket, took my hand trowel from my knapsack, dropped to my knees and began gently probing in the loose dark loam. Suddenly I felt the point strike something that gave forth the unmistakable characteristic tinkle of flint stone. I worked carefully, and soon uncovered and lifted out a beautiful willow-shape double-pointed blade. I have known few such delightful moments. For I held in my hand a blade similar in every particular to the blades discovered seventy or eighty years ago in France, near the village of Solutré, and thenceforth designated by archaeologists *the Solutrean culture*. Similar blades have been discovered at one station in England, others in northern and southern Spain, Germany, Hungary, and near Lake Baikal, in Siberia.

But more delightful surprises were in store for me. I continued hand-trowelling, and within a couple of hours found five more artifacts—or a total of eight, that Sunday afternoon. Three were spearheads or long poniards. One of the latter had been broken in the middle, but I found the remainder of it the following day (Figs. 20, p 67, and 21 b, p 68).

Late the following afternoon, I returned and sank a trench eighteen inches deep anterior to the deposit found the previous evening, then began hand trowelling, and, still in the loose loam, though at different depths, I found nine more artifacts. Some are shown on Figure 19 c-f, p 66. There were two spearheads or poniards and a knife not shown.

Before dark set in I put up a tent I had brought with me near the Ferry road and a spring.

I arose at daybreak, breakfasted, and returned to my digging. By eleven o'clock I had unearthed ten artifacts, nine of them within four feet of the previous lots. None of the nine was at a depth of more than six inches (Fig. 9 d, p 60).

Beyond this area I dug ten or twelve feet, but found nothing save a few scattered firestones and an occasional piece of flint. Now I dug my trench eighteen inches deep at right angles to the former deposits, and at ten inches, in dark sandy loam, found a very large knife, 6 in. long by 3 at the base, which is chipped at an obtuse angle, so that the artifact could be used for a scraper as well as a knife, as in many similar artifacts. It is of grey chert; unusually large flakes had been struck off the face by the artificer, with what one can well describe as effortless sureness (Fig. 22, p 69). There is also secondary chipping along the edges and the rounded base. This small area produced, in all, twenty-eight artifacts of extraordinary beauty. None were patinated, due to the fact that they had been buried, therefore not subject to the sun's rays.

Strange to relate, I had not noticed until now that the ground had been seeded with oats, and, rather dismayed at the discovery, I went to the owner and confessed what I had done. Much to my relief he laughed good naturedly, and said he "guessed I hadn't done much damage." I thanked him and asked if he would allow me to do a little more digging after his oats were cropped. He readily gave his consent, and added that the lower terrace had only been ploughed once before in a hundred years.

I returned to the place October 7th, after the oats had been harvested, in company with Mr William Kesson of Fredericton, N.B., and readily found where I had dug four months previously by landmarks I had observed, consisting of a big boulder on the west side of the river, an elm tree southwards, and a spruce tree to the eastwards. We dug a trench eight feet long and one foot deep parallel with the river, and worked for two or three hours, during which, at ten inches, I found a beautiful double-pointed blade.

We found nothing more until we had reached the base of the ascent leading to the upper terrace, where we found fourteen whole pieces, some double-ended, others with rounded bases, and three broken portions which exactly fitted the broken knives I had found June 4th. All the fourteen pieces were on the same level, ten of them bunched together side by side, ten inches below the top soil. Three about sixteen inches from the ten; one three feet, opposite Mr. Kesson. There are three peculiarities worth noting about the small area in which the forty-three pieces were found: there were no arrowheads, scrapers nor any other objects in the lot, and the artifacts were quite different in shape and material from some I later found on the upper terrace. There was neither bone, ashes, nor flint chippings associated with the artifacts. Perhaps the greater depth of the last deposit was due to the fact that it was at the incline, and subjected to periodic deposits of sandy loam washed down by rains following the ploughing of the upper terrace immediately above; or when the ground was first cleared and the stumps upended, new soil from above would almost certainly find its way to the bottom. It is possible that all the artifacts, or at least those bunched together, were mortuary offerings, although as said above we discovered no evidence of bone.

I do not for one moment affirm that the Bristol blades (and a few other of like pattern found in New Brunswick), were made contemporary with those discovered in France and other European stations; but I do affirm that the European blades, and some found in England, and at Lake Baikal in Siberia, are so similar to the Bristol blades that it might have been my pieces that Osborn depicted in his book.*

The following summer, the late Dr Wintemburg, of the National Museum, Ottawa, visited the province, and being informed of my find by Mr Kesson, he came to Woodstock in company with Mr Kesson and the late Mr R. P. Gorham. After viewing the specimens— of which he made line tracings—he said that during more than thirty-five years of field-work he had never found any quite like them, was at a loss to place them in their true culture group, but thought they might be archaic Algonkian. He made the remark, which at the time I thought strange, that I would never find any others quite like them. But although it is quite true that have not found any similar large blades, I have dug up some very small double-pointed ones; and, as said before, know of others of large lozenge shape from Three Brooks, and one I dug at the Narrows on the Tobique River.

---

* Osborn. *Men of the Old Stone Age.*
  See [Osborn's] Plate 20. Four were double pointed knives, and are depicted on Figure 23.

Also on the Tobique, I have found four quite long shouldered[58] spearheads, or poniards, similar to, but shorter than those from the Bristol site.

To sum up: was this distinct type found on four sites in New Brunswick, as well as in other parts of North America, a transmission from Europe or Asia at some remote period, or was it evolved in this country by people with no knowledge of the Old World forms? If the late Lord Avebury was correct in his opinion that the simple arts and sciences were independently developed by different tribes, in different parts of the world, and at different times, there is nothing more to be said on the matter. But to the present writer, it would seem that it is quite impossible to arrive at a correct answer to the problem. All I can safely do is to state the facts of their occurrences, and let it go at that. Though I can safely affirm that double-pointed blades have been found associated with stemmed and shouldered spearheads or poniards, and with blades of the rounded base type; and, on two occasions, they were found on the surface in association with triangular shape knives and arrowheads where they were turned up by the plough. Anyone seizing upon this latter fact as insufficient evidence of contemporaneity must take into consideration that a ploughshare is seldom set at more than six inches, and often less, so that deposits on the same original level, but not below, would at various times be turned up. It is my belief that frost does not disturb and throw up deposits of artifacts situated below the usual ploughing depth.

The French prototypes of these double-pointed blades were regarded by de Mortilet rather as blades of poniards than as javelin heads, and are known as laurel leaf (broad), and willow leaf (narrow). In some of these French blades, the ends are not symmetrical and contain a small prolongative, like a leaf stem, but set at an angle. This, if the reader remembers is a distinguishing trait of some of the Bristol blades.

---

58   "A type of stone point made on a blade, with a notch on one side of the base and flaked partly or wholly on both sides. Shouldered points are characteristic of some Upper Palaeolithic cultures of Europe, such as the Solutrean…"—http://www.archaeologywordsmith.com.

David Black comments:"GFC is using the term 'shouldered' in a way that is different from how it was used for the Solutrean projectile points from Europe. The Solutrean points are single-shouldered—that is, they have asymmetrical stems that are shouldered on only one side. The projectile points from Bristol and elsewhere in N.B. that GFC is referring to are doubled-shouldered—that is, they have rounded shoulders on both sides tapering to symmetrical stems (what would now be called 'contracting stems'). Thus, while the bi-pointed bifaces from Bristol-Shiktahawk superficially resemble Solutrean 'laurel-leaf' bifaces, as GFC noted, the stemmed projectile points from that site are significantly different from the Solutrean ones. This is an important distinction for two reasons: 1) It ties into the long-standing contentions in archaeological interpretation between 'independent invention' and 'diffusion', which GFC addresses from pg. 88 through pg. 103; and 2) It relates to a continuing controversy in eastern North American archaeology about whether European Paleolithic people contributed directly to the populations and/or technologies of aboriginal America."

The French blades have been observed in "five different shapes: irregular lozenge; oval, pointed at both ends...arrow-head form with peduncle[59]—doubtless for attachment of a shaft."

"The distinguishing implement of the 'high' or middle Solutrean, is the large laurel point, flaked and chipped on both sides, and attaining a marvellous perfection in technique and symmetry. Finest examples are the famous *pointes de laurier,* fourteen in number, discovered at Volgu-et-Loire, in 1873. They were found in a sort of cache, and it would seem probable were intended as a sort of votive offering, for one at least was coloured red, and all were too fragile and delicate to be of any use in the chase. They were all unusually large, the smallest measuring nine inches, and the largest over thirteen and a half inches. In workmanship they are equalled only by the marvellous neolithic (new stone age) specimens of Egypt and Scandinavia."*

By consulting Figure 23, p 128 of this book, it will be seen that the four blades have perfect symmetry, both lateral and bilateral. And, by a strange coincidence, the blade in Figure 23 a had been broken at the precise lower third portion as Fig. 121, page 339 in Osborn's book. I cite this fact not as being of any significance other than as an extraordinary coincidence. (Editor's note: More blades from the Shiktahawk site can be seen on Figure 24, c, d and g, p 129)[60]

Oh!—I almost forgot to tell an amusing incident as Mr Kesson and I were walking down the lower terrace preparatory to coming home. At this time a half barrel stood at the base of the incline and was usually almost full of water conveyed to it by a wooden gutter. We stopped beside the half barrel and I took the large blade and began washing the dark loam from its surface. Suddenly it slipped from my grasp and disappeared into the depths below before my frantic effort to retrieve it. Without pausing to roll up my sleeve I thrust hand and arm to my armpit. All I encountered was black silt—three or four inches of it. No beautiful knife blade. A strange, uncanny sensation swept over me. I felt that the spirit of the ancient owner of the blade was determined that I never would recover it. I glanced at Mr Kesson. He said, in his rich Aberdonian voice: "It might be a good idea to set the gutter to one side and dip out the water." I hadn't thought of such a practical solution of my difficulty, although I had little faith that I would ever find my precious artifact.

At any rate we removed the gutter to one side, and dipped up most of the water from the barrel; at least sufficient to allow me to explore the mucky bottom without further wetting my whole arm. Finally, after several more minutes of effort, my fingers touched one edge of the blade. I drew it up and turned my friend a face from which all fear had

---

59   Stalk. GFC does not list all five of Osborn's shapes. The sentence he quotes, from *Men of the Old Stone Age*, p 344, is: "The explorers of the type station of Solutre have discovered five principal shapes, as follows: (i) irregular lozenge; (2) oval, pointed at both ends; (3) oval, pointed at one end; (4) regular lozenge; (5) arrow-head form with peduncle, doubtless for attachment to a shaft."

60   Figure 24 is not mentioned in the text. For a description of the blades see Appendix 3, Technical Captions.

---

*   Osborn op. cit.

suddenly vanished. I sighed a "Thank God!" Kesson's lips were wreathed in an amused smile, then he said: "I'll never forget this day—the look of utter hopelessness on your face."

"Thanks," I said, "for your suggestion about the gutter."

*　　*　　*

Four or five years ago, Mr Kenyon, the stone-age expert on the staff of The Royal Ontario Museum asked me if I would show a team of archaeologists some of the campsites on the St John River. I gladly said yes. When they came, I first took them to one of the best sites. They dug for a couple of hours, then left and reported that they had found nothing. Then I took them to Medoctec and showed them the site of the old prehistoric village and palisaded fort from which they took two or three hundred pounds of flint chippings, but no finished artifacts. From Medoctec I took them to the Bristol site and secured permission from the owner to do some excavating. First I led them to the lower terrace, where more than a quarter of a century earlier I had found the Solutrean type artifacts. They sunk a short trench, dug for about an hour then repaired to the upper terrace from which, digging in a small area, they took away fully one hundred pounds of chippings, but no finished pieces. (Enough chips to pave the streets of Ottawa!)

I was much disappointed when they left the lower terrace, for I firmly believe it contains more "gold" in the form of more stone objects similar to my finds, for my digging hadn't covered an area of more than twenty by twenty-five feet. However, I am hoping that some time in the near future I may have the privilege of not only extending my former operations, but doing some digging on the upper terrace.

I feel confident that the blades I found were chipped near the site, because I found a large block of black, mottled flint that had had flakes struck off it, quite near the lower end of the terrace, a few rods from the Little Shiktahawk; and, it may be, there are deposits of leaf-shape blades and poniards on the upper terrace.

No similar blades are in the Royal Ontario Museum, the National Museum at Ottawa, the McCord, Chateau Ramezay, New Brunswick Museum nor the richly endowed Phillips-Andover Museum at Andover, Massachusetts. Dr Douglas Byers, of the latter museum (to whom I sent a photograph depicting several of the blades) wrote me that he had never seen anything quite like them from the northeast. There are three similar blades in Harvard Museum, but they came from the southwestern United States.

On Thursday, July 23, 1914, the late Dr Warren K. Moorehead, of Phillips-Andover Museum, in charge of an expedition consisting of eleven archaeological students, in six large canoes, came down the St John River and, among other places, stopped at Bristol. From his book I take the following: "Found an old Mohawk and Maliseet fort across river. Dug in same, but found nothing. Took measurements. No village site. Dug at several points along the river on high hills…"

Dr Moorehead's statement that he found an "old Mohawk and Maliseet fort across (the) river" is possibly a typographical error since he must have well known that the Mohawks were age-old enemies of the Maliseets. He probably meant Micmac-Maliseet fort; though how he could determine such is beyond me to understand. He probably repeated some tradition told him by some of the local residents. But if Dr Moorehead had dug anywhere on the two terraces (the natural terrain for a prehistoric campsite) he would have discovered one of the most extensive along the whole river.

Professional archaeologists have been taught to trench scientifically, but many of them haven't been taught to accept advice from amateurs. So I'd like to have a dozen young men trained in scientific trenching, and chain them to the Bristol site for two whole months, of course with sufficient food, drink, and the privilege of sleeping at least eight hours each night.

*   *   *

On one occasion when I was sinking some test pits on the upper terrace at the Bristol site a tall rangy man approached me and said: "Diggin' for gold?"

I explained my object. He glanced at me pityingly, watched my efforts for perhaps fifteen minutes longer, then walked across the flat in the direction of the small railway station.

A week or so later I was talking to the station agent, during which he said, after a preliminary chuckle: "You remember that fellow who visited you last time you were here?" I nodded, and he continued: "Well, he came into the station on his return, and pointing out the window said: 'D'ye see that fellow digging over there? He digs a hole a foot or so deep, then fills it in, and digs another. Oh...he's quite harmless...not dangerous, but all the same he's got a wicked lookin' spade with a helluva sharp blade.'"

Then there was the aged man who, on another occasion, came to where I was digging and asked me the same question as the first, then told me a yarn about buried treasure on the opposite side of the river and a Viking galley that one night came down the Shiktahawk, and disturbed some treasure hunters (of whom he was one).[61] Finally he suggested that if I wanted odd shaped stones, I could find tons of them along the beach without digging for them.

---

61   This story is told in *Six Salmon Rivers* 4th ed., 2015, pp 103-106.

CHAPTER 11
CAMPSITE AT FORKS OF MIRAMICHI

As I have stated in dealing with the Bristol site, the old Indian portage between the St John waters from the present highway road to Foreston, follows practically the same route as the old Indian portage between the St John and the Miramichi waters. At Foreston the Indian could put in his canoe and paddle down the South Branch to the Forks, named such because here the South and North branches meet and form the Main Southwest Miramichi River. Naturally the Forks would be a camping place in prehistoric times, as it is now. For thence, on the south side, are short portages to Nashwaak, Miramichi and Napadogan lakes. And by going up the North Branch they portaged to the Waps-ke-hegan, and thence reached the Tobique River. All this vast wilderness was then, as now, a good game country, and the rivers and lakes teemed with fish.

The name Miramichi is probably not Indian. Some modern writers have said that in the Micmac tongue it signifies "Happy Retreat", but this is only a fanciful or romantic interpretation that has no basis in fact. Indeed on early maps the name is Lust-a-gouch-chick, and told at greater length in *Song of the Reel*[62] means Little Lustagouche to distinguish it from the more northerly Lustagouche.[63] Many years ago my Indian, friend, Noel Moulton, told me that his people (the Maliseet) knew them as Micmac names. Moreover, he said that in the old days his own people (the Maliseet) had hunting camps far down the river, and at Nashwaak, Miramichi and Napadogan Lakes. The latter he rendered Na-quadonis, and said there was another smaller lake which he called Naqua-don-a-sis, the *sis* being the diminutive in the Maliseet tongue.

*   *   *

On the 28th of May, 1942,[64] my beloved friend, Doctor Nelson P. Grant, general medical practitioner and surgeon, was laid to rest in the churchyard a few hundred yards from his home. Only twice before had I experienced such an overwhelming sense of loss and crushing loneliness. A part of my world had collapsed. For twenty-nine years, along with Charley Clark and Bill Kennedy, we had fished the salmon waters of

---

62   Chapel Street Editions, 2015.

63   The more northerly Lustagouche is now the Restigouche.

64   In the first editions of *Someone Before Us* this reads: "On the 28th of May, 1939." For this edition I have changed it to the actual date of Dr Grant's death, May 28, 1942.

the Miramichi, Restigouche and the Tobique. At the Forks of the Miramichi we jointly owned a small camp.

For a couple of days following the funeral I had no ambition to practice my profession. In the evenings I went to Upper Woodstock where, on a couple of acres of intervale land, he had a summer cottage. Here, on a wooden bench, we had sat the evening before his death, watched the river and the opposite hills and talked of this and that. On the third day I told my wife I was going to the Forks, for I felt that, if in any place on earth, his beloved ghost would be seated in his wicker chair on the broad verandah of our little camp, while he watched the waters of the North Branch silently gliding around the bend to mingle with those of the South Branch.

She helped pack my dunnage and filled a carton with enough food to last a week, and I set off alone. I didn't take any of my fishing rods, but I had a spade and hand trowel in the car trunk. Indeed they are almost always there.

*   *   *

For two days (save for trips to the spring to get drinking water) I remained on the camp verandah, reading or watching the river. Below me, between the cedar pilings that supported the verandah, I had dug eighteen years before, and discovered scores of red jasper flakes, a spear, an arrowhead, and several broken knives which verified my long held theory that Indians had camped here. Then, beside a small brook southwards, I had found a grooved stone axe. Other than these two places and some work in the small clearing in which our camp and two others were situated, most of my archaeological work had been done nearer home.

Shortly after lunch of my third day of my present stay at the Forks, I took a walk down the old tote road flanking the right-hand bank of the river; not only for exercise, but to get a supply of birch bark to use for kindling fire in the cook stove. I didn't get the birch bark on this occasion. The previous year a bulldozer had been used to widen the tote road a distance of four or five miles to facilitate the trucking of logs, cut by an operator for the Flemming-Gibson Lumber Company. Thus I hadn't gone more than two hundred yards from my camp when I found that whole trees of spruce, fir and hardwoods had been uprooted and tossed to either side of the road, as was the centuries-old accumulation of humus; and there, on the yellowish sandy soil, were numerous milky quartz flakes and cracked, fire-reddened beach stones.

A campsite! I retraced my steps to the camp, and soon returned with spade and trowel. First I dug a trench six feet long by one deep, in the middle of the road, and found numerous flakes of white quartz and a few of red jasper. I worked carefully towards a big spruce tree that had been upended. Its upright roots, like the tentacles of an octopus, flanked the extreme northern border of the road; its lower roots were embedded in the soil beneath; its trunk for its whole length extended over a small bit of level terrain that finally dipped at an angle of forty-five degrees to a small bogan or back-water of the river.

The line of flints ceased about four feet from the roots of the upturned spruce, but I continued to work and, slightly to the right of it, and within the area of its roots, both submerged in the soil and upright, I found a perfect arrowhead of near quartz crystal.

It was at a depth of ten inches, notched and shouldered, but patinated with a yellowish stain from its contact with the sandy loam. Later I had to scrub it vigorously with soap and water before it revealed its original translucent beauty.

This find was but a prelude to many more beautiful points, the same shape as the first but of a greyish brown chert. In all, I dug out twenty-three points, all on the same horizon.[65] (Some depicted on Figure 25, p 130.) The afternoon wore away, and I was now digging between the lower roots and hand-trowelling was more difficult, while above me projected the lateral roots. In short, I was in a sort of cave and seated on the cool earth. Soon I discovered that I was not only digging out sandy loam but large quantities of decayed wood, and that the lower end of the spruce was resting on a pine log that lay parallel with the tote road.

The mosquitoes and black flies were most annoying; the former because of their continuous and monotonous singing as they flew in clouds about my face and neck. I had long since established an immunity to their stings, but the black flies bit like bull dogs, drawing the blood. I had my flit-gun with me, and every few minutes had to spray my neck and wide-brimmed hat with the "dope". I also smoked my pipe, but all my efforts were far from sufficient to persuade the pests to let me alone; they got in my ears and at my eyes beneath my glasses; if I removed my pipe for an instant they got into my mouth. When I say that I was attacked by thousands, I am not exaggerating. I even sprayed the cave-like area beneath the roots of the tree.

When dusk began to settle over the forest the murderous black flies disappeared, but, if anything, the mosquitoes increased in number. I worked until I was no longer able to see what I was doing. As I crawled out of the cave, stood up and eased my aching back, the shrill whistle or blowing of a deer, repeated thrice, came so suddenly, so unexpectedly, so near me my scalp seemed to lift, and a chill ran down my back. Then I had only walked a few rods up the tote road when I heard a crash on my right, and for an instant dimly saw the form of a huge bear as it bounded away, looking like a loose bag of bones in a black sack, between the boles of the trees. I heard a heavy splash as it plunged into the river, if possible more alarmed than I was. I am of opinion it had been following the deer, and that I had scared it from its hoped-for prey.

The following morning I was again at the site, and noticed, on the opposite side of the log that rested on the decayed pine, a curious depression in the moss. It was about four feet in length, twenty inches wide, and some eight inches below the surrounding mossy soil. It ran slightly to the right of the trunk of the upended spruce tree and on a line with the arrowheads I had found the previous day. I carefully spaded out the moss, cut away some small cedar roots, and came on yellowish sand which was so wet I at first

---

65 "An archaeological horizon is a widely disseminated level of common art and artifacts at an archaeological site or, more usually, over a larger geographic area."—Wikipedia.GFC follows an older usage, in which "horizon" means layer or stratum—essentially, the depth at which a group of artefacts is found.
David Black suggests that he may also have used the term as a soil scientist would. Cf. Wikipedia definition: "A soil horizon is a layer generally parallel to the soil crust, whose physical characteristics differ from the layers above and beneath. Each soil type usually has three or four horizons."

thought I had chanced on an old spring hole used by lumbermen to water their horses. (I have found such on several occasions.) I began at the extreme lower end farthest from the rotted pine log, gently probing the wet muck with the blade of my spade, and soon touched something that gave the familiar tinkling sound so characteristic of flint stone. Within half an hour, within an area no bigger in circumference than a large dinner plate, I dug out twenty-five arrowheads of white quartz and two of near quartz crystal. (Some of which depicted on Figure 26, p 109.)

During the rest of the day I lengthened and widened the area towards the end or river side of the small terrace but found nothing save flakes. The following day my son-in-law, Ken Homer, came to visit me, and we worked backwards towards the rotted pine log, where beneath it, were more arrow points; one Ken found was of red jasper beautifully chipped and notched. There were no other artifacts, nor ashes, nor firestones. There was one bit of bone about eight inches long by three wide, and though much decayed, I thought it might possibly be analyzed in an attempt to discover whether it was human or animal. I laid it carefully on the top of a stump. It seemed to me possible that I had discovered a grave, for the depression was of such a nature as would result from the decomposition of a body at some remote period. Moreover, the two lots of arrowheads (I include those Ken and I found beneath the pine log with the first lot) were situated near where the head of an interred person would be, and the other lot near the feet. On the other hand, they may have been placed in the wet sand to keep them "green" (less liable to break.) The chert points, as well as those made of near quartz crystal, are equal in manufacture to the best I have seen in New Brunswick or from elsewhere. All are notched, the base slightly convex, with the secondary chipping so minute along the edges it could only be done by using the incisal edge of an incisor tooth of some animal. Digging farther up the hauling road, I found two large knives beneath five inches of tundra[66] and eight inches of yellowish sandy-loam. One of these knives is depicted on Figure 27 b, p 131.

It was now necessary for me to return home, but a week later I was again at the Forks. I got a young woodsman to sever the spruce tree in sections, which we dumped over the brow of the terrace towards the river. We cleared a space some twelve feet by ten of underbrush and small saplings, then lengthened the trench I had originally made in the centre of the roadway and worked westwards. We found nothing but a few chippings until we arrived at the southern extremity of the rotted pine log where, in black humus just below the moss, my son-in-law and I found half a dozen stone knives and a possible spearhead. Save for one knife of greyish coloured chert and a spearhead of the same material, they were all of milky quartz. Below this humus we found hard-packed sand which we dug out to a depth of two feet, and at this level I found a small object of native

---

66   David Black comments: "GFC appears to be using the term 'tundra' here to indicate a layer of forest litter dominated by mosses and/or lichens, though earlier in the book he uses tundra in the generally accepted ecological sense: 'a treeless area beyond the timberline in high-latitude regions, having a permanently frozen subsoil and supporting low-growing vegetation such as lichens, mosses, and shrubs, or a similar area found at high   elevations.'—www.thefreedictionary.com."
Personal communication, 23 September 2016.

26 Arrowheads from different sites, and, in centre, a large knife banded with brown,
from Three Brooks

copper. It is one inch long by one-half inch at the widest part, and conforms to the exact shape of a rabbit sitting on its rear end. Whether its rabbit-like shape is accidental, or whether it was made that way by intent, I know not; but, remembering that the rabbit had some special significance in Indian mythology, I consulted Leland's *Algonkin Legends* when I returned home and learned anew that according to an ancient legend, the rabbit is said to be the father of all the eastern Indians.

At the two-foot depth we also found numerous boulders weighing from three or four pounds each to as much as twenty or thirty pounds. Their use is problematical. Since they seem to be of a hard, flinty material, it is possible they were cached in the damp sand to keep them "green" for future manufacture into artifacts. On the other hand, they may have been used as weights during the making of birch-bark canoes.

Having dug to and over the brow of the declivity, where we found nothing save numerous chippings, we returned to the hauling road, and in the course of the next month sometimes alone, or again Ken with me, extended the digging to its western extremity, as well as beyond it to a thick growth of trees, then both up and down the road a distance of fifty feet. At a depth of eight inches were numerous chippings: quartz, brownish chert, and quantities of jaspery red slate, fire stones, and ashes. At this depth were a few knives, two crude adzes or chisels, and three arrowheads. One of these is of chalcedony, the second of a hard purplish material new to me, the third of translucent,

109

golden agate, peculiar to the Tobique region. On the east side of the highway I found a splendid slate spearhead. This was at the two-foot depth where with great difficulty I dug beneath the roots of a sizeable tree. At first glance the piece appeared to be of a brownish slate, but on washing it, I discovered that subsequent to its original grinding to give it sharp edges it had been partially re-sharpened, thus disclosing the original dark stone of which it had been made.

About ten feet to the right of the "possible grave" I found a deep fire pit, and in it, and scattered about within a three foot area, many pottery sherds. There must have been three or four pots, since several of the sherds have quite different decorations, some of these seem very crude. Others more finely executed in quite elaborate patterns (Fig. 28, p 132). This fire-pit was about on the same level as one excavated a few days earlier by a friend of mine from Saint John. Fifty feet distant I dug up at a depth of eight inches a very fine maul, or war club, of hard grey stone. It weighs three and three-quarter pounds, is deeply grooved, with shoulders above and below the groove. The head is elliptical in shape, the striking end flattened on one side. The time expended in its manufacture must have taken several days and the piece seems too elaborately done to have been meant for the mere driving of stakes. (See Figure 29, p 133.)

At this point, and on the left side of the tote road, is a terrace-like extension of the area that contained the large supply of arrowheads. It runs parallel with the river for about three hundred feet to a small brook and gorge. This terrace, from the side of the tote road to the declivity below, which is the eastern boundary of the bogan mentioned before, is about forty feet in depth. It is covered with second growth hard and soft woods. Beneath the tundra was a line of ashes extending practically the whole area. The ashes covered a deep layer of shale-like rocks, and within the ashes, and the upper rock layer, were thousands of grey, white, and black chippings. Because of the multitude of roots it was difficult digging, but with Ken Homer and Levi Grant as helpers we managed to explore the major portion of this terrain. However, save for four or five arrowheads, and a grooveless axe, we found nothing but chippings. Evidently it was the main workshop of the prehistoric Indians who had foregathered at the Forks.

On a high knoll opposite the Forks pool, still on the south side of the river, is a bit of terrain bisected by a "run-around" of the old hauling road. I dug here, and at four inches found ashes, fire stones, plenty of milky and translucent quartz chippings, and, at a depth of twelve inches, in yellowish sand, a pear shaped so-called plummet (Fig. 30 b, p 134). There were no other artifacts, nor any chippings of fire stone associated with it. It is similar to Fig. 24 A page 43 in Willoughby's *Antiquities of the New England Indians*.

I now have four "plummets". One a friend gave me is about four inches long, ¾ in diameter, perfectly round, of mottled grey and black granite, beautifully polished, and has a hole drilled quite through the piece at one end.[67] It is a superb piece and, so far as I know, is quite unique. It was picked up on the beach near St George, New Brunswick, and given to me by Mr Key of Sussex. It resembles L in Fig. 24, Willoughby's book, but is much more symmetrical. Yet another "plummet" I picked up from a ploughed field on the St John River opposite the Eel River, is four sided (Fig. 30 e, p 134).

---

67   Peter Paul is wearing this artefact in Figure 32, p 219.

These oddly shaped objects have been the subject for many diverse suppositions concerning their probable use. By some writers they are termed fish lures, sinkers, plummets and pendants for personal adornment. They may be any one of these. I would suggest that a possible use was that of twisting strands of the inner bark of trees, slippery elm and certain grasses and rushes, for the manufacture of mats, robes to cover the body, as well as bags and baskets, also for twisting sinews. As an experiment, I took two three-foot pieces of cord, tied one end of both to the small constriction forming the neck of the "pendant," then, holding the other ends of the cord in my left hand, I gave the pendant a sharp turn to the right. As it rotated, the two pieces of cord were twisted together more quickly than it takes to tell. In such manner two or three standards of rawhide, previously stretched, could have been twisted to make a bow-string that would be stronger, as well as last longer, than a single strand.

I have dug along the hauling road at intervals for four miles, and found plenty of temporary camp sites with fire stones, ashes and chippings, but no finished artifacts, save at Crooked Rapids, three miles below the Forks. There, at twelve inches, my son-in-law found a beautiful knife blade, shaped like a beech leaf. It is three and a half inches long, by one and one half wide at the rounded base, and is of the reddish-brown flint so common along the Tobique waters. I found half a dozen knives. We also found scrapers, and Levi Grant, a young helper, found two polished chisels of bluish-grey flint. One is the flaring type, and has a stain that looks like dried blood.

It may have been a flesher. It has a long flake struck from the back of the poll,[68] as though it had been purposely flattened for insertion in a handle. These chisels, as well as stone adzes, could have been hafted[69] in a long pole and used to strip canoe bark from birch trees. There would only be one other method I know: that is, a long piece of wood with one end sharpened chisel shape. I saw my Indian friend use this latter implement a few years ago to peel some bark we needed for mending my canoe.

In concluding this account of the Forks area, I would say that it warrants further and intensive investigation, as there are doubtless other sites—possibly away from the river, where the Indians probably camped. Naturally there would be campsites at Nashwaak lake—reached by a four mile portage—as well as on the North Branch at the mouth of Beddel brook, and at Miramichi and Napadogan lakes.

What interested me profoundly about this Forks of Miramichi site was the fact that some of the artifacts were only three or four inches below the top soil, while others were at a depth of twelve and, in the case of the native copper object, and the slate spearhead, were twenty-four inches—in yellowish sand, indicating that between at least two occupations the river had risen on more than one occasion to a height of twenty feet above normal, and deposited sand that covered up the lower as well as the intermediate level of occupation. One day in June I was at this Forks site digging quite alone, and thoroughly enjoying myself. If the reader remembers, I have recorded that I found a piece of bone and carefully laid it on top of a stump intending to take it home and submit

---

68   "The blunt or broad end of a tool such as a hammer or axe."—http://wwwthefreedictionary. com.

69   A haft is a handle. To haft an implement is to fasten a handle to it.

it to McGill University for analysis. I had forgotten to remove it from its resting place. Now, this day, I found it and put it on a fallen log a few feet from a deep trench I had sunk. About mid-afternoon I walked back to the camp to refill my spray gun with fly repellent. Harley Hannah, who had a camp a few rods from mine, was on his verandah talking to a female whose daughter and boy friend were fishing below the Forks pool. (I learned of this later.)

Back at my digging, I was working down the side of the trench with my hand trowel when the woman suddenly appeared. She cheerfully greeted me, said she was tired talking to a man who was hard of hearing, and said yes or no at the wrong time, and had to be shouted at. However, she had asked him who I was, and finally got from him my name and what I was doing down the tote road; so she thought she'd "like to watch operations and have a little chat".

Little chat! She sat down on the heaped-up sandy loam I'd thrown up, lit a cigarette, and between puffs began her "chat". It was a continual flow—like water going over a dam. Then she lit another cigarette, and the talk flowed on. I asked her to be careful with the butts because the forest was as dry as tinder.

She said "OK," stabbed the butt into the damp sand, and lit another. Her voice was like the droning of a bee in a dark hive. Finally I threw a spadeful of sandy loam on her feet, then apologized. "OK," she chirped. "No hard feelings. You're a good listener." But she got up, moved back to the log where I had cached the fragment of bone, and plumped her two hundred pound carcass upon it, crushing it in a hundred fragments.

I crawled out of the trench, walked down the tote road a couple of hundred yards, then descended the high bank to a small spring brook which vented into the river. I took a long drink, sat down, lighted my pipe, and gradually cooled off, mentally and physically.

An hour or so later I cautiously approached my digging place, determined, if she was still there, to return to the brook. But only fifteen cigarette butts, monuments to her love of the "naughty weed" (as James I was wont to speak of tobacco) stood upright in the sand, and my precious bone smashed almost beyond recognition—eloquent testimonials to her former presence.

*   *   *

One day Ken and I were participants in an amusing incident. We had dug a deep trench, and now hand trowelling along its perpendicular sides, when two little girls, aged eight and nine, came down the tote road and perched themselves on the heaped-up earth about three feet in front of us.

After a while I found a black chert scraper no bigger than my thumb nail. I turned to Ken and said: "I wonder what they (the Indians) used these tiny things for? They're too small to scrape hides." I paused a few moments, then added: "Of course they had finger nails and toe nails. They had to cut them down with something reasonably sharp." Ken nodded. One of the little girls piped up: "I bite mine off," and suiting action to the words, she grasped one of her ankles with both hands, bent it up to meet her bent head, and, the toes at her mouth, her sharp teeth went snip—snip! and the nails were severed as well as any chiropodist could do the job.

To conclude this Fork site: working with Ken, Levi Grant and for the most part by myself, it produced more than one hundred and twenty artifacts, and I feel quite sure that others remain under the ground on the south side of the river as well as the west below the mouth of what is known as the Bogan.

SITE AT MOUTH OF LAKE BROOK

About ten miles from the Forks, on the right hand shore of the Miramichi immediately below the mouth of Lake Brook, we discovered a campsite at which we briefly dug in September 1944, 1945 and July 1946. The source of Lake Brook is Miramichi Lake from which there were trails to Nashwaak and Napadogan lakes.

At this site we found, besides some knives and arrowheads, a very good celt or grooveless axe, an iron spearhead, and a stone gouge about seven inches long with a groove running from end to end; the cutting edges are quite badly marred. It was lying below eight inches of red ash which had patinated the whole piece the same colour.

On the last occasion I dug here I had with me my Indian friend Noel, and Levi Grant. We had sunk a crescent-shaped trench about ten feet from a big flat boulder six feet from the river bank, and were working towards this. Noel was about five feet on my left, Levi the same distance on my right. Oh, I have forgotten to say that Levi had run a trench directly in front of the boulder facing us. He was about to dump the boulder into this trench when Noel said in a commanding voice "Don't do that. My bird it's there." So Levi returned to his side of the crescent. We were all using hand trowels and working with the greatest care. Perhaps a couple of hours passed during which we had found a few scrapers and a spearhead of milky quartz and great numbers of chert, red jasper and white quartz flakes. Now, quite forgetting that Noel had peremptorily ordered Levi away from the boulder, I rose from my knees, dropped my trowel, took my spade, circled Noel, came to the river side of the boulder, shoved the blade of my spade into the earth and with a quick twist dumped the rock upside down into the trench. Even as I heard Noel's voice, in angry tones he had never before used to me: "You spoil my bird's nest!" I saw an arrowhead follow the boulder and drop to one side of it. I picked it up, then apologized to Noel. For a few moments he said nothing; he took a plug of chewing tobacco from his pocket, bit off a sizeable piece with his strong teeth, then: "Fifty arrowheads there I not spoil my bird's nest!" I was humbled by his broad humanity, his love of all little harmless creatures which took precedence over the buried relics of his remote ancestors. He explained that when he first began digging he had noticed a bird fly from the nest.

Yes—there had been five eggs in the nest!

The arrowhead was more deeply barbed along the edges than any I have seen. On this occasion we found, near the river bank, a deep hole half-filled with leaf mould, which we dug out but discovered nothing save some black ash and burned stones. Back from the river two hundred feet were many flint chippings. Doubtless there are other deposits across the river, as well as up the brook and at the lake itself. The area certainly merits further intensive investigation. The foregoing was written twenty years ago. Since then, while on a salmon fishing trip with Bill Gillalpin as guide, we stayed here several days, did considerable digging, found some important pieces of stone work, and caught several panfuls of nice trout from the pool directly opposite a big granite boulder that rears its flat top above the surface of the river. This was a wonderful occasion which I have dealt with quite fully in *Song of the Reel*.

CHAPTER 12
THE BIG CLEARWATER SITE

During the latter part of September 1939, and the first two weeks in September, 1940, I visited the old Indian campsite at the mouth of Big Clearwater on the Main Southwest Miramichi River. Big Clearwater is the most important branch of the Main Southwest, and according to the late Dr Ganong, heads from a large central plateau within a few miles of the Gulquac that flows into the main Tobique River, twelve or fourteen miles above the town of Plaster Rock. "Big Clearwater," as its name signifies, is a cold, clear and rapid stream, with two falls; one three miles from its confluence with the Miramichi, the other six miles up. Salmon go up in large numbers, and it is said that at the Big Falls there is an old Indian campsite." Big Clearwater is twenty-eight miles from the Forks and twenty-two miles from Boiestown.

This stream, according to Ganong, is called by the Micmac Indians *Pichiamek* on the Franquelin de-Meulles map of 1686. By the Maliseets it is known in their more euphonious dialect as *Pes-Ki-o-min-ek,* which is proof that the latter tribe were familiar with this lower part of the river, probably coming overland from the Gulquac, or down the main river as far as the "Sisters", and perhaps as far as Rocky Brook. It would also seem to indicate that the hunting and fishing areas of the two tribes often overlapped.

Mr William McInnis, of the Canadian Geological Survey, visited Big Clearwater stream in 1882, if I remember correctly, and described his observations of certain Signs near the mouth of the stream. To quote a portion of his letter to Dr Ganong: "In the angle on the left bank of these streams (Big Clearwater, and the S. W. Miramichi) there are to be seen some interesting remains of old defence works, consisting of a cellar-like excavation with elevated rim towards the Miramichi, and several smaller shelters of heaped-up large boulders extending down the bank of the river at intervals of fifty yards or so one from the other, each capable of concealing two or three men only. There was also a mound about five feet high by eight in diameter, which, through lack of tools, we were unable to properly examine. On the opposite bank of the Clearwater I dug up one large spearhead, with several broken arrowheads of quartz and jasper." Dr Ganong also quotes information given him by Mr. John Hayes, of Hayesville, as follows: "At the mouth of Clearwater is an old camping ground. There have been holes dug in the ground from ten to fifteen feet across and about six feet deep. I helped dig some of these holes out and found a number of stone axes and lots of stone arrowheads, whose colour is dark red or white. These holes are nearly filled with leaves and other stuff that has collected in them, but one can tell where they are quite easily. They have all been walled up from the bottom with rough stone..."

On the 20th of September, 1939, my companion, Levi Grant and I tented on the lower side of Big Clearwater on a little cleared spot flanking the Miramichi. We inspected and dug out three or four small holes among the bushes, but found no artifacts. There were ashes and charcoal in the bottom, and I am of the opinion that these, at least, were fire holes.

About fifty yards below the mouth of Clearwater is a small clearing fifty or sixty feet in length, by thirty in depth from the river bank to the forest beyond. There were tent stakes driven into the ground where evidently some river drivers or anglers had set up a tent. We began excavating at the extreme edge of the bank and almost immediately found, among a layer of ashes at a depth of ten inches from the surface, chippings of red jasper, white quartz, broken and whole knives and spearheads. My companion dug out half of a broken slate gorget. It had evidently been broken in three pieces. A little later he found another portion which exactly fitted the first and larger piece. When fitted together they made up two-thirds of the original artifact. It had been drilled with one hole from either side, as can be readily seen (Fig. 31 b, p 135).

According to the late Dr Wintemburg, gorgets are rare in New Brunswick. Besides the one noted above, there is one in the Fisher Memorial Library, at Woodstock, and I have two of banded slate (Fig. 31 c and d, p 135), both found by Sandy McArthur along the shore of Hazy Point, Chiputneticook Lake, opposite Davenport's Cove, whence an old Indian portage led to the Baskahegan, a branch of the Mattawamkeg, which in turn flows into the Penobscot.

To revert to the Clearwater: we had sunk our trench to a depth of twenty inches. The artifacts we found were all about ten inches from the surface in sandy loam. Below this was hardpacked sand, and, eight inches below the artifacts noted above, was a second line of ashes and firestones that contained plenty of red jasper chippings, but no artifacts.

Associated with the broken gorget were bits of broken pottery, some with a very fine decorative motif I had never seen before. Five feet from the gorget, to the left, and three feet from the edge of the river bank, I dug out a beautiful semi-lunar knife of banded agate. (See Figure 34 e, p 136.) When first found it was almost wholly red, but after a few weeks it assumed, for the most part, a milky colour. Beneath the upper portion, which was left about one-half inch thick for a hand-grip, are a series of curved bands extending about three-quarters of an inch, with the deepest part of the curves extending towards the cutting edge, which is beautifully chipped with secondary conchoidal fractures. I feel that the source of this piece was far distant, and that it was worked at the place of its discovery, since we found no flakes of this material, large or small, during intensive digging at this Clearwater site.

Six feet distant from this knife, at the same depth of ten inches, I found a spearhead or knife of very hard brownish flint, seven and one-half inches long, by two and a quarter at its greatest width. Both the agate knife, and that of brown flint, were lying in the sandy loam, and were not associated with ashes, but there were many chippings of jaspery slate. I have one similar, though smaller, found on the beach two miles above Woodstock. Both pieces are made from flint rock characteristic of the Tobique. Ten feet distant, below the grass roots, my companion found the remains of what had been a copper or brass kettle, and below it, again, lying on top of fire stones and ashes, a large stone axe of hard sandstone.[70] It is deeply grooved, and plainly shows numerous indentations where it had been shaped by pecking.[71] Near the bank, he had already found a small tomahawk. The latter is three and a half inches long by one-and-a-half inches wide. The bit had been ground to quite a sharp cutting edge. Near the poll it is indented on either edge, but not grooved across the face. Some archaeologists claim that these tiny objects, when hafted, made quite formidable weapons for striking an enemy. I have found one—but not as well made—near Florenceville, and another near the Forks of the Tobique. My own belief is that these small tomahawks were made for, or probably by, children, just as youngsters today imitate the products made by their elders. (See Figure 30 a and f, p 134.) Near the big stone axe, we found a knife at the same ten-inch depth and a small spearhead of apple-green flint I had never seen before. Some of the knives we found on this expedition in 1939 are well made, others of indifferent workmanship. The better ones compare favourably with most of those I found on the St John River and its tributaries. There were few arrowheads among the hundred artifacts.

Going down river, we dug a test pit near the base of a very ancient pine stump, and found a small scraper of that translucent quartzite of which Willoughby says the source is no nearer than Labrador, and Ritchie of the New York State Museum, suggests is probably near Lake Albanel, in northern Quebec.

Among a second growth of saplings, about one hundred feet north of our first digging, we found plenty of red jasper, or jaspery slate chippings at a four inch depth, also about a dozen whole, and several broken knives. Although we spent five days at this Clearwater site, the area we dug over did not exceed twenty by fifteen feet. From my notes I quote the following: "The whole area both above and below the mouth of Big Clearwater seems to be a rich and practically unexplored field for further archaeological research." I have heard that several specimens were found a few days ago, by an American, near the Big Salmon Falls six miles up the Clearwater.

As before stated, I again camped at the mouth of Big Clearwater in September 1944. As on the previous occasion, I was told by my canoemen who have lived all their lives at or near Boiestown—some twenty-two miles downriver—that French Acadians once lived on the flat above and below Clearwater stream. One of the above mentioned guides said that the French had only resided with the Indians for two or three years, and then departed. He stated that near the base of a high hill (readily seen from the mouth of Clearwater) and about five hundred yards from the confluence of the latter stream with the Main Southwest Miramichi, there are several graves with stones placed at the head and foot of each. I was told by another guide that in recent years a rude cross of

---

70   "A clastic (composed of fragments of pre-existing minerals and rock) sedimentary rock composed mainly of sand-sized minerals or rock grains… The most common colors are: tan, brown, yellow, red, grey, pink, white, and black."—Wikipedia

71   Pecking "involved hitting the stone with a hammerstone or pecking hammer to crush or crumble a small amount of stone from the potential artifact." — http://www.ou.edu/archsur/OKArtifacts.

wood had been placed at the head of one of the supposed graves. The same account was independently given me by my canoeman, Milburn Price of Juniper. He said he had seen the "graves" several years ago. He tried to guide me to the place but failed to find it.

It is quite conceivable that, following the Acadian expulsion from Grand Pré, the River St John, and later from the settlements at the mouth of the Miramichi, some of the French at this latter place may have made their way up the swift and tortuous river, and sojourned with the Indians at the mouth of the Big Clearwater. There is a persistent tradition that they did so. At any rate, whether done by Indians or French, the Flat, for a distance of about three hundred yards above and below the mouth of the stream, had been cleared of big timber. Save for a few sizable spruce, the area, to a depth of seventy-five yards, is covered with small second-growth hardwoods, softwoods and a plentiful supply of alder and hazel bushes. The curious circular pits, and the "smaller shelters of heaped-up boulders extending down the bank of the river" described by Mr McInnis in a letter to Dr Ganong, as "defence works," cannot, I feel reasonably sure, be definitely determined as such. On the contrary, from careful excavation of the space within these "smaller shelters capable of concealing two or three men" (I quote Mr McInnis), I proved, to myself at least, that they were fire-places. Within the area of each were the usual fire-stones, deep layers of ashes, black cinders and plentiful deposits of red jasper, white quartz and whole or broken artifacts. The only remains of European manufacture found in any of these fire-places were portions of a copper kettle, before noted, an iron spear point barbed on one side, and two concentric pieces of brass. These latter resemble the silver gorgets given the Indians by both French and English and were found just below the moss. They are pierced at either end, and in two of the holes yet remained a bit of rawhide. The inner side of these brass objects is slightly concave and covered with black ash; the obverse side was so finely polished that it shines like pure gold, despite the many years it had remained in the soil. I can think of no purposes for these pieces save that of decoration. (See Figure 35 c, p 119.) The bits of rawhide would suggest that they were attached to an upper garment, much as modern costume jewelry is worn today. Pring described some of the ornaments worn by some of the Maine Indians as "thin plates of Brasse a foot long, and half a foot broad before their breasts."

One of my canoemen, Lawrence Sweet, carefully dug out one of the large circular depressions. This depression is on the bank of the Main Southwest Miramichi about thirty-five yards below the mouth of Big Clearwater. It is five feet in diameter and walled up on three sides with big boulders; the crest, flanking the river, is slightly higher than the rear. It was filled in with leaf mould and small roots to a depth of four feet, proving that many years, perhaps centuries, had elapsed since it was last used. Beneath the mould was hard packed sand. The pit contained no chippings, ashes, cinders, nor artifacts of any kind. It *would* serve as a defence work, since its position commands a view of the river both up and down. On the other hand, it could well serve as a storage for food. It is similar in every respect to other pits, not only along the bank flanking Clearwater and the Main River, but at numerous points twenty-five, fifty, and seventy yards in the woods away from the river. I found and dug out similar pits at Burnt Hill Stream, three miles above the mouth of Clearwater; at the Forks of the Miramichi; at Rocky Brook, and the

35 Knife, pendant, metal objects
a. Large knife or meat chopper, Tobique Narrows; b. perforated pendant,
Medoctec Flat, St John River; c. metal objects, Big Clearwater, Main S.W. Miramichi

mouth of Lake Brook. In some of the holes big trees were growing, making excavation impossible. They were clean holes; that is, they contained no chippings, artifacts nor ashes. It would appear that they were cellars for food storage, described by John Gyles in his memoirs as "*Indian barns*" (1736).

There were still other depressions scattered over a wide area that definitely *were* fire holes, since they contained deep layers of blackened ash and cinders. I have wondered if they could have been fire holes around which winter wigwams were built. A fire built thus would not only be confined in a small space, but would heat the ground within the wigwam for hours after the fire had gone out. My Maliseet Indian friend, Noel Moulton, told me that on hunting trips in the dead of winter in the Moosehead Lake region, in Maine, his father cleared away the snow with his snowshoes to the bare ground, then built a great fire. When nothing but a bed of red cinders remained, they were all carefully raked to the front of the proposed camp against a back log; evergreen boughs were next placed over the warmed earth, the blankets over the boughs, and the wigwam hastily constructed—the front facing the campfire. My friend told me that the ground thus heated remained so all night.

We discovered many ordinary fireplaces at Big Clearwater—that is, large boulders arranged in a half circle. Some were close to the river bank, many others back in the woods. In most cases the soil had *made*[72] around them, and they were covered with a thick growth of moss, so that they appeared as mere mossy hummocks. It was only by striking them with a spade that we could prove them to be boulders. Within each space formed by the half circle of boulders, were ashes and flint chippings. Some contained broken knives and spearheads, but generally the whole artifacts were a little remote, that is, several feet from the fireplaces. An interesting feature, in some cases however, was that when we had removed the boulders, we discovered artifacts and chippings from four to ten inches below the soil upon which the boulders had been placed, this proving an earlier and a later occupation.

Yet another interesting formation of boulders we discovered in a small clearing about fifty yards from the Main River, in the angle above the mouth of the Clearwater. These boulders, all about the same size, had been placed in two seven-foot parallel lines about six feet apart. It occurred to me that they had been placed there by whites to hold down the sides of a tent. At yet another place, below the mouth of Clearwater, and about one hundred and twenty-five feet from the river bank, was a line of boulders ten feet long, forming a rectangular space corresponding to Number 2, figure 2, described by E.W. Hawkes in No. 14—1916, Anthropological series—*The Labrador Eskimo*.[73] A few feet distant we unearthed the broken butt-end of a knife of so-called Labrador flint, already described by me elsewhere.

When first discovered by the French, the Eskimo inhabited the northern shore of the Gulf of St Lawrence as far west as Mingan, which is, I believe, opposite West Cape, on Anticosti Island, whence, at the beginning of the seventeenth century, they were driven northward to the Belle Isle mainland by Montagnais, possibly assisted by the Micmac of Gaspé Peninsula.

Some archaeological writers have maintained that the Eskimo once occupied the Maritimes and as far south as the State of New York. This is postulated on the few spear-points, knives and arrow-points of so-called Labrador quartzite found here, and the presence in New England of the semi-lunar knife; there are few pieces of the former in Peabody Museum, half a dozen in Phillips-Andover, Andover, Mass; one knife in the collection of Indian artifacts in Chateau Ramezay, Montreal, and a few pieces from

---

72 "made" appears to be a misprint. David Black speculates that: "GFC's intended meaning is that 'soil had *formed*' around the boulders. He was certainly perceptive enough to understand the significance of this: that the boulders had been in place, unmoved, for a long period of time. This may have struck him as significant because these boulders differed in this respect from other (smaller?) fireplace stones he had observed."

73 David Black comments: "This must be a reference to Hawkes' Figure 11: Camp Circles in Labrador: 2. Oldstyle camp for the ancient double deer-skin tent, on page 62 of *The Labrador Eskimo*."

campsites in Ontario. Ritchie describes a "Killed"[74] blade found at Muskilonge Lake about eight miles east of the St Lawrence River in New York State.

I have found but eight whole and four or five broken artifacts of this material in central and northern New Brunswick, but no chippings until five years ago. At this time John McClement and I were working on the campsite opposite the mouth of Gulquac stream which vents into Tobique River twelve miles above the town of Plaster Rock. Here we dug out three quite large flakes of this "Labrador—Lake Albanel" stone, on the same horizon as hundreds of unlike material chippings characteristic of the whole Tobique River system. Later I showed the three flakes to my friend Ernest Hale, professor of Geology at the University of New Brunswick, and he said he could show me rocks of the same material native to New Brunswick: I have not yet written to Dr Ritchie about these finds. But perhaps there are deposits of this dark-banded greyish quartzite in New England, and even in New York State from which the artifacts found there were manufactured, and that their original source was neither Labrador nor the Lake Albanel region. Although, let me make haste to add, the diffusion of the finished objects of which Ritchie speaks cannot be ruled out. On the other hand, the flakes we found on the Tobique, and Dr Hale's assurance that the material is native to New Brunswick, would seem irrefragable proof that they didn't originate anywhere but here.

What we know is only a fraction of what we don't know, and it behooves professional and amateur archaeologists alike to proceed with caution in making categorical statements which time may disprove.

To sum up: the numerous fire-holes and what seem to be food shelters or barns at Big Clearwater (similar to those discovered by Wintemburg at the Lawson site), would indicate that a considerable number of Indians had made this site their headquarters over a long period of years prior, as well as subsequent, to the coming of the white man. It was then, as now, in the heart of a great game country and the river abounding with salmon, trout and other fish. The Indian could with little difficulty construct weirs and stretch nets across the mouth of Big Clearwater, up which even today salmon go in great numbers. On foot (hardly by canoe) he could reach the great central plateau at the head of the Miramichi waters, finally the Tobique River by way of Big Gulquac.

This Big Clearwater site both below and above the stream is one of the most interesting of many I have yet visited. It certainly warrants further and intensive investigation. There is a small flat, or terrace, on higher ground on the south side of the river directly opposite Clearwater stream. Here was formerly a camp owned by a New Yorker. There is a good spring brook, and very likely the place was inhabited by prehistoric Indians.

Whether the artifacts found at this Big Clearwater site are wholly of Micmac manufacture, or a mixture of Micmac and Maliseet, is difficult to determine. People of both tribes very possibly visited the place. The large knife-blade, already mentioned may

---

74 "The term 'killed' typically refers to a ceremonial object that has been purposefully broken and placed within or near a burial." Mandy Melton and Al Luckenbach, "The Ritual Killing of Slate Gorgets at the Pig Point Site," *Maryland Archeology*, Vol. 49 (2): 21-27, September 2013.—http://www.losttownsproject.org.

have been brought from the Tobique region—where a large number of the artifacts are of the same material. We found no chippings of the material at Big Clearwater.

Most of the knives found here are triangular in shape, quite thin, not more than an inch wide at the base, many less, and from two or three and a half inches in length, with convex edges and straight bases, which are wedge-like. Some of these knife blades are slightly curved; two or three are notched and may have been used as arrowpoints.

Since the above was written, I have again visited the place, and found many knives, broken and whole of jaspery slate, and a very fine double-pointed willow-shape blade of grey chert. We extended the first site we had worked three years before, and I found a bone spear-point about six inches long. We also dug on the upper side of Clearwater stream, and among the trees and bushes found a few crude knives and several pottery sherds. The latter were not in a fire pit, but scattered about in the dark loam and associated with ashes and bits of flint.

CHAPTER 13
THE LANE'S CREEK SITE

Two miles north of Woodstock, Lane's Creek—formerly known as Trout Brook—vents into the St John River. There is a quite large flat below, and one much smaller above it; the latter, at its widest part being no more than one hundred feet, and extends about three hundred feet northward parallel with the river. At the northern extremity the width is contracted to a mere two or three yards, along which is a path formerly made by cattle. Originally this portion, as well as the whole flat, was much wider; but in recent years ice-jams have torn away some thirty feet of the bank.

The whole area shows abundant signs of prehistoric occupation. There were three distinct horizons: one at eight inches; the second twenty-four; and the third exactly four feet five inches—as measured by my Indian helper Noel Moulton. At the first two levels were chert chippings, and a few whole and broken knives. At the greater depth was a thick line of ash and a layer of the same greyish chert as the artifacts found at horizon eight, and twenty inches. There were no artifacts, whole or broken, at the four-feet five-inch horizon.

Edwin Tappan Adney, whose scale models of birch-bark and other Indian canoes have justly won him international recognition and fame, had asked me to show him the Lane's Creek site, so in late June I took him with me. While I was digging a short distance away, he found in a small area where the terrace narrows to a few feet, a line of ash, and below it an unfinished stone axe.

A little later, to the left of this, the ground sloped downwards at an angle of forty-five degrees to the beach. This slope was the result of the previous spring freshet, which had forced huge cakes of ice almost to the top of the terrace which, during the summer, is all of twenty feet higher than the normal river height; the ice had torn away a considerable portion of the terrace, and the wash of the strong river current had helped create the sharp incline above noted.

About six feet from the base of this hard-packed sand, I had noticed a two-inch dark line that I was quite sure was ash. I pointed this out to Adney. He ridiculed the idea, said the dark line was only darker soil, and suggested that I save myself work that would lead to nothing of interest. I didn't heed him, but began digging, and soon found that the dark line was getting blacker and deeper. Finally, five or six feet in, I came on a greater bed of intensely black ash and fire stones. There were two layers of these, which had been set one upon the other with meticulous care, and occupied an area about three feet by two. The interstices between the stones were filled with ash so black I was quite sure it would make ink. Some of the stones had been cracked by the fire. There were no artifacts or flint flakes.

Adney immediately declared the stones marked the site of a sweat lodge. Indubitably it was a fireplace; whether it had been a sweat lodge no man could positively say and be sure that his theory was correct. It was on the same horizon as the line of ash and flints my Indian friend, Noel, and I had discovered a week before.

I now wanted to excavate beyond the line of firestones to find out if there was anything behind them, but Adney said he first wanted to make a sketch of what he insisted was the site of a sweat lodge. I said all right, but asked him not to disturb the rocks, since I wanted to inspect the area further the following day.

It was now time for me to go home. Adney said he'd return in the morning and make the drawing, and accompanied me to my car. I let him down at his place at Upper Woodstock.

Late the next afternoon I went to the site, and to my surprise and resentment found that the rocks and the soil beneath them had entirely disappeared.

Today, in one of our Maritime museums, there is an exact reproduction of the fire-place (partly enclosed with birch-bark) and labelled I understand; "Sweat lodge formerly above Lane's Creek, Upper Woodstock, New Brunswick, reconstructed by E. T. Adney"!

*   *   *

Later in the summer, to the left of the fire-place, but at an eight inch depth below the top soil, I dug out a semi-lunar knife, two scrapers and an arrowhead, all of the smoky quartzite termed by one archaeologist *Labrador Stone,* and by another Lake Albanel product. But, as I have said previously in this, it is native to New Brunswick (Fig. 6 e, p 58).

Thirty feet northward, at the base of a big butternut tree, where the bench is only about six feet in width, the late W. E. Hale, who was with me at the time, dug out the butt-end of a large knife of sugary grey stone, lying near reddish ash and many flint chippings. (Six years later, near by but slightly northward, I found the remainder of this knife.)

Two weeks later, at eight inches, slightly to the left of the butternut tree, I found six knives; the materials being black flint, red jasper, and a bluish chert. They were all bunched together in a twelve-inch area near the edge of the high bank, which at this point drops a sheer twenty feet to the beach. In shape they are oval, pointed almond, and triangular, similar to some depicted on p. 178 of Osborn's *Men of the Old Stone Age,* and designated by him as late Acheulean, from one of the prehistoric stations on the Somme, at St Acheul, France.

A very significant fact about this Lane's Creek Site is that the artifacts of "Labrador" quartzite were on the same horizon as the foregoing deposit of blades, and the stone axe found by Mr Adney.

Digging at the extreme lower end of the flat, near the brook, we found several deposits of ashes, firestones, chippings, knives, and arrowheads at a twelve-inch depth, while at three feet were firestones, ashes, and many chippings, but no finished artifacts. This latter area seems to have been the main workshop of the inhabitants who frequented it, as literally bushels of large broken and chipped flint stones were abundant. All the stones save a few were of greyish-blue chert, which is the material from which most of the finished artifacts had been made.

Twelve years ago, in the early spring, I visited the flat, just after the ice had run out of the river, and the water was within six inches of the top of the terrace. In earlier times it is quite probable that the river was much narrower than now, and the whole terrace was periodically overflowed, with a consequent deposition of silt and a gradual buildup of the bench.

Three hundred yards above this small flat, and separated from it by a high bluff, is a long flat about a mile in length, and on the average four hundred yards wide. The lower, or southern, portion is occupied by my daughter Mrs K. C. Homer,[75] the northern portion by Mr Robert Speer. One finds flint chippings and burned firestones along practically its whole course contiguous to the river. At one point I uncovered a campsite about sixty feet in length by twenty-five in depth. It contained bushels of flint chippings, ash and firestones at twelve inches. On top of the line of ash, I dug out fifteen knives and arrowpoints and one spearhead, within a radius of six feet. The arrow-points are long and extremely thin; the spearhead is notched and shouldered, and of black chert. (See Figure 6 c, p 58.) Among the ashes was a lower third molar tooth, the cusps entirely worn away, showing that it had belonged to some very old person. As there were no others, and no evidence of bone, I concluded that it had loosened in the owner's mouth, and he had picked, or pried it out, and tossed it among the ashes of his campfire. I also found at this site two very long and thick crudely chipped blades, that may have been used as meat choppers, or possibly they were big knives in the process of manufacture. But if found in some parts of the continent, they would very probably be assigned to some very remote period: "before the art of chipping had been perfected."[76] As it happened, they were on the same horizon and associated with well-finished artifacts, and is one more proof of how little we can rely on the supposition that such crude objects indicate an extreme antiquity.

The following spring, while walking along the shore, below this particular site, I picked up a beautiful little scraper of "Labrador" quartzite from the sloping bank to which it had fallen from the terrace above following an unusually high spring freshet. The Mactaquac dam has flooded all this lovely intervale. What a pity!

---

75 This flat is where Dr Grant spent his last evening talking with GFC, who in 1946 bought the house and land (about 40 acres in all) for his daughter Dees.

76 Source not found.

PHOTOGRAPHS
PART 2

23 Solutrean-like blades from Bristol, St John River

a   b   c

d   e   f   g

24   Similar to other blades in the book

a=6.0 cm

25 Arrowheads from different sites

a

b

c

27 Gouge and knives
a. Stone gouge, Pokiok Stream, St John River system; b. chert knife,
Forks, Main S.W. Miramichi; c. knife from Smith Flat, Tobique River

a

b

d

c

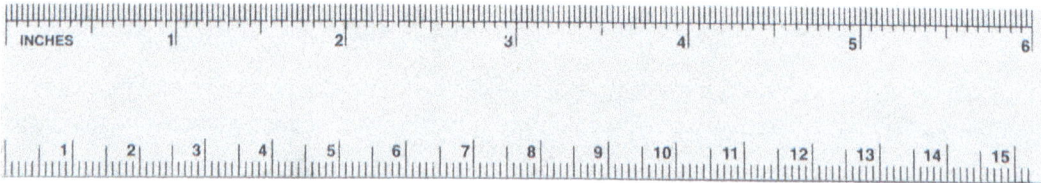

28 Pottery sherds

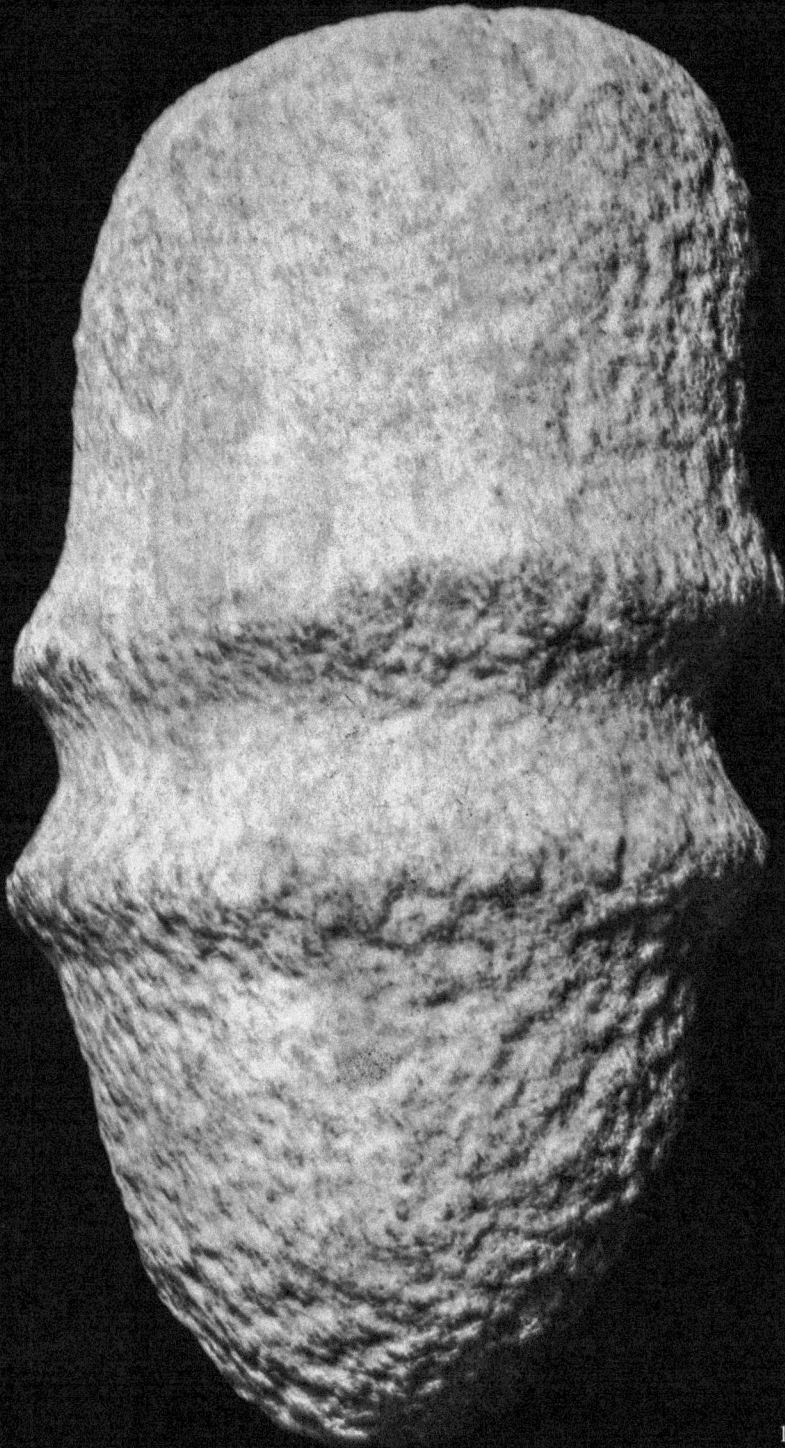

29 Maul, the Forks, Main S.W. Miramichi River

30 Paint bowl, plummets, toys

a. Small tomahawk, Big Clearwater, Main S.W. Miramichi River; b. plummet (so called) Forks, Main
S.W. Miramichi River; c. paint bowl (?), Bristol, St John River; d. polished adze, Three Brooks, Tobique
River; e. plummet, and f. small tomahawk, both from St John River opposite Florenceville

31 Ornaments
a. Perforated pendant (probably ceremonial object), Hazy Point, Grand Lake; b. broken gorget, Big Clearwater, Main S.W. Miramichi; c. slate ornament, Grand Lake; d. butterfly pendant, (slate), Grand Lake. (Note GFC's repair to d.)

135

34 Knives and spearheads
a. Spearhead, Tobique Narrows; b. knife, Clearwater, Main S.W. Miramichi; c. Wapske; d.
spearhead, Wapske; e, agate knife, Big Clearwater, Main S.W. Miramichi; f, g and h, knives,
Three Brooks, Tobique River

36 Knives
a. Quartz knife, Three Brooks; b. unfinished knife, Bristol;
c. broken knife, Red Rapids, Tobique River

37 Double-grooved stone axe, Wapske, Tobique River

38 Large black chert knife, Wapske, Tobique, actual size

a. moose lying down

width=3.5 cm

c. moose standing

width=c. 3.4 cm

d. doe deer lying down

b. pipe bowl

width=4.6 cm

e. pipe howl with
Polchies' daughter

40 Stone objects carved by Dr Peter Polchies, c. 1914-1917
a. to e., above, are shown at actual size, with e. enlarged below

a. and b. fabric fragments from
cedar-bark robe, Sunny Comer, N.B.

c. stone pipe bowl

e.

f.

9.8 cm

d. Micmac stone
pipe bowl

e. and f. European clay tobacco pipes, Medoctec flat

41 Fabric and pipes
a. and b. Portions of cedar-bark robe, from near Sunny Corner, Northwest Miramichi; c. small stone
pipe from Medoctec; d. Micmac stone pipe bowl; e. and f. European trade pipes, Medoctec Flat

42 Rock maple decorated paddle, showing both sides, made by
Dr Peter Polchies, Indian Reserve, Woodstock, N.B.

a. Fur trade canoe. Model is 178 cm (5.83 foot). Original was 890 cm (29.2 foot)

b. Algonquin canoe with paddle, salmon spear and bundle of ribs.
Model is 104 cm (3.42 foot). Original was 521 cm (17 .1 foot)

c. Athabascan skin canoe. Model is 109 cm (3.6 foot)
Original was 545 cm (17.9 foot)

d. Shuswap-Chilkat spruce-bark canoe. Model is
83.8 cm (2.75 foot). Original was 419 cm (13.75 foot)

45 Model canoes made by Tappan Adney, all at 1/5 scale, early 1290s to early 1940s

46 GFC and Peter Paul, c. 1961, repairing a birchbark canoe made by Peter Jo in the 1890s. The kettle hanging from a stick tripod contains pitch for caulking the seams.

a. Mary Clarke, early 1930s

b. George Greer, Jane Clarke (GFC's elder daughter) and GFC, c. 1919

47 Family members in birchbark canoes

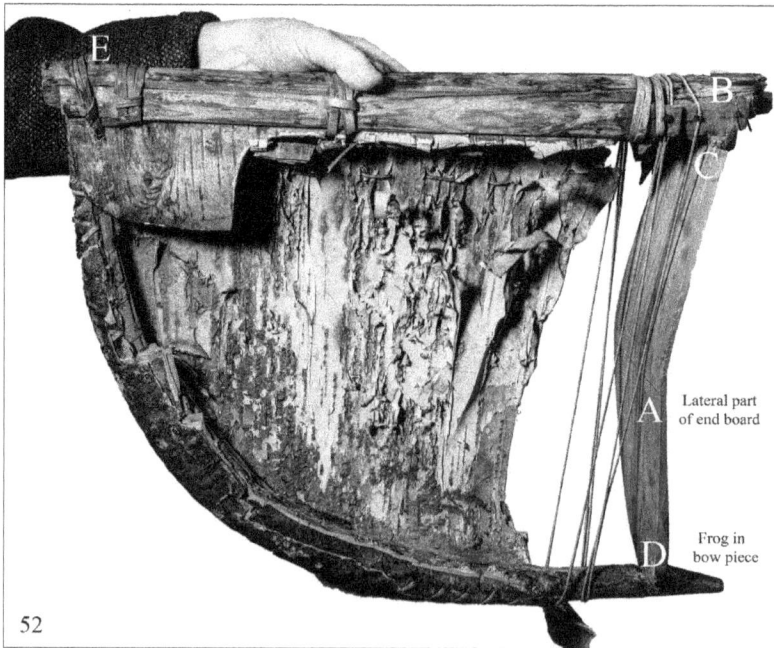

51 and 52 Bow end of birch-bark canoe showing construction of end boards, which are in proper positio

53 Canoe models, 1/5th scale of natural size, made by E.T.Adney,
probably photographed outside Adney's bungalow in Upper Woodstock

CHAPTER 14
THE WAPSKE SITE

Come with me now to the Wapske site, for I have some interesting things to tell about this place whose full Indian name is Waps-ke-hegan but shortened to its present form by the early white settlers, as have so many Indian place-names been mutilated.

Wapske Flat, then, is less than a mile below the town of Plaster Rock, on the west side of the Tobique River—the most important tributary of the St John. It is about three-quarters of a mile in length, its lower end opposite Wapske stream, which heads from a high plateau separating it from the Miramichi waters. The Flat cannot be seen from the highway road leading to the town. The lower half of the Flat was then owned by Mr Sidney Linton, the upper by Mr Otto Lawson.

I had heard that some Indian "tools" had been picked up on these properties, and was most anxious to visit them. The last three days of May, 1937, there was a heavy run of salmon in the Tobique, and, with two of my angling friends, I was at Gulquac Lodge (twelve miles above Plaster Rock), and enjoying splendid fishing. Early after lunch, on the last day of our stay, I stole away from my chums and drove downriver to make a hurried reconnaissance of the Flat, which I had heard had been partially ploughed the preceding autumn. Arriving at the home of Mr Lawson I was told that a hauling road, near the lower end of his house, led to the Flat, more than half a mile distant.

I found that this road, which led through a thick growth of trees for some distance, led to a barn on the Linton property. A well-defined terrace runs in a curve from below the barn, and continues to the extreme upper end of the Lawson property. This terrace dips gradually ten or twelve feet to the lower Flat. Evidently the river was much higher in the remote past, and covered the Flat to the border of the upper terrace. At its widest the properties extend as much as five hundred yards from their western border to the river, which makes a wide bend, like a bow, and, of course, the contour of the Flat conforms to it. The western border abuts the forested upland which extends almost to the highway road. Thus the Flat is a quiet, secluded place—an archaeologist's paradise. For not only its remoteness appeals; practically every yard of it is rich in evidences of a prehistoric past covering untold centuries. This is why I have been at such pains to describe it—for future "treasure seekers."

*   *   *

To the left of the barn, about fifteen acres had been ploughed the previous autumn. Walking over it I saw hundreds of spalls[77] and chips of chert, rose and white quartz, besides some of a brownish hard stone peculiar to the Tobique region. They were even lying in the ruts of the hauling road, and between them. At this time I picked up an unfinished knife and a few broken tips of arrowheads.

The following late September I drove to Tobique, accompanied by my Indian friend, Noel Moulton, secured accommodation in a cabin owned by Mrs Linton, two miles from the Flat, to which, next morning, we drove part of the way. We found that the area near the barn had been sown with buckwheat, which had matured, been cut, and was now in stooks.

We began excavating to the left of the hauling road, near the barn, and soon found chippings, ashes and firestones, a few broken knives and two whole knives of the rounded base type, and one of the straight base, triangular form. We dug out a twelve foot square area to a depth of twelve inches, but, save for the artifacts mentioned above, discovered no more. Then we sunk another trench to a depth of two feet below the first, beginning as before at the margin of the hauling road. We were near the centre of the square area when, at a depth of thirty inches from the topsoil, we found a fireplace containing burned stones, ashes and chippings of greyish chert. Among the ashes were three small knives, known as the willow pattern, and diminutive examples of the large double-pointed blades I had found at Bristol on the St John River.

Oh—this is really precious. I have told it in *Six Salmon Rivers and Another,* and an author isn't supposed to repeat a story in a subsequent publication. But the story is mine. *Six Salmon Rivers* may never be read by the reader of this, so listen.

Noel was in the bottom of the wide trench shovelling out some loose earth, and I was hand trowelling down one side, when a man and a boy came catercorner across the Flat from the river bank, where they had been gathering wild cherries. When they got close to us they paused, and the man said to me: "What you diggin fer—gold?"

I told him no; explained that we were digging for the arrowheads, knives, spearheads and other stone objects used by the Indians long ages past.

"Got any?" he asked. "Yes."

"Show 'em to me?"

"Certainly," and I took a handful out of my little basket and held them before his eyes.

He gazed at them a few moments in silence, then said: "There was three fellers come up the river last week. They crossed the bridge down there" (pointing to the railway bridge a few hundred yards below us) "They went up Wapske stream. *They was huntin' fer gold too.*"

I made no comment but restored my finds to the basket.

For a little while longer the man and boy watched us working. Finally the man said to Noel: "Hey, feller, just what do you expect to find down there, anyhow?"

Noel pushed his felt hat back from his brow, spat out some tobacco juice and leaning on the handle of his spade, looked up and said: "Well, I tell you. My great— great—great—

---

77   "Small fragments or chips especially of stone." —www.merriam-webster.com/dictionary.

great—great grandfather, he leave my great—great—great—great—great grandmother round here somewhere—I try to find her." Then he resumed his work.

The man made no reply. There was a puzzled expression on his dull countenance, as though he were grappling with a conundrum beyond his capacity to unravel. His mouth opened and closed several times, then he roughly grasped the boy by the arm, and said gruffly: "Come on!"

Noel looked up at me, a droll look in his dark eyes, and said: "I guess that hold'm, Doc."

A quick wit and a keen sense of humour were both inherent parts of Noel's makeup. If ever I am in the blues, I only have to recall that little episode, and Noel's delightful reply to the wild-cherry man, who, if he is still alive, must even yet be puzzling his brains in the effort to find out just *what* Noel meant.

In mid-October we excavated about seventy-five yards beyond the left of the hauling road. At twelve inches we found two laurel-shape knives heavily patinated on both sides. At ten inches, a very fine spearhead (Fig. 34 d and h, p 136). At this latter depth we found two knives of rose quartz of the rounded base type, three oval-shape knives, two inches in length, of translucent red material, and many scrapers of various size and form (See Figure 16, p 64.) All these pieces were lying in sandy loam beyond a fire-place which contained ash and burned stones. There were many chippings of jasper, rose and white quartz, black and grey and brown chert, besides many partly blocked-out forms of the same materials.

We now had to leave for the season. The following year this particular portion of the Flat was sown with oats and seeded with clover. Conditions like this, where fields are only occasionally ploughed, and then for years in grass, necessarily limit digging operations at many important sites.

The following autumn we excavated a small area close to the upper end of the barn, and at a depth of eight inches found blades similar to the willow shape type we had dug up at site A at thirty inches. They were not as well made, perhaps due to the fact that the material—a hard brown stone—is of a more refractory character than the ordinary chert of which the first blades were made.

At this same time, we made a reconnaissance near the river, on the lower terrace, and, sinking a test pit, discovered a cache of quartz stone of various colours that had been roughly broken into pieces of all sizes, from a quarter of a pound to two pounds in weight. There were probably a couple of bushels in the lot. It looked as though they had been brought to the place and stored for future working into finished shapes.

Yet again, the succeeding spring, with Noel as helper, I was at the Wapske site for two days. The portion of the Linton section, beyond the barn, to the right of the hauling road, had been ploughed the autumn before, and on the slope leading down to the lower terrace I picked up a chert knife. It is bluish on one side, with slightly greyish patination on the other. It is three inches long by three quarters wide at the base, which is wedge shape. (See Figure 6 f, p 58.) It is similar to a cache of several blades found on the northwest Miramichi, and now in the collection of Mr William Kesson of Fredericton. Beyond this, a few rods (on Mr Lawson's section of the Flat), were the remains of a very old barn. Most of the boards had been hauled away or otherwise disposed of, but the huge sills and beams were lying on and partly embedded in the soil. We dug between these as best we could, and at twelve inches came on a great bed of ash and fire-stones, among which were broken and whole artifacts: knives and arrowheads of chert, rose quartz, a spearhead of creamy chalcedony, dozens of scrapers, and some pottery sherds. We would have excavated deeper but for the fact that below the twelve-inch horizon the ground was yet frozen hard. We found here a knife of transparent quartz that, if it were found in Europe, Asia (or even in some parts of the United States) would be assigned to a period contemporary with primitive man's first crude efforts to make a cutting implement. For it was made by simply taking a block of translucent quartz, and striking it at an angle with a hammer stone, thus producing a wedge-shape cutting tool; the top, by which it can be grasped, is an inch and a quarter wide. Oh—yes, the top, to a depth of one quarter of an inch, is a smooth reddish-brown colour, the remainder of the stone is greyish. It weighs exactly sixteen ounces, is depicted on Figure 36 a, p 135, and for cutting tough steak would be more efficient than most steel knives![78]

This find—which is only one of many of like nature—is yet another evidence how little dependence we can place on the classifications so often dogmatically used by "experts". If any of them read this book, I can imagine them giving me hell! Be that as it may, I found it on the same horizon as beautifully chipped blades, so I assume that all had been made by the same people.

Mr. Lawson told me that, several years before I met him, he had ploughed up an object he thought was black flint. It was, he said, about a foot long, slightly larger in circumference than a railroad spike, perfectly round, straight, pointed and sharp at one end. From his description I have no doubt it was similar to an object found at the southern end of Chisuncook lake about 1890 by Arthur E. Marks.*

Mr Lawson related to me that he had "carefully" put the object he found on a shelf in his tool house, but it had later disappeared: One of those disappointing and vexatious losses about which we all too frequently hear.

The two ungrooved hatchets we found at this place are long and narrow with finely polished butts, and are similar to those depicted on Plate 10, Moorehead's *Archaeology of Maine*. In the same book, on Fig. 48, are depicted some projectile points from various so-called "Red Paint" cemeteries in Maine; and in Fig. 49 other types said to be of the same culture group, though not of "Labrador" quartzite. Precisely similar forms of the same material have been found on the St John River and the Tobique. The ungrooved hatchet seems to be pretty well distributed all over New Brunswick. The same holds true of the gouge and adze blades, and are similar to the so-called "Red Paint" or "pre-Algonkian" artifacts, but may be designated such with the same absence of definite proof as that so positively adduced by the proponents of a pre-Algonkian culture group.

All we definitely know is that these artifacts are distributed over a wide area, that without doubt Indians made and used them, but to assign them categorically to some

---

78   GFC sometimes demonstrated its sharpness by using it on steak or chops at dinner.

---

*   Moorehead. *Archaeology of Maine*. fig. 116.

remote era of prehistoric man, is to arrogate to oneself an omniscience which is hardly justified in the light of our present knowledge of the subject.*

I may say here that I picked up on the Lawson portion of this Flat, as a surface find, quite a long spearhead, or poniard, identical in shape to some I found three miles south at the Three Brooks Site, and to several at Bristol (on the St John River) already referred to.

Two years ago,[79] in early May, I took John McClement, my grandson Stephen Homer, and his young friend Garfield Saunders to Wapske Flat. We found it had been ploughed the previous autumn. We walked over its lengthy and wide expanse, on which, at several places many years before Noel and I had spent such wonderful and productive hours.

The barn was now gone, but near its site John picked up a very nice grooved tomahawk; and, a little later, I found a double-grooved axe of large size; the only double-grooved axe I've seen from New Brunswick. (Figure 37, p 138. I have painted the grooves white so that they will show up better in the reproduction.)[80]

On the lower terrace, about one hundred yards from the river, I found two stone knives of large size. They had been turned up by the plough and deposited point down, in the earth of the turned-up furrow. (Figure 38, p 139—This piece, actual size, is boldly chipped from the periphery towards the centre.) Later, at my home, a friend who saw it said, a note of suspicion in his voice—as though he doubted it had been shaped by man): "You say Indians struck off those grooves with another stone? How?"

"Oh," I said, "this knife was once in plastic form. The Indian held it in both palms, and with his thumbs worked across the face of it. Then he put it aside to harden."

On the occasion I found this and the smaller blade I called to John McClement, some distance away, who joined me, and presently he found a larger blade, but badly marred by the plough.

In concluding the chapter I must say that the Wapske site deserves much more attention than I have been able to give it.

---

79   Probably 1963.

80   Mercifully, he painted the grooves on only one side. Figure 37 shows the other side, as photographed by Rob Blanchard and David Black.

---

*   Moorehead. *Archaeology of Maine.* fig. 116.

CHAPTER 15
THE TOBIQUE NARROWS SITE

Tom Moulton, elder brother of my Indian friend Noel, was born on the Maliseet Indian reserve, which stands on a point of land where the Tobique River vents into the St John. The aboriginal name for the Tobique is *Na-goot-tuk*; Tobique possibly being from an old Indian named Tobit, who in the late seventeen-hundreds lived in a wigwam on the site of the present village.

For many years Tom had lived alternately at Moosehead Lake in northern Maine, and at Tobique. In both places he acted as guide, both hunting and fishing; and later in the season trapped fur-bearing animals. Many times he had portaged his canoe over the Northeast Carry, and had to make two trips to lug the dunnage and supplies of his sportsmen to the St John waters. He had guided on the Restigouche, Upsalquitch, Tobique and their furthermost tributaries. Wherever there was canoeable water he had poled or paddled his canoe. As a mere lad he had accompanied old Noel Bear (of the famous Bear family), on a caribou hunt, and beaten a snow-trail over the height of land to the great central plateau, between the Tobique and the Miramichi waters, reached Burnt Hill Brook, which pours its tribute of waters into the Miramichi, and had run a line of traps as far as Little Southwest Miramichi Lake.

Thus his ancestors had explored every stream and lake and dead-water, untold centuries before ever the white man dreamed there were such continents as North and South America.

Thirty-five years ago, when Tom was past middle age, he bought a small frame house on a crescent-shape terrace about one hundred yards above the suspension bridge which at that time spanned the Tobique River Narrows. The terrace comprised some fifteen acres. It was somewhat the shape of a saucer cut in half, and extended westwards about three hundred yards to a high tree-covered ridge.

The house stood on the right of a paved highway leading up the valley. The eastern side of it was only a rod from a high bank, which descended abruptly some sixty feet to a narrow intervale bordered by the Tobique River.

From the lower end, or horn of the crescent, a gravelled road wound up and over the ridge, then down to the village of Maliseet.

Thus Tom and his wife abode in peaceful isolation, for the only other visible dwellings were on the opposite side of the river.

The view upriver from Tom's house was superb beyond description. Enclosed by rolling hills or ridges, the river rippled over many shallows, swirled around the humped backs of exposed slate ledges, deepened, then again raced over more shallows between yet more ledges of rock.

An American angler termed it the *million dollar view*. That directly opposite, and below Tom's house, where both shores converged to a bare one hundred feet, was equally awe-inspiring. For the whole force of the river plunged between high palisades of slate rock as perpendicular as a plumb-line; and had attracted untold numbers of tourists since first the valley was settled by the white man.

Tom had married a Passamaquoddy Indian woman named Eva (I don't remember her family name). When I first met them I was with Tom's younger brother, Noel, who had told me, what I had long suspected, that the crescent had been a very old campsite and should contain stone relics of his ancestors. I later found that few other places I have explored contained so many evidences of prehistoric occupation.

The month was late September. We were invited to have dinner, which was almost ready for the table. We had fried pork chops, potatoes boiled in their jackets, creamed carrots, delicious home-baked bread, home-made butter (for Tom had a cow), and whole cucumbers pickled in brine with a few spices. Then, for dessert, pumpkin pie with cinnamon dusted over the top. It was ambrosia, and I ate two wedges of it. Oh, yes, and tea—none ever better!

Tom had a little vegetable garden, which began about fifteen feet from his front door, was sixty feet in length by twenty-five in width. The east, or river-side of it flanked the high terrace on which the house stood. A small area, but it produced enough vegetables for their need, which were now gathered for winter use. Besides these Tom had a patch of potatoes up the hillside near the road leading to Maliseet.

After the meal, I asked Tom if he had ever seen any stone arrowheads, axes, or other objects made by his remote ancestors.

"No," he said in a slow, measured voice. "I make that garden fourteen year, and never find anything like that."

Then I asked him if I could do some digging.

"Yes," he answered, "dig all you want."

So Noel and I began digging a trench at the lower end of the plot. It was slow work, for we dug with care, and soon I found a beautiful spearhead of whitish chert with longitudinal blue lines its whole length. (See Figure 34 a, p 136.) Then Noel found a long slate spear or knife of red jaspery slate. Close to the edge of the declivity I dug out a long chert knife that originally had been bluish-grey, but was now painted a rich cream colour (Fig. 18 a, p 65). Tom gave me a long look and asked if I was able to see under the ground.

We found arrowheads, numerous scrapers of milky quartz, red jasper and black chert, and a big grooved axe. There was a deep fire-pit which we dug out, and at the bottom found a chert knife, the point of which had been broken. I neglected to say that, some distance below the garden plot Tom had a barn. At the end facing the river he kept two pigs in a pen. I am always interested in livestock, so I walked over to have a look at his porkers. Soon my eye was attracted by a beautiful black double-pointed knife blade, with Solutrean characteristics, lying on the dark earth. I wasn't long climbing over the sty and picking it up. Doubtless it had been upturned from some unknown depth by the snout of one of the pigs. A couple of weeks later I had the same experience, a similar knife of black chert. And I wanted to turn the pigs out and do some excavating myself.

On this occasion, Noel and I did some trenching below the barn contiguous to a small spring brook which came from the hillside across the highway road. We found hundreds of flint chippings of different size and colour, and several scrapers, and I dug out the most beautiful little arrowhead I have in my collection, and a stone axe. Then, climbing over a low cedar rail fence, where the ground sloped abruptly to the intervale below, I picked up, from the surface among some trees, another stone object which might be termed an axe in the making. It is an irregular-shape beach stone, grooved on both sides, but hadn't been sharpened.

On another visit we crossed the highway road to the field, opposite Tom's house, and found numerous burned and cracked fire-stones where wigwams had stood. Scouting along the southern periphery of this field, we picked up, among the alders that bordered it, five grooved axes. Evidently they had been ploughed up by Tom, or the previous owner of the place, and, not recognized as Indian tools, had been tossed among the alders where we found them.

The following year I dug up another axe near Tom's house, so now I have nine stone axes from this area. And only the Almighty knows how many more lie buried there.

For the next three years I did occasional digging at this place, often with Noel, and on one occasion Peter Trueman, son of the then president of the University of New Brunswick, was with me. And on every occasion I have been there I have found abundant evidences of prehistoric occupation. Indeed to dig out the whole area would have consumed half a score of years, working every summer until freeze-up.

I cannot remember when I enjoyed myself more thoroughly, though I didn't always dig the whole time I was at Tom's "retreat". Often I took time off and sat beside him in a deck chair, and, my eyes drinking in the *million-dollar view*, listened to his slow voice as he relived for himself, and for me, his experiences shooting Big Black Rapids, on the Upper St John; his trips over the Miramichi waters; of climbing Sagum mountain (near Lake Nictau), on a bear hunt; of a trip through more wilderness to the Upsalquitch; from this fascinating salmon stream to the Restigouche, and up the Kedgwick until he was in the very heartland of Quebec province.

Fascinating tales. I have two snapshots of Tom: one manoeuvring his canoe through white water on the Restigouche; the other of him and Pete Loler seated near a high, rudely fashioned wooden cross at a place called Little Cross Point. He was then a young man—looking not more than twenty. On one of the last occasions, I visited Tom, and did some excavating, he was ill—how seriously I didn't then know. And across the Narrows a concrete dam was being constructed to impound the waters of Tobique to provide electric energy for northern New Brunswick and the State of Maine.

From where Tom and I sat, we heard the roar of bulldozers, the rattle of cement mixers, the movement of trucks hauling gravel—all the noisy clamour which goes with construction work. With a wide sweep of his brown hand that included the upper part of the Narrows, and the whole glory of the river as far as the eye could reach, he said in his dispassionate voice (so characteristic of his race which scorns to betray unseemly emotion) and with no note of anger: "Soon white man will spoil all."

And even as he spoke the fatalistic words, there came from along the shores, below the Narrows, the drone and the scream of power-saws, that might have been the protests of the trees sacrificed on the altar of man's insatiable demand for more and yet more electric power to drive the wheels of Progress.

*   *   *

Tom died a few months before the dam was completed. Perhaps the immortal gods, knowing his disease was fatal, had taken pity on him, and saved him the anguish of being forced to move from a place where he had known such happiness.

There were many friends and relatives at the service in his little home: some from as far away as Moosehead Lake, Old Town, and Passamaquoddy. For it is a custom of long standing on such occasions. Then I followed the cortege up the hill and over the height of land, and down to the village of Maliseet, and into the Franciscan chapel in which (though not a Catholic) I had accompanied him several times while he was alive. Then to the cemetery where all that was mortal of Tom Moulton was consigned to Mother Earth.

But did his spirit—when he breathed his last in the little house overlooking the *Million-Dollar View*, go to the heaven of the white man, or to that Valhalla of his ancestors, where game and fish and corn abounded and there was no hunger any more?

A few months later the rising waters covered the crescent-shape terrace where for untold centuries his forebears chipped their weapons of war and chase, made their birch-bark canoes, and boxes decorated with dyed porcupine quills, and baskets of black ash splints. And lived much the same sort of life as did our own white ancestors only two thousand years ago.

The dam didn't involve the destruction of any other house. But the view up the long pond, when I saw it from the top of the dam, gave me somewhat the same sense of irreparable loss I would experience were some modern vandal to tear a painting by Turner or Rembrandt from its frame, and mutilate it for all time to come.

But the *Million-Dollar View* was more vital than any painting done by mortal hand. For none could capture and immortalize the song of the waters that, ever since the glaciers had retreated, had rippled over the bars and washed the reflected moon and the stars, and the jewelled rays of the sun.

All was now a huge pond as far as Red Rapids, twelve miles distant; as voiceless as the lips of a dead man. And I remembered Tom's dispassionate words as he said:

"Soon white man will spoil all."

Perhaps he was *me-tà-o-lin* like certain medicine men of his tribe, and like his old grandmother, who foretold that his brother Noel would never be drowned. For so far as the St John and Tobique waters are concerned, man's ever accelerating demands have ever since been engaged in fulfilling his prophecy.

CHAPTER 16
NICHOLAS DENYS

Writers of aboriginal life in Acadia are fortunate in having access to the works of Marc Lescarbot and Nicholas Denys, both in the original and in translation. For as I have said earlier in this; without them we would know little of native life and customs of the native Americans in what is now New Brunswick and Nova Scotia.

John Gyles, the New England lad who lived among the St John River Indians at Medoctec for six years (1689-1695) gives a far from complete account of them; his memoirs, published 1736, being mostly concerned with his own adventures. But what he does give us is invaluable.

The earlier historians wrote about the Micmac, but I believe that in large part it also applies to the Maliseet or St John River Indians. For the two tribes were in close association, their hunting grounds often overlapped, and no doubt then, as well as now, there was some intermarriage between them.

When Acadia was returned to France in 1632, Isaac de Razilly was sent out as Lieutenant-Governor, and Nicholas Denys came with him. He first engaged in the fisheries at Cape Rossignol, then had stations and fortified posts at Miscou, St Anns, and St Peter's—on Cape Breton Island.

He must have been a close observer, and made voluminous notes during his thirty-five years truck with the Indians, for his *Historie* published in 1672, gives us intimate word pictures of their culture and way of life.

No man in New France underwent more vicissitudes of fortune at the hands of some of his own contemporaries than did Denys. Through their machinations he twice lost all his properties in Acadia; then when these were restored by the Crown, and he was made Lieutenant-Governor of all the territory comprised in the coasts and islands of the Gulf of St Lawrence and Gaspé to the Cape of Canso, fire destroyed his fort at St Peter's, and all his trading goods. Financially ruined, he went to Paris where he lived in great poverty. But finally he returned to his beloved Acadia, and spent his last days with his son Richard, at Miramichi.

Nicholas Denys was a man of the highest integrity, kindly, compassionate, returned good for evil even to those who had wronged him. And, while their very names are anathema to most writers of Acadian history, Nicholas Denys stands out unblemished, honourable and wholly magnificent.

He tells us (contemporary with the period of which he wrote) that "the Indians had as yet changed their customs but little, (although) making use of kettles, axes, knives, and of iron for their arrowheads there were still but few of them who had firearms.

"Their chief food consisted of fish and meat, roasted or boiled, To roast the meat they cut it in fillets, and put it on a split stick, which, if the time was summer, they inserted one end in the ground, if in winter the snow in front of a fire. When one side was cooked, they turned the opposite to the blaze. Each person, men, women, as well as children of suitable age, cooked his own meat. When it was done, they put one end between the teeth and cut off a piece with a knife. When they had chewed and swallowed this they repeated the process. Before they got iron knives they used knives of bone which they sharpened on rocks." (Probably sandstone.) The foregoing method of cooking meat on wooden spits was used by our St John River Indians when on hunting expeditions up to seventy years ago. The cover-jacket of this book (the original painting by Edwin Tappan Adney) depicts more clearly than words, a Maliseet Indian of the Tobique region (I think one of the Bear family) cooking his meat. It is especially interesting in that it shows how old customs persisted. Denys tells us of another method used by the Micmac: "They tied a cord of bark (doubtless cedar) to a stake and the other end to the top of a wigwam, or from tree to tree, or two forked sticks stuck in the ground. The meat was attached to the lower end of the cord, through which was thrust a stick with which it was twisted several times. After it was let go, the string and meat revolved first one side then the other, next the fire. This was repeated until the meat was cooked.

"Fish was roasted on split sticks which served as a grill, or frequently upon coals, and was thoroughly cooked before eaten."

Tom Moulton had a favourite station or pool at Red Rock, a short distance from his house above Tobique Narrows, to which he took some of his salmon fishermen guests. When a fish was caught, Tom often split it down the back, pinned each portion to a separate board, spread butter, and a little salt and pepper over the fish, then set the boards upright in front of the fire. This novel method of cooking no less delighted his guests than did the luscious golden salmon taken only a little while before from the fast-flowing river. Denys informs us of yet another method of cooking meats: "They took the butt of a large tree that had fallen. They did not cut it down, for they had no axes, and with stone axes, well sharpened, and set into the end of a forked stick, they cut a little into the top of the wood, at the length they meant to make the kettle (as he called it) in the shape of a trough. Then they made a fire in this hollow until the wood was burned to a depth of about four inches, then with knives of stones (gouges) and huge pointed bones they removed the burned wood and repeated the process until it was the desired depth. Then they filled it with water, placed therein the meat. Then, having heated stones red hot, they put them in the water. In this manner they cooked their meats."

They were great lovers of soup. "They drank little raw water formerly, as indeed they do at present. Their greatest task was to feed well and go hunting. They killed animals only in proportion to their need of them. They ate fish (seals) to obtain the fat oil (which they do) as much for greasing themselves as for drinking; and whales which frequently came ashore on the coast, and on the blubber of which they made good cheer. Their greatest liking was for grease, and they ate it as one does bread, and drank it liquid." This love of fat was a characteristic of my Indian friend Noel Moulton, and, I believe, other Indians on the St John River at the present time as it was in olden days. Many times, when Noel was at my house, my wife had hot roast pork, or sometimes cold, for dinner! Now I much like the fat part of pork, but it doesn't like me, so I always cut it off and eat the lean portion. Seeing this, Noel would say: "You not eat the fat?" And when I said no, he would say: "You give it to me. I eat it. It keep me warm." He pronounced it "woohm".

"The men," says Denys, "have three or four wives, sometimes more. If any of them proves to be sterile, they can divorce her and take another." They were more humane than our Henry VIII, who for one cause or another removed the heads of some of his wives!

"The children," he says," are not obstinate, since they (the parents) give them anything they ask for, without letting them cry for what they want. The greatest persons give way to the little ones. They love their children greatly. They are their wealth.

"After they have lived in one place," says Denys," they go to another fifteen or twenty leagues[81] distant. Then the women and girls must carry the wigwams (he means the bark which covered them), dishes, bags, skins, robes, everything they can take, for the men and boys carry nothing. The woman who is mistress, that is she who has given birth to the first boy, takes command, and does not go into the woods for (poles) or anything. Everything is brought to her. She fits the poles to make the wigwam, arranges the fir boughs for beds. If the family is large they make the wigwam long enough for two fires, otherwise they make it round, like military tents. (Rain never enters the wigwam.) The round ones hold ten or twelve persons, the long ones twice as many. Fires are made in the middle of the round kind, and at the ends of the long sort."

Denys tells us that they obtain bark by cutting all around the tree with stone axes (as high as they can reach), then low down all around, then split it from above downward, and with knives of bone separate it from the tree, which ought to be in sap to loosen readily. (This bark is for wigwams. For canoes winter bark is best—that is bark before the sap rises in the spring).

Of their marriage customs, Denys says: "When a boy wished to marry a girl he was obliged to serve her father several years. It was his duty to go hunting to prove that he was capable of supporting a wife and family. He had to make bows, arrows, the frames of snowshoes, even a canoe. Everything he did at this proving time went to the father of the girl; nevertheless, he had use of it himself in case of need. His mistress corded snowshoes" (filled in the webbing, Denys means), "made his clothes, moccasins and stockings as evidence that she was capable in work. The father, mother, daughter and sisters all slept in the same wigwam, the daughter near the mother; the suitor on the other side with the fire between them. Other women and children also slept there.

"When the term of probation had expired it was time to talk of marriage. The relatives of the boy visited the girl to see if she was pleasing to them. If the father of the girl was favourable, it was necessary to learn from the parties concerned if they were content with it, and if one of the two did not wish the marriage, nothing further was done. They were never compelled to marry. But if all were in agreement, the day was chosen for making

81 70-95 km.

a banquet. Meantime the boy went hunting and did his best to treat the entire assembly as well to roast as to boiled meat, and there must be abundance of soup good and fat.

"When the guests were assembled there was eating and drinking, war songs were sung, speeches made, genealogies recited, admonitions not to become degenerate, but to be worthy of their ancestors. Thus it had been from generation to generation from the most ancient times.

"In summer the men wore robes of mooseskin dressed white, and ornamented with embroidery two fingers in breadth at the bottom, both close and open work. Others three rows at the bottom, some lengthwise, others across the bottom in broken chevrons, or studded with figures of animals, according to fancy, red, white and blue colours were applied to the skins of their robes with some isinglass. They had bones fashioned in different ways which they passed quite hot over the colours, in a like manner somewhat like that in which our guilds gild the covers of books. Nor do these colours come off with water."

Denys, like Lescarbot before him, is enthusiastic about their beautiful colours, especially flame colour which he says: "surpasses any seen in France."

He tells us that their grave offerings sometimes were of the value of £2,000. This, he says, "caused pity, and perhaps envy among the French; but they did not dare to go and take the furs, for this would cause hatred and everlasting war, which was not prudent to risk. It would have ruined trade we had with them.

"Their most valued possessions were the copper kettles they got from the French, and these too they put in the graves with their deceased kindred for use in the spirit world. On one occasion they consented, after appeals from the French, to open one of their graves. Of course the idea of the French was to prove to them that the kettle and other things were still there. The kettle was perforated and covered with verdigris. An Indian struck against it and it no longer sounded. He began to make a great cry, and said someone had wished to deceive them. 'We see indeed,' said he, 'the robes are all rust, and it is a sign that the dead man has no need of them in the other world, where they have enough of them because of the length of time that they have been furnished with them.

"'But in respect of the kettle,' he went on, 'they have need of it since amongst us it is a utensil of recent introduction with which in the other world he cannot yet be furnished. Do you not see,' said he rapping again upon the kettle. 'No longer any sound and no longer says a word, because its spirit has abandoned it to go to be of use in the other world to the dead man to whom we have given it?'"

"It was very difficult," says Denys, "to keep from laughing, but much more difficult to make them see their error. For being shown another kettle worn out from use, and being made to hear that it spoke no word (when struck) more than the other—'Ha!' said he, 'that is because it is dead, and its soul has gone to the land where the souls of kettles are accustomed to go.'"

Denys tells us about an Indian sent by Governor De Razilly to Paris (in company of a Frenchman who had some of the Micmac dialect. Passing along the Rue Aubry they saw copper smiths at work and many copper kettles displayed. The Indian was astounded, and said to the interpreter: "Are they (the coppersmiths) relatives of the king, and is this not the trade of the greatest seignior of the kingdom?"

And so I leave Denys, although loath to part with him, for he has so much else to tell about the Indians of Acadia. But in retrospect I recall the poignant picture he draws of the marriage feast; of the genealogies recited; of the admonitions not to become degenerate, but to be worthy of their ancestors. Then of Denys' comment: "Thus it had been from generation to generation from the most ancient times." And I wonder if possibly it doesn't stem back countless centuries before Joel's warning to his people; "Tell ye your children of it, and let your children tell their children, and their children another generation." (Joel 1-3).

And this brings to my mind what Marc Lescarbot tells us about the care the Micmac Indians of Acadia observed for their deceased friends and kindred, keeping the place of their sepulture secret so that no enemy would disturb their bones. And I remember, with loathing, how some of our present white people in New Brunswick have, within the last year and a half, allowed the bones of the old pioneers and their descendants to be removed and their cemeteries destroyed.[82] And that only quite recently it was suggested that the old Loyalist cemetery, in the heart of Fredericton, where lie the bones and ashes of its first citizens, be made into a parking lot.

So I come to the conclusion that the white man, in his scramble for material things, has forgotten those things of the spirit which the "poor Indian" took such pains to observe and made such an important part of his life.

Then I recall what Joseph Howe wrote many years ago: "A wise nation preserves its records, gathers up its muniments, decorates the tombs of its illustrious dead, repairs its great structures, and fosters national pride and love of country by perpetual references to the sacrifices and glories of the past."[83]

---

82 By the headpond of the Mactaquac dam.

83 From an address Howe gave in Framingham, MA. "The Howe family gathering, at Harmony Grove, South Framingham, Thursday, August 31, 1871," ed. Elias Nason.

Chapter 17
Polychrome Of Bird

Several years ago a rounded beach pebble, containing a polychrome painting of a bird, was picked up from a ploughed field by the young daughter of Mr George Clark, on his farm on the Rosedale Road, four miles north of Woodstock. The stone is dark grey in colour, water-worn quite smooth, as are so many beach stones, is about five inches in diameter and about one half inch thick. What bird the drawing is meant to typify I know not. The top of the head is a vivid scarlet, as is the breast, with black streaks along the wing over a ground-work of scarlet. The tail feathers are indicated by four black lines edged with scarlet; the remainder of the body is black. The mouth is open, the bill, above and below, coloured a faint yellow. The feet rest on what was meant for the branch of a tree, which is a vivid dark green. The colours are almost as bright as though painted yesterday. The field from which the object was picked up is quite some distance—perhaps two hundred yards—from the Clark homestead. Old residents of the locality say there never was any house nearer than the present Clark dwelling. Whether the polychrome was executed by an Indian, Frenchman, or an English settler, no one, perhaps, will ever know. On the whole, this polychrome drawing is a most interesting relic. If prehistoric, it is unique among archaeological finds in this part of the continent (Fig. 39, p 165). If of European craftsmanship it is singular that the artist picked a beach stone, rather than paper, canvas, or a wooden plaque, on which to express his artistic impulse. At any rate I have

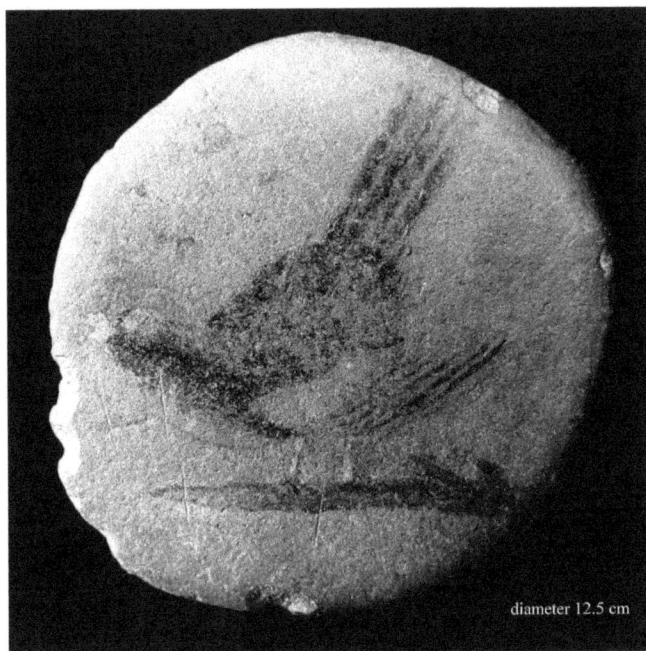

diameter 12.5 cm

39 Polychrome of bird, St John River, above Woodstock

photographed the pebble, and though of course the colours do not show, they are as I have described.

Apart from Lescarbot's statement that the Micmac of Nova Scotia did paintings and carvings equalling those in France, we know from the marvellous polychrome drawings discovered on the walls of the great Castillo Grotto in northern Spain, as well as those of the cavern at Fort-de-Gaume, Dordogne, France, what prehistoric man in Europe was capable of executing; and we also know, from irrefutable evidence of early writers of the 17th century, that polychromes were produced by our Indians along the New England coast. According to Daniel Gookin's *Historical Collections,* the Indians manufactured many baskets, some of rushes, some of coarse grass, maize husks, wild hemp, and some barks of trees, many of them with portraitures of birds, beasts, fishes and flowers upon them in colours. Josselyn in *Two Voyages to New England,* described baskets bags, and woven mats, dyed blue, red, and yellow. And Wood, in his *New England Prospect,* described the same art "with intermixed colours and protracture of antique imagerie." Rossier, in his *True Relation of Weymouth's Voyage To Northern Virginia* says: "They have excellent colours, and having seen our Indico, they made shew of it, or of some other like thing which maketh as good a blew." Wintemberg, in his *Roebuck Prehistoric Village* site quoted Van Corlear as saying that the people of Oneida painted all sorts of beasts on the fronts of their houses, and that around the entrance of the grave houses they painted dogs and deer and snakes and other beasts.*"

Perhaps only a few whites know that the Indian had his primary native colours. (See Speck's *Penobscot Man,* p. 137). His dyes he made from roots, leaves, rotten wood, red, and yellow clays, the strawberry blight—called Indian paint; powdered cuprite and haematite. These red and yellow clays were mixed with water, fish oil, or animal fats. The roots, leaves and rotten wood were put in a pot with water, boiled, and the resultant dye used to colour fabrics, bark or porcupine quills. If it be the latter, it generally takes two or three days for the dye to permeate them, and give a fast colour, according to my informant, the late Mrs Mary Moulton, a daughter of the late Dr Peter Polchies of the Maliseet Reserve below Woodstock.

Rotten wood gives a dark blue (indigo); white maple a light blue; ash bark and its ashes and the roots of the gold-thread give yellow. Hemlock bark or pine a rich olive green, and by adding more and more cedar lye one gets black. Alder gives a dark red; the stag horn sumach a dark pink.†[84]

It is doubtful if today these native dyes are much used, since it is much less trouble to purchase the ready-made products from the drug stores.

The point is that we are all too prone to belittle the artistic ability and ingenuity of primitive man in North America and often, to our shame be it said, place him in a

---

84   GFC wrote an article about First Nations dyes: "Dyes of the Maritime Indians." *The Herbarist,* no. 36, April 1970: 12-15.

---

*   Dr William Wintemberg F.R.S.C. Anthropological Series No. 83, 1936.

†   For some of these dyes I am indebted to Dr Speck's *Penobscot* Man, who gives credit for some to the late Mrs. Fannie Eckstorm.

category on a level with, or just a little higher than, the brute beasts, which is a gross libel on a people whose intelligence was equal to that of our not so remote prehistoric ancestors. I have reproduced on Figure 40, p 140 some of the stone pipes and animals executed for me, forty years ago, by the late Dr Peter Polchies, of the Maliseet reserve below Woodstock. Using whetstones I purchased for him at a hardware store as his medium, and with only a jack-knife for a tool he carved out these small objects with a masterful fidelity to detail that is astonishing. On the base of the pipe (Fig. 40 e) is a lizard, and on the front of the bowl is an almost life-like portrayal of one of his daughters when she was a small child. The face is true and Mongoloid. The whole piece is a marvel of consummate craftsmanship. The moose standing upright, and the one lying down, are equally amazing (Fig. 40 c and a); even the hair is indicated by minute incised lines along the back and sides of the creatures. I also have a paddle, six feet long, on the blade of which he made splendid carvings. Figure 42, p 142 shows both sides of the blade. Then I have a wooden shield he made me to support a pair of Caribou antlers, which contains a life-like portrait of King Edward VII; and, a few months before he died, Dr Polchies laboriously fashioned a beaver about four by two inches in size, out of a small block of white marble. I sent it to my literary agent in London, and she uses it as a paper weight. She said it represented a symbol of perseverance and hard work. (Editor's note: Other examples of First Nations crafts can be seen on Figure 41, a-d, p 141.)[85]

But Dr Polchies has not been the only modern Indian on the St John river to do excellent carving. His brother, Noel, and his nephew—I believe—William Polchies, of Kingsclear, above Fredericton, were both possessed of no mean artistic ability. One of Noel's pieces, a woman's hand carved for the handle of a so-called crooked knife, is, or was, in Pennsylvania Museum, and, along with other St John River Indian work, labelled Penobscot.

---

85   These items are not mentioned in the text. For a description see Appendix 3, Technical Captions.

CHAPTER 18
VARIOUS SITES

Although on many occasions I have been able to take enough time off from my practice to open up portions of several important campsites, on other occasions I have been limited only to making reconnaisances of ploughed areas. My hope is that other workers may profit from my investigations, so I am listing a few, some of which are quite far distant. Although I prefer to excavate and find *one* artifact rather than several surface objects, this too has its fascinating side. The fresh-turned furrow in late autumn; the same field after the snows have departed and the rains have washed the face of the brown earth, and the discovery of ashes, fire-stones, and flints marking the site where some ancient artificer sat and worked, tells a story as old as the human race... And in these evidences of the past I am almost oblivious to the facts of the present, or that the pendulum of time swings inexorably forward to new inventions, some of which, too, in a few years, will become obsolete.

So I suggest that you accompany me for a little while, and, as we walk over ploughed fields, drink in the sunshine and the wind and the smells of the brown soil until the light of day begins to fade; and then—home again.

THE ODELL FLAT

From a ploughed field owned by Armstrong brothers forming the upper extremity of the great flat opposite the mouth of the Odell stream, on the west side of the Tobique River, I picked up a grooved stone axe, and what seems to be an unfinished gouge or adze blade. The latter is nine and a quarter inches long, of grey chert, and has two well defined knobs two inches from the poll. The part meant for the blade is two and five-sixteenths inches wide. The front had been pecked slightly gouge-shape. The back is pecked off to form an acute angle. The sides, an inch and a half from the bit, curve inward and run practically straight to the knobs, beyond which they taper to the poll, which is three-quarters of an inch wide. On the whole, it is one of the most interesting pieces in my collection, since it so plainly shows the myriad hammerstone marks of the artificer, and one naturally wonders what caused him to leave his work unfinished (Fig. 43 a, p 170).

There were also plenty of chert and quartz chippings in this field, even close to the fence flanking the highway road and extending several hundred yards almost to the river.

Below the Armstrong site, and contiguous to it, is the Fred Smith farm. Below the house, the ground slopes to a flat terrace about two hundred yards in depth and three

43 Gouge, chisel, scraper
a. unfinished knobbed gouge, opposite Odell Stream, Tobique River; b. chisel,
Crooked Rapids, Main S.W. Miramichi; c. scraper, Gulquac site, Tobique River

hundred and fifty yards in width. One finds here many chippings of hard, dark brown stone. My son-in-law and I picked up several broken artifacts that had originally been very long and wide knives or spearheads. My son-in-law picked up a large blade of this material that had been turned out by the plough. (Figure 27 c, p 131—The gouge, Figure 27 a, is from Pokiok, St John River.)

This terrace finally ends in a short incline to a much larger flat extending to the river and five or six hundred yards long. Here too, one finds numerous chippings of quartz, chert, and others of a dark brown flinty stone similar to the chippings and broken artifacts on the upper terrace.

My Indian friend and helper later dug for a couple of hours on the upper terrace at one spot, and though we found no finished artifacts, we did uncover plenty of chippings. The site certainly deserves more intensive work than we had time to devote to it.

THE THREE BROOKS SITE

The Three Brooks Site is one of the most important of the many I have investigated. It is below the stream of the same name and about four miles below the town of Plaster Rock, on a farm formerly owned by Carter Edgar. From near the river bank the flat is level for a few rods, then ascends gently to a level beach or terrace.

Over a period of fifty years, Carter Edgar and his son Charles ploughed up and recovered upwards of a hundred very fine artifacts, including half a dozen grooved axes, a good gouge of hard sandstone, arrowheads and knives; among the latter being several similar to the double pointed laurel shape blades I discovered at Bristol. One also picks up at this Three Brooks Site triangular-shape knives, and long slender blades of the rounded base type, of the same variety of flint as that found on other sites all up and down the Tobique.

A few years ago, after the autumn ploughing, I picked up a small celt, or grooveless hatchet. It is a fine piece and polished from the bit to and including the poll (Fig. 30 d, p 134).

During the autumn of 1948, while showing Mr Hadlock the place following the potato harvest, I picked up a long narrow gouge of hard sandstone. It was standing upright in the sandy loam where it had evidently been deposited by the potato digging machine. It is twelve inches long. Yet another was picked up two weeks later by my son-in-law, K. C. Homer. Two years after this, the field again having been harvested of potatoes, I found another but smaller gouge which, as were the others, is of sandstone. They would seem to be of little use for cutting anything save charred wood. Hence it would appear quite evident that they were used for hollowing out wooden bowls and trays that had first been charred by fire. This site has produced more gouges than any other on the Tobique or the St John River.

At this time I picked up, besides a couple of knives and a broken arrowhead, a large chert knife. The point is missing, and because it was a fresh break I concluded that it had been broken off by the potato digger or the piece had been stepped on by one of the "pickers".

This field, especially the gentle slope from the terrace to the river bank, as well as the terrace itself, is rich in chippings of quartzite, agates of various colours, chert—black and bluish-grey, and the dark brown and very flinty stone already mentioned as characteristic of the Tobique River region. I have several knives of this material, whole or in part. From this Edgar site I picked up a four-sided object evidently intended for a knife. I believe these four-sided objects to be preliminary forms struck off by the artificer in preparation for subsequent chipping into finished artifacts.

For various reasons I cannot reveal, I have been able to excavate only at two or three places on this Three Brooks site, but if it were possible to investigate further I am sure the results would be satisfactory and most interesting.

On one occasion, John McClement, who was with me, opened up a fireplace and found fully a hundred pottery sherds.

On the flat below, the area close to the riverbank shows abundant evidence of prehistoric occupation; also the high terrace on the farm above Three Brooks.

The site was evidently a permanent, or semi-permanent, village, and occupied over a considerable period. There is a good salmon pool at the mouth of Three Brooks, while up the stream itself, on which, I believe, is a long dead-water, big game as well as fur-bearing animals must have been plentiful in the old days. (Figure 26 h, p 109 shows a large knife ploughed up at Three Brooks by Carter Edgar.)

George Bernard Site

Below the Tobique narrows, on the right hand side going with the stream, is a small flat divided by an old road once used to get to a bridge that formerly led from the Indian Reserve at mouth of Tobique to the mainland a couple of miles above the Village of Perth. This small flat, which flanks the highway road on its left leading to the reserve, was until recently worked by George Bernard, an Indian living at the Tobique Point Reserve. I found several fine artifacts at this place, including arrowheads, spearheads, knives, scrapers, part of a stone gouge, and a stone axe of reddish sandstone. The latter was partly embedded in the ploughed and harrowed soil. The other artifacts were at a depth of from six to twelve inches.

Most of the artifacts here were large, and of very dark flinty stone similar to many found at the Three Brooks and Wapske sites. Near the river end of the high terrace, I dug out, at four inches, a very large object, Ovate in form, with rounded base, probably a chopping knife. It is covered with creamy-coloured patination (Fig. 35 a, p 119). We saw no evidences of pottery sherds.

The Sadler Site

On the farm of Horace Sadler, at Maple View, about four miles above Plaster Rock, is a very extensive campsite flanking the west side of the Tobique River. Here I dug up, at eight inches, a very nice spearhead and several knives; one six inches long of red jasper was a surface find. I was told by Mr Sadler's father that across the river, near a brook, were several fireplaces or heaped up boulders. Since I had no canoe to make a crossing, I was unable to inspect the place. Indeed, all along this river, on practically every cleared intervale, one finds evidences of Indian occupation in times past.

Site Above Red Rapids

Two miles above Red Rapids, on the left side of the river, is an interesting campsite. I found here a long water-worn spearhead, or knife, of grey chert. It is about seven inches long, an inch and a quarter in width, and plainly shows the numerous conchoidal fractures struck off by the artificer.

Some years ago I briefly inspected a field opposite this site on the left of the highway road, which had recently been ploughed, and found the upper third of a very thin and wide knife, beautifully flaked across its whole surface on both sides, and with minute secondary chipping along the edges. In October, three years later, the field again having been ploughed, I picked up the middle portion. It is deeply patinated a rich creamy colour on both sides, the patination reaching almost to the centre of the piece, while the first portion shows but very little on its bluish-grey surface. Why the heavy patination on one piece, and so little on the other? The answer, I believe, is that the patinated piece had been in contact with a deposit of lime and chemical fertilizer put on the field during the years following my discovery of the unpatinated portion of the knife (Fig. 36 c, p 135).

Mr Wendell Hadlock, director of the Abbe Museum, at first doubted my contention that the two pieces were from the same artifact; but finally, after he had juggled with them for several minutes, he said: "You're right; they fit!"

Gulquac Site

Opposite the mouth of the Big Gulquac, and flanking the famous salmon pool of that name, is an important prehistoric campsite. One finds here thousands of chippings, those of the reddish-brown stone, peculiar to sites on the Tobique, predominating. Most of them are directly below the thick growth of moss, but there are many leading down to a depth of eight and ten inches. I found several broken spearheads (or knives?), scrapers and a few arrow-points. Some of the artifacts were clinging to the soil about the roots of trees blown down by wind storms. I had no time to dig more than thirty or forty feet from the river bank, but doubtless chippings and artifacts extend a considerable distance inland among the trees. John Ogilvy found a beautiful arrowhead of translucent red quartz lying on the beach, and his brother Hendry gave me a long object of black slate, beautifully polished. Very probably it was in process of being manufactured into a pendant. It has no hole, but there is a small rounded depression near one end, suggesting that the artificer intended to drill it at that place. The piece was half embedded in the river bank near a small brook. He also gave me an iron tomahawk he had found at an earlier date near the same spot.

This site may have been only a temporary place for hunters and fishermen, but all evidence points to it having been used over a long period of years.

I have a large copper kettle given me by Hendry Ogilvy, who found it at Trousers Lake, eighteen miles from the Tobique river. It was embedded in and almost covered with moss, is in good state of preservation, and would hold about five gallons. I have no doubt that one would find prehistoric campsites at this lake, as well as at Long Lake and many other waters only a few miles distant.

The Big Gulquac site certainly deserves more intensive work than I was able to devote to it, and I trust that other investigators will sometime give it a thorough going over.

There is a campsite on the Everett farm, at the lower end of the village of Riley Brook; one on the old Miller farm, now owned by Ralph Hayden, and a very important site on the big flat opposite the home of the late Mr Roy Stevenson at Nictau. On this latter flat I picked up a very fine adze blade of hard black stone. It is seven inches long and polished on all sides from bit to poll (Fig. 21 a, p 68).

There was also a small hatchet which I gave to Roy's son. In return he gave me a tiny thumb-nail scraper of quartz crystal he had found at the same place along with several knives.

All along the bench which flanks the river, one finds firestones, ash, and a great number of chippings. This place, too, deserves intensive working.

Campsite On Bert Shaw's Flat

Four miles north of Woodstock, on the Bert Shaw farm, are the remains of a campsite that must have been quite important in prehistoric times. The site is perhaps six hundred yards in extent, and is made up of a lower, and upper terrace; the former terrace at one time extended one hundred feet nearer the river than at present.

Some splendid artifacts, such as spearheads, knives and arrowheads have been turned up by the plough; chert, red jasper chippings, and fire stones litter the soil. I have found no pottery sherds. There persists a legend that Indian graves were formerly to be seen at the extreme lower end of the flat, opposite the upper end of Pine Island.

It is very rarely that artifacts of bone are found in Central New Brunswick. However, in the spring of the same year, Bert Shaw, while excavating a fire hole on the lower flat of his farm, discovered several pieces of bone, two of which, due to the fact that they contain incised lines, he thought might be portions of an earthen pot. Another object is a portion of a tanged spear for taking fish, which he correctly identified as such. He carefully saved all the pieces he had found, and showed them to me when I visited the place a week later. I recognized the decorated pieces as bone. They are flat, about two inches long, by half an inch wide, and one quarter inch thick, and may be portions of what was once a comb. The incised lines form a series of conical wigwams. There is also an interesting object of bone one inch in length, shaped like the nib of a pen. This is similar to some objects depicted on page 215 of Willoughby's *Antiquities of New England Indians,* and described by him on page 214 as a bird spear.

Mr Shaw deserves much credit for preserving these objects, for although he had picked up many surface artifacts from his flat covering a period of thirty years, he had not, to my knowledge, done any digging prior to the date he found the bone objects we have described. A less careful and observant worker might have discarded them as unworthy of preservation.

More recently, I was given a perforated stone pendant by a Mr Keye of Queen's County, N.B. It was found by employees of the New Brunswick Telephone Company while excavating for the placement of a line pole. On one side it is decorated with incised lines of the same pattern as the bone object found by Mr. Shaw. These two pieces were found more than a hundred miles apart. Later—1950—Mr Robert Currie, of Woodstock, gave me a flat slate-stone which contains a similar series of incised "wigwams". They are, however, enclosed by an incised line that has the form of a semi-lunar knife. Mr Currie found this object on the beach close to the bank, about one hundred feet east of the old Indian burying ground at Meductic Flat, St John River.

Site Opposite East Florenceville

Opposite the upper end of the village of East Florenceville is a flat, or intervale, owned by a Mr Hume, that contains abundant evidence of prehistoric Indian occupation. There are two terraces, the upper one being more extensive in area than the lower. I have been unable to do any digging save on a small portion near the lower, or southern end. Here I found a grooved hatchet, and a crudely formed but serviceable tomahawk. At this time I also found a plummet or pendant (Fig. 30 e, p 134).

This Hume flat, as well as the field north of it, that extends to White Marsh brook—on which the Fish Hatchery is situated, and the larger flat north of the brook, warrants extensive digging. On the latter flat, which is owned by Mr McCain, one finds numerous flints and fire stones. After it had been ploughed in 1950, I picked up a very finely made stone drill. It is about an inch and a half long, but unfortunately the point is missing.

Noddin, Saunders, And Mcguire[86] Sites

Below Clark's Brook, six miles north of Woodstock on the west side of the St John River opposite Grand Bar, is a quite large intervale, or flat, that is perhaps fifty or sixty feet above high freshet level. The flat extends southward from Clark's Brook about five hundred yards. The lower one third portion is owned by Mr Harry Boyer, the upper by a Mr Noddin.[87] A line fence divides the two properties. That owned by Mr Noddin contains the greater number of evidences of prehistoric occupation, which must have covered a considerable period—possibly on account of the fact that Grand Bar was then, as it is now, especially good salmon water.

I have dug up arrowheads and knives at this place, and found on the surface, after it had been partially ploughed and harrowed, two stone mauls. Also, late one evening while returning from partridge hunting, I picked up a long object that had been partially worked, either for a knife or spearhead (Fig. 18 b, p 65).

The *Saunders* site is perhaps a mile northward. I discovered it several years ago, after a small portion had been ploughed and harrowed. It is an ideal camping site; for not only is there a fine sandy beach for canoe landings, but within a distance of three hundred yards half a dozen small cold rivulets enter the St John River. Although I have dug up some notched arrowheads at this place, the shouldered long-stemmed variety predominate. Some of these latter were at a thirty-inch depth in sandy loam on a low bench contiguous to the beach, from which it runs level for about thirty feet, then rises gradually to another bench.

The great depth at which these shouldered and long-stemmed points were found, as well as the fact that I had been told that this type was much older than the notched variety, at first inclined me to concur in this belief. But later, on the upper bench, only thirty feet distant, I found the notched type at eight inches and then, to the right a few yards, on the same horizon, long-stemmed points similar to those found at the thirty-inch level on the lower bench! Which fact would seem to be yet another proof of how little we can rely on depths as a determinant of age.

This flat was formerly all under cultivation, and about eighty years ago the then owner—a Mr Dickenson—ploughed up a large copper or brass kettle, in which were two stone pipe bowls and several stone "darts". Mr Dickenson gave one of the pipes to a son living at Canterbury, and the other to a son then living at Hartland. About twenty-five years ago, the Canterbury Dickenson told me about the finds and a week later brought me his pipe bowl. It is of soapstone, vasiform in shape, and was classified by the late Dr Wintemburg as Iroquoian.

---

86 The text does not mention the McGuire site. In a surviving page of the monograph, p 209, GFC describes finding chippings and a triangular knife on the Lee McGuire site.

87 Charles Noddin died in 1938. His flat is described in a surviving page of an unpublished article (in the GFC Collection at UNB), "Discovery of Prehistoric CampSites on the Saint John River, by Dr George Frederick Clarke." GFC there speaks of him as still alive.

What became of the stone darts Mr Dickenson didn't know. I asked him if there had been any bones in the kettle, and he replied that, if there had been, they were scattered when the ploughshare turned it over and not noticed by his father.

There is also a tradition that on this same site was ploughed up portions of a skeleton wrapped in a moose hide bound about with spruce roots.

Chapter 19
Eight Pieces Of Black Ash

It is to be hoped that the reader will not think that I am being sentimental about the Indian. I merely desire to accord him his just due, which is far greater than a good many of us think to concede. We are all too prone to think of him as a wholly barbarous creature, devoid of love, affection, or kindliness; but the facts of history, as I have shown, prove the contrary. In his consideration for his women-folk during the child-bearing stage he was often vastly our superior. In war it was his custom to send notice to those he intended to attack. This Cannonicus did to the white settlers of Plymouth, sending them a sheaf of arrows enclosed in the skin of a rattlesnake. The white race, as well as the yellow, were not so courteous during the last two great wars.

The white has been the historian of the red man, consequently he has often been depicted as wholly treacherous and bloodthirsty. However, the very writers who have been his detractors have unwittingly, it seems, given quite another picture to those of us who have a passion for the truth. Cartier and his men were greeted as veritable gods by the Indians of Hochelaga; likewise the early English explorers to north and south Virginia. They requited the kindness shown them by treachery and kidnappings, and, on their return voyage, marvelled that they were regarded with suspicion and enmity. The Indians learned all too quickly, and the white man was hardly justified in heaping condemnation on his pupil. The ruthless act of Hunt, who seized upon several of the confiding Indians of Massachusetts, and sold them into slavery, sowed the seeds of distrust among all the Indians of the Atlantic coast, and was one of the many reasons for the hostility shown the early colonists of Massachusetts, Rhode Island, and Connecticut.

We have only to read the unbiased history of *one* noted American writer to realize that the spirit of the times prevailing among Puritan New England historians—such as Hubbard and Mather, was quite as barbarous, if not more so than that of the Indians of that period. In regard to the son of Philip (last chief of the Wampanoags) then a lad only nine years of age, the authorities seem to have been greatly exercised in spirit. There were so many nice precedents for his execution to be found in Scripture, and security as well as vengeance, would be satisfied by the destruction of the whole of the house of their dreaded enemy. Nothing can better show the venomous spirit of the times, or the depraving influence of a barbarous theology, than the following extract from a letter written by the Rev. Increase Mather* of Boston, to his friend Mr Cotton: "If it had not

---

* Rev. Increase Mather 1639-1723, pastor of North Church, Boston.

been out of my mind, when I was writing, I should have said something about Philip's son. It is necessary that some effectual course should be taken about him. He makes me think of Hadad, who was a little child when his father, the chief Sachem of the Edomites, was killed by Joab, and had not others fled away with him, I am apt to think that David would have taken a course that Hadad should never have proved a scourge to the next generation." In the case of Philip, however, more humane counsel (than that of the Rev. Mr Mather), prevailed, and the poor child was *only* shipped as a slave to the Bermudas!

And after the burning of the Pequot fort, the Pequots from other villages, on hearing of the disastrous tidings, hastened in numbers to the scene, and their very natural anguish is mocked at by the Rev. Cotton Mather* in a strain of satire as dull as it is wicked: "When they came to see the ashes of their friends mingled with the ashes of the fort, and the bodies of their countrymen so terribly barbikewed, where the English had been doing a good morning's work, they howled, they roared, they stamped, they tore their hair, and though they did not swear (for they knew not how,) yet they cursed, and were the pictures of so many devils in desperation." Is not the feeling which prompted this truly diabolical sentence identical with that which animates the red warrior when beholding his foe consuming at the stake, or running the gauntlet through innumerable blows?

Another picture: Several hundred of the broken Pequot nation were on one occasion taken in the Narragansett country. "The men among them," says the Rev. William Holland, "to the number of thirty, were turned presently into Charron's ferry boat, under the command of Skipper Gallop, who dispatched them a little without the harbour." "Twas found," says the Rev. Cotton Mather, "the quickest way was to feed the fishes with 'em." The women and children were enslaved.

*   *   *

We took from the Indian his rightful heritage, uprooted him from a way of life that had been his for untold centuries. We cajoled him with specious promises, broke solemn treaties. He was assured that he would be allowed to take fish from the rivers, game from the forests, birch-bark for his canoes, black ash for his basketry. In short, he was to continue to pursue the same sort of life as his ancestors.

In 1779 English contractors were engaged cutting pine logs on the St John River for masts for the Royal Navy. Col. John Allen, of Machias, Maine, tried to induce the Indians to obstruct the workmen. Hearing of this, Governor Franklin, of Nova Scotia (of which New Brunswick was then a part), wrote from Windsor, N.S. to Pierre Tomah—perhaps the most influential chief of the St John river Indians—in these words:

"Brethren, King George needs masts for his ships, and has employed people to provide them *On Your River* (the italics are mine) and depends on you to protect the workmen cutting them and conveying them to Fort Howe..."

Naturally the Indians considered the words *On Your River* as an admission that the St John River was theirs, and that the Nova Scotia government made no claim of suzerainty over it. But when the Revolutionary war ended, both the newly formed United States,

---

*   Cotton Mather, D.D. son of Increase. John Cotton 1585-1652. Puritan divine.

and the loyalist English of Nova Scotia, promptly forgot their fine promises to the Indian. They were no longer needed by either party!

The years passed, and finally the St John River Indian was segregated on Reserves (concentration camps, some modern Indians have termed them). Living conditions were terrible, the houses mere shacks. Many of the people developed tuberculosis and other diseases. Their spiritual needs were looked after by ministers and priests, their bodies allowed to languish; possibly from a theory that what happened to his physical body was of little moment so long as his soul was assured of going to heaven.

Thirty-five years ago I wrote the Department of Indian Affairs, Ottawa, and suggested that a small building be erected on each reserve in New Brunswick; that some light machinery; power driven saws, planers and sanding machines be installed, and a white man put in charge to instruct the Indians how to use them. I suggested that the Indian could then manufacture hoe, peavey,[88] rake and pickaxe handles, and these be made available for the wholesale and retail trade. I said that a consequence of this product by their own hands would be to give the Indian a feeling of independence as well as a living wage. I was not accorded the courtesy of a reply. Possibly the Indian Department heads felt that the implementation of my suggestion would interfere with the white man's manufacture of the same products.

Of late years, in this province of New Brunswick, there has been much talk of equal opportunity for all. I cannot help wondering whether this is meant to include the Indian. We hear of an immense sum of money being voted by the federal government for the purpose of building new homes for the Indian. It isn't only new homes he needs. He needs to be recognized as a human being with the same yearnings as the white man for the amenities of civilisation; and, above all, the right to have a job and receive a living wage.

As the descendant of a race which developed our first democracy on the shores of America, he must be made to feel that he has an equal part to play with the descendants of the French, English, and other races which constitute the Dominion of Canada in building our country's future.

We prate of democracy, of justice. A few years ago my friend, Peter Paul, took eight pieces of black ash (which he considered his right) from a thousand-acre farm in Carleton County. He was arrested by the police and charged with theft.[89] I went his bail. He hired a lawyer to defend him. I personally prepared the brief, and had four or five old treaties, made between whites and Indians, in support of my arguments. Neither brief nor treaties were used.

On the day of trial, I was called (about eleven-thirty in the morning) by the defence lawyer to give evidence. The judge immediately declared a recess of an hour. On resumption of the trial I was not called upon to give my evidence; nor—to my surprise and indignation—during the rest of the proceedings, although every few minutes I

---

88 A lumberman's hook with a spike at the end.

89 This was Peter Paul's second trial for taking black ash in accordance with ancient treaty rights. The first was in 1945. After the second trial he went on cutting black ash, hoping that, if he were again charged, a third trial would definitively establish his treaty rights in the matter. But the tide was beginning to turn; he was not arrested again.

expected to be called. Peter Paul was found guilty, and bound over to keep the peace for one year. The presiding judge told him that, because of his misconception of what constituted his legal rights, he was imposing only a light sentence.

The facts are these: There had been several cases over a period of years during which Indians had exercised what they had considered their inalienable right to take black ash wherever they found it. Indeed, many owners of wood lots recognized their claim. But others resented any infringement of their title deeds to their lands—even though black ash is practically worthless, either as lumber or firewood. Magistrates had been much exercised in their minds about the legal rights of the Indian in this respect. Several had ruled in favour of the Indian; others had taken the opposite course. It was hoped by everyone that Peter Paul's case would settle the matter.

Before I left the court, the judge said to me: "I was disappointed that you weren't recalled this afternoon, because I felt that you had something interesting to say." I had!!

It has always been my opinion that both the trial and the verdict constituted a negation, not merely of traditional rights, but of the inherent and inviolable rights of the Indian as implicitly expressed by Governor Franklin's letter to chief Tomah, and so understood by the whole tribe then as well as now.

*   *   *

Let us go farther afield: According to Sir Thomas Pownall, Governor and Commander-in-Chief of Massachusetts Bay and South Carolina, and Lieutenant-Governor of New Jersey, whose book *The Administration of the Colonies* (4th edition, 1769) is before me from which I quote:

"In the year 1726, the Seneccas, Cayougaes and Onada-agaes acceded to the same terms of alliance, in which the Mohawks and Oneidas were already—So that the whole of the dwelling and hunting lands of the Five-nation confederacy were put under the protection of the English and held by them in Trust, for and to the use of these Indians and their posterity. To which these nations affixed their marks (totems).

"Instead of executing this trust faithfully and with honour, by extending to the Indians our civil protection against the frauds of the English, and our military protection against the attempts of the French, we have used this trust only as a pretence to assume a dominion over them—We have suffered the English settlers to profit of every bad occasion to defraud them of their lands— We have never made any effectual regulations to prevent their being defrauded in their trade; and until our own interest appeared to be affected, we abandoned them to their own chance and force, opposed to the strength of a powerful enemy. Nay, when at last we thought necessary for the sake, not of national faith and honour, for the sake, not of these our faithful allies, but for the sake of our own safety and interest to interfere, in opposing the French encroachments, we took it up as disputing the empire of America with the French; not as protecting and guarding the Indian lands and interest to their use, agreeable to the sacred trust by which we were bound. And thus these savages (as we to our own shame call them) repeatedly told us, 'That both we and the French sought to amuse them with fine tales of our several upright intentions; that both parties told them, that they made war for the protection of the Indian rights, but that our actions plainly discovered that the war was only a contest who should become masters of the country, which was the property neither of the one nor the other.' Since we have driven the French government from America, we have confirmed this charge of the Indians against us, by assuming that dominion which in faith and justice we cannot say we have gained over the Indians, which, in fact, we have not gained, and which, be it remembered, will cost more blood and treasure before we do gain it, than it is for the honor and interest of Great Britain to expend in so bad and useless a cause."

THE END

Appendix 1
How To Make A Birch-Bark Canoe
by E. T. Adney Edited By G. F. Clarke

The birch-bark canoe was the most perfect product of the native American's creative genius; and the Maliseet, or St John River canoe, was, I believe, the most beautiful of any made by the various tribes inhabiting Canada. It is a poem in wood and bark. The steps in its construction are so complex that mere words are inadequate to convey a clear picture to the reader without illustrations. And even with these to aid his understanding, he may find it difficult to grasp all of its varied features.

44 Edwin Tappan Adney, 1897

No craft of comparable size was as light, or could carry as much freight. Indeed the rapid progress, comparatively speaking, that marked exploration of the vast hinterland of the North American continent, after the coming of the white man, would have been retarded for a hundred years had he not utilized the birch-bark canoe of the aboriginal inhabitants.

No white man ever knew more about the canoes of the various tribes than did Edwin Tappan Adney (Fig. 44, p 183). I'll correct or amplify the foregoing and declare that he knew more about them than any other man, or any combination of men the world over. This remarkable genius was born at Athens Ohio, in 1868, came to Upper Woodstock, New Brunswick, during his nineteenth year, to make a study of the material culture of the St John River Indians. He made the acquaintance of old Peter Jo, one of the last of the great canoe builders on the St John. Jo lived (as did a few other Indians of the Maliseet tribe), on the intervale just below Lane's Creek where it vents into the St John. It was lucky for Adney that Jo was just about to start building yet another of his birch-bark canoes, for which he always had a ready sale to young whites who used them as pleasure craft on the river, and for hunting and fishing on nearby lakes and streams.

Adney visited Peter Jo practically every day during this summer stay at Upper Woodstock; and watching, often assisting Jo, he became familiar with all the different phases inherent in the construction of the birch-bark canoe.[90] Being an artist and draughtsman of rare ability, he made sketches of the several parts, and wrote an article "How To Build A Birch-Bark Canoe," which was published in *Harper's Young People,* issue of June, 1890.

Adney's life was a romance in itself. A biography of his various activities would fill half a dozen volumes. He was the son of Prof. W. H. G. Adney and Ruth (Shaw) Adney. His mother took him to New York while he was in his early teens. He studied at the Art Students' League, often got up at daybreak to study birds in Central Park, did pen and ink drawings for Chapman's *Handbook of Birds in Eastern North America*; did work for *Outing* and other magazines, was on the staff of *Harper's*; staff of Museum of Natural History; covered the Klondike gold rush for *Harper's* and the *London Chronicle,* 1897-98, and for *Collier's Weekly* at Cape Nome, 1900. He married Minnie Bell Sharp, 1899, issue one son, Glenn. About 1907 he returned to Woodstock; later (1916), he joined the Royal Canadian Engineers. At end of the war he remained in Montreal seven or eight years, during which time he was consultant in heraldry for Henry Birks and Sons. He designed the seal for the Royal College of Physicians and Surgeons, did the coat of arms of Cardinal Richelieu for Manoir Richelieu and (but I must be brief) began constructing models of birch-bark canoes (Figs. 45 a-d, p 143 and 53, p 147). About 1932 he returned to Upper Woodstock, opened up the little bungalow he had built with his own hands sixteen years before, and continued work on his canoe models until a few years before his death in 1950.

In all he made more than a hundred models, (which included models of the *Master Canoe* of the Hudson Bay Company, originally 36 to 40 feet in length); spruce-bark canoes, moosehide canoes; the umiak and kayak of the Eskimo—all built to one-fifth scale of actual size. Most of these models he later sold to the Newport News Marine Museum. Why this museum? you may ask. I answer: because none of the several wealthy men he approached in Canada possessed enough sense of their historical value—that in these models rested the whole early story of inland water transportation in North

90 In a letter written c. 1961 (editor's collection), GFC makes it clear that the canoe in Figure 54 a is the one Adney and Peter Jo built in that summer of 1888. The racing canoe in Figure 54 b was also built in 1888, by Jim Paul and Peter Polchies of the St Mary's Reserve near Fredericton, for Colonel Herbert Dibblee of Woodstock. In 1892 Dibblee and Adney paddled it (or possibly a similar canoe made by Peter Jo) in the annual canoe race at Woodstock.

America—to pay the very modest sum his industry was entitled to! Thus, one by one, Canada continues to lose her historical treasures.[91]

*   *   *

Now I must again roll back the years more than three-quarters of a century to Peter Jo, and the canoe he was about to build; of which I will give a "simplified" description. For the most part I shall use Adney's text as in *Harper's Young People*; but, because I know a good deal about canoes, having owned three of full size,[92] as well as several models; and, moreover, helped Adney restore a 16½-footer (Fig. 54 a, p 192) also made by Peter

48 Maliseets of the St Mary Indian Reserve, opposite Fredericton, building a canoe, 1890s

Jo, (which I now own),[93] I am rearranging the matter to suit myself. But first, I must tell you that usually a whole family (including the women), or several men, assisted in the work (Fig. 48, p 185). For one man could hardly accomplish it alone; or at least not without great difficulty.

---

91   Two books record Adney's great lifework. The first is his own notes and drawings, put in order for publication as: Edwin Tappan Adney and H. I. Chapelle, *The Bark Canoes and Skin Boats of North America* (Smithsonian Institution Press, 1964). The second is a picture book by John Jennings: *Bark Canoes: The Art and Obsession of Tappan Adney* (Firefly Books, 2004). It has large, beautiful colour photographs of a hundred and ten of the canoe models in the Marine Museum.

92   Until the 1930s GFC regularly used birchbark canoes. Several snapshots survive that show them in use, such as Fig. 47 a-b, p 145.

93   GFC and Peter Paul further restored this canoe c. 1961; see Fig. 46, p 144.

The bark has been selected from a big birch (called Masqua by the Maliseet Indians), free from low-hanging limbs, and with as few knots as possible. Jo peeled the bark in the early spring, before the sap began to flow upward. For at this time the bark is more free from bubbles, and tougher in every respect. This is known as "winter birch-bark," and is preferred to summer bark. He rolled it up like a rug or bed-roll, tied it about with spruce roots, and lugged it home. Then he put it in the little creek to keep it supple until he was ready to use it, otherwise it would dry out and crack. The canoe is to be about 19 feet long, and thirty inches wide across the middle, gradually tapering towards the ends. The woodwork (all except the cross bars, which are of rock maple) is split from the heart of a straight-grained white cedar log, free from knots. Long stringy roots of the black spruce, peeled and split in half, some in quarters, are used for lashings and sewings. At present these are in deep water to keep them supple. The ribs, forty-eight in number, 2½ in. wide, one-half-inch thick and tapering slightly at the top, were bent, two at a time, one within the other (for if bent separately they would be sure to break) to the desired shape. When five or six had been bent, they were placed, one within the other, and tied across the top with a rope made from the inner bark of the cedar, to keep them from losing their shape, and put under cover to dry thoroughly. Then more ribs were bent until the desired number was confined within cedar-bark ropes. The greatest care was taken in bending these ribs, since their shape determines whether the bottom of the finished canoe is to be flat or rounded. If flat it is more stable on the water; less "crank", some have expressed it.

The gunwales, which serve as a building frame, resemble two bent bows, held apart by five cross-bars. These bows are each whittled square, with a bevel on the lower outside edge, and tapering towards the ends. These ends have been rabbeted about 2½ inches on their inner surface facing each other (Fig. 49 i, p 187). The purpose of these notches or rabbets will be explained later. Mortices have been cut out of the gunwales, each facing the other, of which we have ten altogether, wide enough to receive the ends of the crossbars. First the middle bar, 28½ inches long, was inserted into the middle mortices in the gunwale, to which it was secured by round hardwood pegs, driven through holes drilled through each part. Then the next cross-bars, 21½ inches long, were stepped in their separate mortices and pegged; finally the shortest bars, 11½ inches long, were inserted in their respective mortices, and the ends of the gunwales bent together, nailed and tied with spruce roots. But not until later will the cross-bars be lashed to the gunwales.

Peter Jo has also made thirty-eight wooden stakes from two to three feet long, flat on one side. The stakes, as you will soon see, play a most important part in building a birch-bark canoe. Indeed they are indispensable. He has also cut enough cedar boards about ¼ in. thick, nine feet long, with which to sheath the inside of the canoe.

As you already know, the gunwales have been bent and secured each in its proper mortice. Jo has already scooped, with the greatest care, a shallow bed out of a flat piece of ground where he is to continue building his craft. This bed is a little over nineteen feet long and three and one half feet wide. It is slightly higher in the centre than at the ends.

With several big flat boulders, which Jo had used on many such occasions, and a few short boards, he is now ready to assemble all the prepared parts above described, and some to be described later, into a beautiful and serviceable canoe.

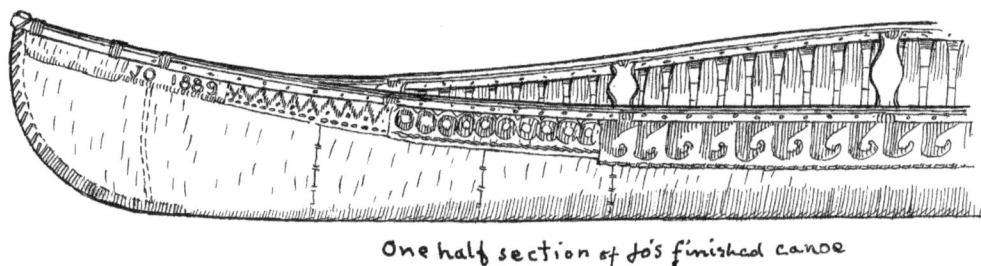

One half section of Jo's finished canoe

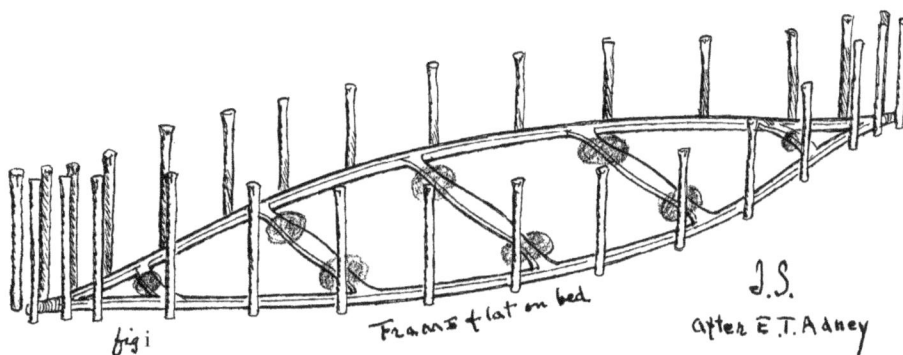

fig i

Frame flat on bed

J.S.
after E.T.Adney

49 Sketches of construction of Peter Jo's birch-bark canoe. John Stevens (after E. T. Adney)

First the gunwales, or frame, are set exactly in the centre of the bed, and heavy boulders put on the cross-bars to keep the frame securely in position. Now Jo begins pounding the stakes, already described, into the ground, the flat sides snug against the frame on each side. They stand in perpendicular positions. Three pairs of these stakes, each pair an inch apart, are also driven into the ground beyond each end of the frame so that the last pair are 9½ feet from the centre cross-bar, but they are not yet tied at the tops (Fig. 49 i, p 187).

The stakes now all in place, they are removed and each one laid on the ground beside the hole it formerly occupied. The boulders on the cross-bars are next removed, and the frame lifted from the bed and laid to one side. The birch bark, which has been taken from the water, is now laid flat in the bed, the outer, or curly side, up, and the frame set on top of it, each extreme end of the frame resting on a short square post about two inches high. Short boards are laid upon the gunwales, and the heavy boulders put on top of them to keep the bark perfectly flat and immovable in the bed.

Now the bark, which, of course, extends beyond the sides of the frame, is split from above downwards a few inches opposite each cross-bar. Then the bark is bent carefully upwards along the sides of the frame, and as this is done each stake, with the flat side against the bark, is inserted into the hole it formerly occupied. The tops of each opposite pair of stakes are connected by a strip of cedar bark, as in Fig. 50 ii, p 188. This keeps them snug and perpendicular.

Since the bark is not always of sufficient width to cover the entire bottom and sides of the canoe, it is necessary to piece out the sides with strips of bark sewed with small peeled spruce roots. It is also necessary to cut gores at certain places in the bark to keep it from buckling; these edges are also sewed together with roots (Fig. 50 ii).

In order to keep the bark from bending too far forward, the chisel-shaped end of a stake, called an inner stake (Fig. 50 iii), is slipped into the crack or space along the outer edge of the frame, just opposite each outer stake, and these are tied together at the upper end. Long thin strips of wood are now pushed in outside, between the bark and the outside stakes (see stripes marked A along the upper side of bark in Fig. 50 ii) and similar boards are placed between the bark and the *inside* stakes Fig. 50 iii). Thus on all sides the bark is held perfectly straight up and down.

The reader must not forget that the frame is still lying flat on the floor of the bark, only upheld at each end by two short square posts. But now the boulders that held the frame solid are again removed, and the frame is lifted up just enough to allow two stout square posts 7½ inches long to be set upright upon the bark, and engage each end of the cross-bar (Fig. 50 iii, marked "post"). Over this part a short board again is laid, and the heavy boulders again set on top of it. Similar posts, 9 inches long, are placed upright under each end of the next cross-bar, and the weights replaced. Two other posts, twelve inches long, are in the same manner placed beneath the shortest cross-bars, of which there are also two. Finally, a single post, 16½ inches long, is placed under each end of the frame, and all the weights replaced. By this method, the frame has assumed the shape seen in Figure 50 ii.

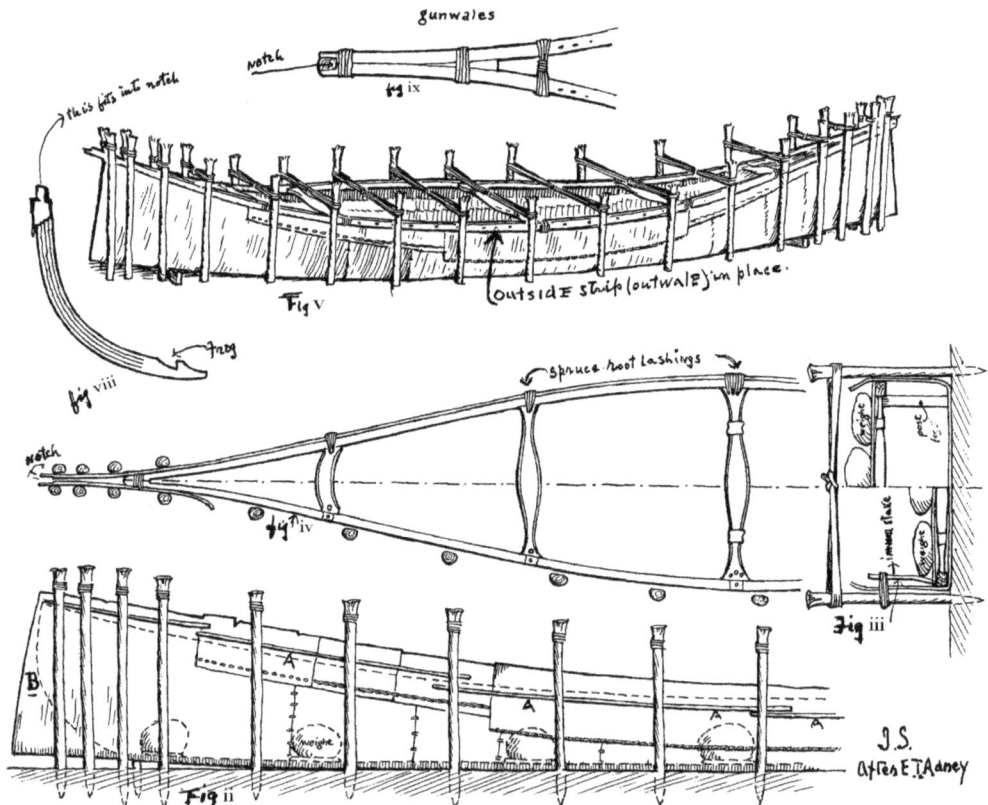

50 More sketches of canoe construction by John Stevens (after E. T. Adney)

The temporary strips of wood outside the bark are now removed, and a long one, over 19 feet long and half an inch thick, is put in its place. This strip is, of course, the outwale, and is bent to the same shape as the frame, and secured to it by slender nails which clinch on the inside. (See Figure 50 v, "Outwale".) Thus the bark is held secure. The cross-bars are now lashed to the outer woodwork by roots which pass through holes drilled in the ends of the cross-bars, and similar holes, punched with an awl, in the bark. The projecting edges of the bark are folded over and down and tacked to the top surface of the frame, so as to offer a smooth surface for the top strip of wood (the upper wale) that is to be put on afterward (in some cases the bark is only brought up to the upper edge of the frame and tacked on). This is when bark and frame are to be lashed together with group-ties of spruce roots. The excess bark is cut away with a sharp knife.

The stakes are again pulled up, and the canoe is laid bottom-up upon two benches about three feet high. It is now somewhat the appearance of a flat-bottomed, double-ended boat, for the beautiful shape of the finished canoe will not be taken until the ribs are put in.

With a pair of dividers, or by the eye alone, the curved line of both bow and stern are marked out, and following this curve the bark is cut away with a knife. (See Figure 50 ii, p 188 for curved dotted line B.)

To strengthen the bow and stern, two pieces of cedar wood, three feet long and 1½ inches wide, have been shaped somewhat triangular, or wedge shape, the top notched on each lateral side leaving a one and one-eighth inch projection. Then the pieces were split part way into at least four strips (laminated) to facilitate bending, then steamed and bent with the thin edge outward, exactly as shown in Figure 50 viii, so as to correspond with the curved line just marked out with the dividers, and wrapped tightly with a length of string (twine or cord). The lower ends were notched or frogged. The purpose of these notches will be explained later. These bow and stern supports have been dried under cover. Now one of these is placed between the curved edges of the bark, a splint of spruce root next covers the crack, and the whole are sewed together by an over and under stitch with spruce roots. Then the opposite end is treated likewise. (I may say here that instead of twine to bind the laminated bow and stern pieces, the model I have was tightly bound with half-inch-wide very thin strips of basket ash or some other wood.)

A much better way to do this latter part of the work, is to put the curved bow and stern pieces in place inside the bark, with the thin edge outward, engage the upper notched end in the rabbeted sides of the gunwales, have a helper hold the lower part firmly on the floor of the canoe, then pare off the excess bark with a sharp knife. Canoe builders didn't always use the same methods.

I have had made two slightly different views of the bow portion of a derelict canoe I found among the ruins of Adney's bungalow a few years after his death. (See Figures 51 and 52, p 146.) The end board is one of two I salvaged from a canoe stolen from me forty years ago and left, right side up, in the woods across the lake from my camp. Three winters of snow and ice had destroyed the canoe beyond repair. These end boards were too long and wide for the bow parts of the Adney reclaimed portion, but I slightly reduced one of them and inserted it in position as shown in Figures 51 and 52. I have marked this end board "A". "B" shows the 1½ inch projection which fits *between* the two inner sides of the gunwales. The two "C"s show the *shoulders* of the end board in position *beneath* the two *under* portions of the gunwales supporting and strengthening them. "D" shows the notch in the extreme lower centre of the end board engaged in the notch, or frog, near the *lower* end of the curved bow piece. "E" shows the *upper* end of the curved bow piece (which is inserted in the rabbeted part of the ends of the gunwales and projects about ½ inch above them).

The whole development by our native Americans of the parts described is ingenious and too complex to portray adequately to the reader by mere words. The marvellous thing is that the men who worked out the various steps in the construction of the birch-bark canoe had not, at the same time, developed better housing than bark wigwams and cabins in which to dwell.

You will notice that I have removed one side of the bark in order that you may see the construction as, with words and pictures, I have described them. The removal of the bark clearly shows the inner curly bark of the opposite side. This curly side, as I explained before; forms the outer side of the tree.

*   *   *

Now let's get back to Jo. The canoe is next laid top-side up, and a pitch prepared of spruce gum and grease melted together in an iron pot, either one or the other of the ingredients added in the making until the pitch will neither crack off in cold water, nor melt easily in the sun. Long strips of cloth are saturated with the hot pitch, and forced from the inside into the cracks along the curved bow and stern pieces, that have just been assembled and sewed into place. The edges of the slits along the sides may now be sewed together. Each crack is covered with very thin pieces of birch-bark over the inside of the cracks, and pasted down with hot pitch.

The canoe is now ready for the thin strips of sheathing that lie edge to edge and extend to within a foot of each end of the inner surface of the bark, and will soon be held firmly in place by the ribs. These pieces of sheathing are in nine-foot lengths; their ends are slightly bevelled, and overlap about 2½ inches where they meet in the centre of the floor and sides of the canoe. First a piece of sheathing is laid exactly in the centre of the floor, and one end is gently but firmly slipped between the bark and the lower straight end of the bow-piece, a little beyond the V-shape frog. At this juncture, two or more men (or women) are needed to assist in the work. Sometimes these helpers hold the sheathing in place with their hands while a few ribs are inserted. Sometimes temporary ribs, of ash or alder saplings shaped flat on one side, are inserted under the gunwales to hold the sheathing in place while some of the permanent ribs are being put in. The pieces of sheathing extend on either side of, and about four inches beyond, the frogged bow and stern pieces.

The ribs, as you know, have all been bent the proper shape, and are now thoroughly dry. Commencing at one end, the space that each rib is to occupy is carefully measured with a splint of basket ash, (or a measuring stick which Jo's forefathers handed down to him) and each rib, purposely made a little longer than seems necessary, is inserted under the inner border of one of the gunwales and the other end driven into place under the opposite gunwale with a long stick and a mallet; thus holding the sheathing yet more firmly against the sides and floor. Each rib, therefore, is driven into the exact place for which it had been fashioned beforehand, and, as the stiff ribs yield but little, the bark is forced out to the proper shape—the shape of the ribs. Between the middle cross-bar and the next, there may be ten ribs, between that and the shortest one, eight ribs, and between the shortest one to near the end, six ribs—forty-eight in all.

Next the bow and stern are stuffed as full of shavings (or moss) as possible. Jo has prepared an end board in this wise: he split two pieces of white cedar to the thickness of ½-inch, and shaped them to a long oval, the centre of which was ¼-inch in thickness. From the lower end he cut a rounded notch; and from each of the lateral sides of the upper part, he cut away one inch of the wood, leaving a projection 1½-inches high and ¾-inch in width. Then he steamed the pieces and gave them a slight bend, which reduced their length to 15 inches, as you have seen in Figures 51 and 52, p 146.

Now the end boards are put in place. To do this, the notched end is stepped into place in the frog of the bow and stern pieces lying on the floor of the canoe at bow and stern. Then the upper part is forced backwards until the shoulders are underneath of and support the gunwales on each side. These rest against the ¾-inch-wide projection already mentioned as forming the upper end of the end board. Thus it will be seen that the sides of these end boards also act as ribs, since they support and hold in place the ends of the sheathing.

Next, two long strips of cedar, half an inch thick, two inches wide in the middle, and tapering to one inch wide at the ends, are nailed along the upper surface of the gunwale. These are the same length as the outside strips. The ends of these, which extend slightly beyond the frame itself, are next securely bound together by roots that pass through the bark and around the four loose ends. But before this is done, the ends of these upper strips (called the upper wale) have been notched on the inside to fit the projecting end of the bow and stern pieces (Figs. 51/52 e). A piece of bark, with rounded corners, is also usually folded down over the upper edges of the bark underneath both the top and sides of the gunwales before they are lashed together. (See Figure 52 f. Part of the piece has been cut away.)

Every crack and seam must now be stopped with hot pitch, plastered on outside with a small wooden paddle, and swathed down with the moistened finger. A piece of stout canvas, three or four inches wide, and two feet long, is pasted with pitch over the sewed edges of bow and stern. Adney depicts several different designs he says were put on the bows of birchbark canoes, as well as the maker's name. (See Jo's finished canoe, Figure 49, p 187.) As I have already related, I have owned four birch canoes,[94] three of which had neither decoration nor name. The fourth, depicted on page 75 of *Bark Canoes and Skin Boats of North America,* by Edwin Tappan Adney and Howard Chapelle, belonged to me (Fig. 54 b, p 192), and Adney made sketches of it. It was decorated, but had no maker's name. I also owned the very old Maliseet model with high ends on page 81 of the

---

94 He says above that he has owned *three* birchbark canoes. He certainly owned at least four.

same book, and a beautiful model of an Ojibway canoe. These models I gave to Adney in 1925. (The canoe models on Figures 45, p 143 and 53, p 147 were made by Adney).

At present, I have a 16½-foot Maliseet canoe (Fig. 54 a, p 192), with group ties of spruce roots along the gunwales; and a 24-foot Micmac canoe with hogged centre, known as a *heavy water* or sea-going canoe.

Nicholas Denys briefly describes a Micmac canoe, and gives its width as two feet. I feel quite sure that he was in error about the width, or else his text was mistranslated, because Lescarbot, writing more than half a century earlier, tells us that the Souriquois (Micmac) canoe was four feet wide in the centre.

a. Maliseet canoe, length 512 cm (16.8'), built by Peter Jo and Tappan Adney, 1888

b. Maliseet racing canoe, length 600.5 cm (19.7'), built by Jim Paul and Peter Polchies, 1888

54 The birchbark canoes GFC owned in the early 1970s

The Spruce-Bark Canoe

The initial steps in building the spruce-bark canoe are much the same as those for its more aristocratic cousin, the birch-bark. First the bark is peeled; the gunwales—merely round poles of saplings—are bent the proper shape, and held apart by cross-bars, the ends of which are bent around the gunwales, project backwards underneath six or eight inches, and are bound securely with cedar bark or spruce roots. On top and sides of these gunwales are two extra wales to give added support to the craft. The gunwales, or frame, are laid on a flat piece of ground, and a few stakes are pounded into the earth on either side of them. Then the stakes are pulled out, the frame removed, and the bark, with the inner or smooth side down, is laid on the bed. The frame is set on the bark, then raised to the proper height and the bark is bent upwards to the frame, and secured to it with spruce roots passed through holes punched in the bark and then over the tops of the gunwales. The bark at bow and stern is brought together so they look like the ends of a bateau.[95] Both bow and stern are supported on both sides by stout cedar withes, and lashed together with spruce roots, or basket ash, and pitched. The ribs are merely hoops of alder fastened to the inner sides of the craft, and the gunwales, with roots. For greater support, these ribs (if they can be called such) were supported at intervals with round poles of cedar or some other wood, running longitudinally. These craft were makeshift affairs, hastily constructed by hunters to cross a lake, or travel a deadwater, and then abandoned. One model described by Edward Jack in *Acadiensis* for June-July, 1905, and found by his party near Little Southwest Miramichi Lake, was sheathed on the inside of the bottom by some twenty pieces of cedar (ash splints may also be used). "This canoe," he says, "was evidently made by some solitary hunter, for it was only capable of holding one person. The model was good." The little model illustrated in Figure 45 d, p 143 is one-fifth scale of a Shuswap-Chilkat Indian canoe, on the west coast. Reverse the shape of the bow and stern and it would serve as a model of a Maliseet spruce-bark canoe, though the Maliseet would add strips of cedar or ash on the floor and sides.

*   *   *

The moosehide canoe follows the general line of the spruce-bark. That is, the frame was made in the same manner, then three or more moose hides (each one overlapping the other two or three inches and sewed with small roots) were stretched over the frame.

Sometimes the hides overlapped the gunwales on either side and were sewed to them the whole length with an over and under stitch. Then the seams were daubed with pitch. These canoes were made and used by hunters and trappers to return home in the spring. Then the hides were removed from the frame and utilized for clothing, moccasins, or webbing for snowshoes. In the old days (I mean after the white traders came to the mouth of the St John River and moose hides were in demand) the hides that had filled their duty as canoe coverings were sold to the truck houses.

Note to the reader: Figure 48, p 185 depicts a birch-bark canoe under construction by St John River Indians, of the St Mary Indian Reserve opposite Fredericton, about the close of the last century. Note that the ribs have not yet been inserted, and fewer stakes used than in the Peter Jo canoe as depicted by Adney (Figs. 49, p 187 and 50, p 188).

---

95   A long, low, flat-bottomed boat with heavily flared sides and sharply pointed ends, much used in river drives.

To The Birch-Bark Canoe

I like to think this thought of you:
    That first as gift for Indian maid,
Her father made a toy canoe,
    Before your larger form was laid.
And you were subject to his whim,
    And limpid lake and gentle stream,
Great rivers with swift rapids grim,
    You floated feather-light as dream:
Long years, ere searching for Cathay
    By westward passage at fortune's beck,
Led by the gallant Cartier,
    The men of France first saw Kebec.

Thenceforward you new masters served,
    And so the years sped by, and they
No longer by ambition spurred
    To reach the realm of old Cathay:
But north, and south, and west now sped,
    Trader, explorer, warrior, priest,

55 Master canoe, 36-40 ft. long, used by Hudson Bay Co. and Nor-West Fur Co. (courtesy Royal Ontario Museum). Original painting by Arthur Heming. The conteur is gesticulating as he speaks.

194

Who urged you as the spirit led,
    And recked not hardship nor defeat:
Champlain, Hennepen and Marquette,
    Brébeuf, and Jogues, and André,
Du Lut, La Salle, and Nicollet,
    Le Moyne, Le Caron, and Jamay.

Perrot, Tonty, and Saint Lausson,
    Jacques Beauchamp, Francois Beaulieu
Hearne, and Thompson, and Radisson,
    MacKenzie, Fraser, M'sieur Rioux.
Nelson, Albany, Montreal—
    You knew all these, oft did convey,
In regal state to ports of call
    The governors of the Hudson bay:
What songs the paddlers sang as you
    Swept downward on the spring's brown flood!
What brawls with some old rival crew,
    And not a little flow of blood!

Or, arms relaxed, and pipes aglow,
    The *Conteur* told of Loup-garou,
The Phantom Walker of the Snow:
    The Thunder Bird, and Windigo.
Where gone explorers and fur brigades
    Who charted the waters sea to sea,
And served a future day and age,
    Theme for a greater Odyssey?
Over the Grand Portage they go—
    La Loche, Des Chats, and Chaudière,
Gros Roche, La Cave, and de Rideau:
    Wraiths of a long-dead yesteryear.

O Birch-Canoe, could I imbue
    My eager hand in fitting praise,
I'd give you all that is your due
    Now you have ended your glad days!
Yet trees, like those that gave you birth,
    Still spread their splendour to the blue,
Near lake, on hillside, big of girth—
    Fit for many a birch canoe.
And do they lean, and tell anew
    To wayward saplings, wind a-dance,
How in the long ago that you
    Had played your part in High Romance?

G.F. CLARKE

195

APPENDIX 2
NOTES FROM LESCARBOT

I have before me a huge book of early eighteenth century vintage containing 931 pages, excluding the index, entitled *Early Voyages*. Indeed the faded brown leather covers contain several books. But the one that more nearly concerns the subject matter in the preceding pages is the second part of *Nova Francia, Containing the Fashions and Manner of Life of the People there: and the Fertility of the Lands and Seas, not mentioned in the former Book.* (Translated out of the French by P. E.)

Although it doesn't give the author's name, I know the original text was by Marc Lescarbot—that lovable Paris attorney who was poet, philosopher, historian, and so familiar with the classics of ancient times that all he writes is sprinkled with long excerpts from them. These, for the most part, I shall delete from the following pages. I must say that he wrote and produced what was, I believe, the first play to be performed in North America, as well as a poem entitled, *A Farewell to New France*.

Lescarbot's *History of Acadia* is, so far as I know, the first detailed description of the Micmac Indians (whom he calls Souriquois) and their way of life; which we can take for granted was similar to that of the Maliseet or St John River Indians, with whom they were in close contact. The following pages, then, contain some excerpts from this fascinating book.

Says Lescarbot, in his quaint phraseology:

"The author of the book of Wisdom, called Solomon's, witnessaith unto us a most true thing, that all men have a like entrance into the world, and the like going out, but each several people hath brought some ceremonies after these were accomplished: for some have wept, seeing the birth of man upon this worldly theatre; others have rejoiced at it, as well because nature hath given to every creature a desire to preserve his own kind, as for that, man having been made mortal by sin, he desireth to be in some sort restored again, to that lost right of immortality, and to have visible image issued from him, by the generation of children. I will not here discourse upon every nation, for it would be an infinite thing, but I will say that the Hebrews, at the nativity of their children, did make some particular ceremonies unto them, spoken of by the prophet Ezekiel, who having in charge to make a demonstration to the city of Jerusalem, of their own abomination, doth reproach unto her, saying, that she is issued and born out of the Cannaneans' country, that her father was an Amorite, and her mother an Hittite; and, as for thy birth, says he, in the day that thou wast born, thy navel was not cut, neither was thou washed in

197

water to soften thee, nor salted with salt, nor, anywise swaddled in clouts. The Cimbri did put their newborn children into the snow to harden them; and the Frenchmen did plunge theirs into the river Rhine, to know if they were legitimate; for if they did sink unto the bottom, they were esteemed bastards, and if they did swim on the water they were legitimate; meaning, as it were, that Frenchmen ought naturally to swim upon the water. As for our savages of New France when that I was there, thinking nothing less than on this history, I took not heed of many things, which I might have observed; but yet I remember, that as a woman was delivered of her child, they came to our fort, to demand very instantly for some grease or oil, to make the child to swallow it down before they gave him the dug (breast) or any food. They can render no reason for this, but that it is a custom of long continuance: whereupon I conjecture that the devil, who hath always borrowed ceremonies from the church, as well in the ancient as in the new law, would, that his people, so do I call them that believe not in God, and are out of communion of saints, should be anointed like to God's people, which unction he hath made to be inward, because the spiritual unction of the Christians is so.

*   *   *

"As for the imposition of names, they give them by tradition, that is to say that they have great quantity of names, which they chuse and impose on their children; but the eldest son commonly beareth his father's name, adding at the end some diminutive; as the eldest of Membertou shall be called Membertouchis, as it were the lesser or the younger Membertou. As for the younger son, he beareth not the father's name, but they give him such name as they list, and he that is born after him shall bear his name, adding a syllable to it."

*   *   *

Describing the feeding and care which the Indian women observe for their young, the usually mild Lescarbot waxes censorious of the society women of France. Says he: "Almighty God, showing a true mother's duty, sayeth by the prophet Isaiah, '*Can a woman forget her child and not have compassion on the son of her womb?*' This pity which God requireth in mothers, is to give the breast to their children, and not to change the food which they have given unto them before their birth. But at this day, the most part make their breasts bare to serve for allurements to whoredom; and being willing to set themselves at ease, free from the children's noise, do send them into the country, where peradventure they be changed, or given to bad nurses, whose corruption and bad nature they suck with their milk... The savage women beareth a greater love than that towards their young ones; for none but themselves do nurture them... Now our savage women do give unto them, with the dug (breast), meats which they use, having first well chewed them; and so little by little bring them up... Now our savage women, after having given birth, do observe without law that which was commanded in the law of Moses touching purification. For they shut themselves up apart for thirty or forty days and knew not their husbands, during which time they do not leave, for all that, from going here and there when they have business, carrying their children with them and taking care of them.

"As for their swaddling of them, they have an even smooth board, like the covering of a drawer or cupboard, upon which they lay the child wrapped in a beaver fur, unless it be hot, and tied thereupon some swaddling band, whom they carry on their backs. Their legs hanging down. Then, being returned into their cabins they set them, in this manner, up against a stone or something else. And, as in these parts, (France) one gives feathers and gilt things to little children, so they (the Indian mothers) hang a quantity of beads, and small square tangs painted diversely coloured, in the upper part by the said board or plank, for the decking of them."

Of course the board or plank is the cradle-board, in which all the natives of North America carried their young children (Fig. 11, p 26).

This cradle-board had a strap of tanned leather, or rope of cedar bark, fastened to the upper part which the mother passed her arms through (as we do pack baskets), and carried it with the child on her back.

Nicholas Denys, in his history of North America (1672) says that the mothers used moss for diapers for their female infants. "As for the males, a small hole was left in the swaddling and supplied with a half-round pieces of birch bark one side of which fitted beneath the penis and carried off the urine."

Roy Stevenson, who spent some time at Telegraph Creek, in Yukon territory, told me the Indian women there used moss for diapers.

Lescarbot says, "The savages are very kind to their children, alleging the reason that their offspring will be more likely to care for them in their old age."

I feel quite sure that the good Lescarbot misinterpreted the Indians in this particular. For from my close association with the Indians of the St John River for more than sixty years, I have found them consistently kind and attentive to their children, and not for the selfish reasons which Lescarbot records. Moreover, even though often encumbered with a large family, they will readily adopt orphans, be they Indians or unfortunate white children.

∗   ∗   ∗

Most early European writers dwell on the improvidence of the Indians in failing to provide for the morrow. "They will," says Lescarbot, "eat all they have, sharing with others who have not, be they kinsmen or strangers. They will eat all the beasts of the forest excepting the wolf; eggs which they gather along the shores of the waters, and take their canooes with them when the geese and outards (ducks) have done laying in the springtime, and they use all, as well those that be old as new. When eating with the French they use modesty and eat very soberly; but at home in their own houses (wigwams or cabins) they stretch out their bellies as much as they can and do not let off eating as long as there is meat; and if any of ours (French) be at their tabagie (feast) they will have him do as they do. They do not wax fat, but they are nimble and swift. If it happens that our savages have venison, or other food, all the company have part of it, a mutual charity and hospitality. They smoked tobacco almost every hour, and say it warms their stomachs. 'When the belly is full, then comes mirth', saith the proverb. Our savages have time out of mind the use of dances for the purpose of pleasing their gods;

or to cheer up somebody, or to rejoice after some victory, or to prevent sickness. In all their dances they sing; some of their dances and songs to the honour of the devil which sheweth them their game and that they think to gratify him. They dance also when they feast anybody as a thank-offering.

"All," he tells us, "do generally believe in the immortality of the soul and that after death they, the good men, are in rest, and the wicked in pain; now them that they esteem to be wicked are their enemies, and they the good men; in such sort that, in their opinion, they shall all after death be well at ease, and especially when they have well defended their country and killed many of their enemies. And as touching the resurrection of the bodies, there are yet some nations in these parts that have some glimpse of it."

I believe Lescarbot should have said it was a universal belief, not only among all the natives of North America, but a belief shared by all people in all climes and in all ages. For both written history and archaeological investigations have disclosed grave or mortuary offerings, which are irrefragable proofs that prehistoric man believed in the resurrection of the body.

Lescarbot gives a most interesting account of the death, the preparation for burial and the funeral of Penoniac, a Micmac chief from Cape Sable, who camped near Port Royal contemporary with, and following, the arrival of the French under Sieur de Monts and Baron de Poutrincourt. In 1605 Penoniac had accompanied Champlain and others on a voyage along the coast of what is now New England. He had for truck some kettles, hatchets and other things he had got from the storehouse at Port Royal, but was killed by some Indians, called by Lescarbot Armouchiquois (a name that, like Souriquois—applied by the French to the people we call Micmac, didn't long survive). The Armouchiquois turned the body of Penoniac over to the French, and Champlain brought it to Grand Manan. Here it was wept for and embalmed by the Indians with Champlain. This was in November 1605.

Says Lescarbot: "Of what kind this balm is, I could not know; not being able to enquire of it upon the places. I believe they jog the corpse and made them to dry. Certain it is, that they preserve them from rottenness, which they do almost throughout these Indies.

"From the river St Croix, the said deceased Penoniac was brought to Port Royal, where again he was wept for. But because they are accustomed to make their lamentations for a long continuance of days, as during a month, fearing to offend us by their cries, (for as much as their cabins were but five hundred paces from our fort) Membertou came to entreat Mons. de Poutrincourt not to dislike that they should mourn after their wonted manner, and that they should be but eight days in the performing of it, which he easily granted them; and then afterwards they began the next day following at break of day, their weepings and cryings, which we did hear from our said fort, taking some intermissions in the midst of the day; and they mourn by intermission, every cabin his day... That which is the mourning apparel of our Souriquois do paint their faces all with black, which maketh them to seem very hideous.

"After our Souriquois had wept for Penoniac, they went to his place where his cabin was whilst he lived, and there they did burn all he had left; his bows, arrows, quivers, his beaver skins, his tobacco (without which they cannot live) and other small belongings, to the end that nobody should quarrel over his successions. The same sheweth how little they care for the goods of this world, giving thereby a goodly lesson to them, who by right or wrong, do run after this silver devil, and very often do break their necks, or if they catch what they desire, it is in making them bankrupt with God, and spoiling the poor, whether it be with open war, or under colour of Justice... This Penoniac, of whom we have spoken, was kept in the cabin of *Niguiroet,* his mother, until spring-time, when that assemblage of savages made for to go to revenge his death, in which assembly he was yet wept for. And before they went to the wars they made an end of his funeral, and carried him (according to their custom) to a desolate island, towards Cape Sable, some four and twenty or thirty leagues[96] distant from Port Royal. Those isles which do serve them for churchyards are secret amongst them, for fear some enemy should seek to torment the bones of their dead.

"After they have brought the dead to his rest, everyone maketh him a present of the best thing he hath; some do cover him with many skins of beavers, of otters and other beasts; others present him with bows, arrows, quivers, knives, matachias (ornaments) and other things which they have in common."

*   *   *

The revenge which his relatives and friends took for the murder of Penoniac was in this wise: first their great sagum, Membertou, who was at this time more than one hundred years old, had sent messengers to all the villages of the Micmac nation, which extended from Cape Breton to the northern coast of what is now New Brunswick, and the Gaspé peninsula. He sent envoys to his allies the Maliseet of the rivers St John and St Croix, and to the Penobscot on the river of that name.

I have previously in this book told how the Indians of Gaspé came by way of the river St John, and were encamped with the Maliseet under chief Chkoudun at the mouth of this river, and for what purpose they had congregated: "to go with Membertou in his war against the Armouchiquois."

So in the late summer of 1607, some four hundred warriors from the various villages on the peninsula of Nova Scotia had gathered at Port Royal. After the usual feasts, songs, dances and speeches, they embarked in their canoes, arranged in divisions, each under its leader, and the whole flotilla sped out of the basin and over the great *Baie de la François* (Bay of Fundy) to the island of Grand Manan, where they were to rendezvous with the Maliseet of the St John and the St Croix, and then pick up the warriors of the Penobscot.

It was a long journey of eighty leagues[97] to the country of the Armouchiquois, where a great battle was fought and won. Bassebez, chief of the Armouchiquois, was killed, along with several lesser chiefs and many of their tribesmen, and the Micmac lost several of their own warriors. But Penoniac was avenged, and then these fearless Argonauts, with old Membertou in their midst, swept back to Port Royal singing their paeans of victory.

---

96   115-145 km.

97   385 km.

*   *   *

Not only was Membertou a redoubtable warrior but, as Lescarbot tells us: "a kind of soothsayer, or magician or medicine man." Our author calls him "a learned Aoutmoin, a name signifying the virtues of his craft. He carrieth hanging at his neck the mark of his profession, which is a purse triangle-wise, covered with embroidery work—that is to say Matachias, which in what there is I know not what, as big as a small nut, which he saith to be his devil called *Aoutim*.

"If any be sick, he is sent for, and he maketh invocations on his devil; he bloweth upon the part grieved, he maketh incisions, sucketh the bad blood from it; if it be a wound, he healeth it by the same means, applying a round slice of the beaver's stones.[98] Finally, some present is made unto him, either of venison or skins. If it be a question to have news of things absent, having first questioned with his spirit, he rendereth his oracles, commonly doubtful, very often false, but some times true; as when he was asked whether Penoniac were dead, he said, that unless he had returned within fifteen days, they should not expect him any more, and that he was killed by the Armouchiquois; and for him to have this answer, he must be presented with some gifts (for there is a trivial proverb among the Greeks, which beareth (says): 'that without money Phoebus' oracles are dumb.') The savage Membertou rendered a true oracle of our coming to Mons. Du Pont, when that he parted from Port Royal for to return into France, seeing the 15th day of July passed without any news. For he did maintain still, and did affirm, that there should come a ship, and that his devil had told him.

"When the savages be hungered they consult with Membertou's oracle, and he saith unto them: 'Go ye to such a place and you will find game.' It happeneth sometimes that they find some, and sometimes none. If by chance that none be found, the excuse is that the beast is wandering, and hath changed place; but so it comes to pass that very often they find some, and this it is that makes them believe that his devil is a god; and they know no other, to whom, notwithstanding, they yield not any service nor adoration in any form of religion.

"When that these Aoutmoins (magicians) make their mows and mops, they fix a staff in a pit, to which they tie a cord, and putting their head into this pit, they make invocations or conjurations in a language unknown to the others that are about, and then with beatings and howlings, until they sweat with very pain; yet so I have not heard that they foam at the mouth as the Turks do. When their devil is come, the master *Aoutmoin* makes them believe that he holdeth him back by his cord, and holdeth fast against him, forcing him to give an answer before he lets him go. By this is known the subtelty of this enemy of nature, who beguileth thus these miserable creatures, and his pride withal, in wielding that they which he calls upon, yield unto him more submission than even the holy prophets and patriarchs have done to God who has only prayed with their faces toward the ground.

"This done, he beginneth to sing something (as I think) to the praise of the devil, who hath discovered some game unto them; and the savages there do answer, making

---

98 Testicles.

some concordance of music among them; then they dance after their manner, with songs I understood not, neither those of ours that understood their speech best. After their songs," says Lescarbot, "our savages make a fire and leap over it, as the ancient Canannites, Ammonites, and sometimes the Israelites did: but they are not so detestable, for they (the Souriquois) do not sacrifice their children to the devil through the fire."

Lescarbot informs us that the Souriquois were subject to scurvy, "but having not the tree called Annedda, they have resources to sweat baths. They dig a hole in the ground, covering it with wood and big flat stones, they put fire in it by a hole, make a covering with poles, cover it with skins and other coverings, so that no air entereth, then they cast water on hot stones, then enter the place, and with motions, the *Aoutmoins* singing, and the others saying (as in their dances) 'bet, bet, bet,' they put themselves into a sweat. If the Aoutmoins do not heal them always, one must consider that our physicians do not always cure their patients neither.

"But," continues Lescarbot, "they live to a great age. Membertou was well over one hundred years old, and had not one grey hair on his head, and so ordinarily be the others. They have all their teeth, and go bareheaded, not caring the least to make any hats of their skins, as they did that used them in this part of the world." (He means France.)

Lescarbot attributes their good health and longevity to "the concord they have among them, and the small care they take for the commodities of their life for the which we French torment and vex ourselves. I dare also, and that very well, attribute the cause of this disposition and long health of our savages to their manner of life, which is after the ancient fashion, without curiosity; for every one doth grant that sobriety is the mother of health, and although they sometimes exceed in their *tabagies,* or feasts, they diet themselves afterward well enough, living very often eight days, more or less, with the smoak of tobacco, nor returning to hunting until they be hungry; and that beside being nimble, they want no exercise one way or another... For, goes on our philosopher: '*Sorrow,*' saith the wise man, '*hath killed many, and there is no profit in it. Envy and wrath shorten the life, and care bringeth old age before the time; but the joy of the heart is the life of man, and a man's gladness prolongeth his days.*'

"They hunt," says Lescarbot, "mostly in the winter. For all the spring and summer time and parts of autumn they have abundant fish for them and their friends, without taking any pains, so they do not much seek for other food. But in winter, when fish goeth away, the Indians, feeling the cold, they forsake the seashore and cabin themselves in the woods where they know game is sure to abound." He tells us that "the ellan, which they call *Basques Orignac* is a tall creature that is next to the dromedary and Camel, for it is bigger than the horse." (He is speaking of the moose.) "It is the most plentiful thing they had next to fish. Being well clothed with a cloak furred with beavers, and sleeves on the arms tied together with a latch; stockings made with the leather of the ellans, like to buff, which they tie at their girdles, and shoes (moccasins) on their feet of the same leather, very finely made, they go with their bows in hand, and their quiver on their backs, that way where their Aoutmoin hath shown them (for we have said heretofore that they consult with the oracle when they are hungry) or somewhere else where they think they shall lose not their time and labour. They have dogs or hounds almost like to foxes in form and bigness, and of hairs all colours, which follow them: and although they do not spend or call, nevertheless they can very well find the haunt of the beast they seek for, which, being found, they pursue her courageously; and they never give over until they have her down; and for to follow the game more closely, they tie under their feet rackets thrice as great as ours with which they run swiftly upon the hard snow without sinking, if it be not hard enough yet they give not over hunting, but will follow the chase three days together, if need be. Finally, having wounded her to death, they so tire her with their hounds, that she is forced to fall down; then they cut and rip up her belly, give relief to the hunters, and take their share of it. One must not think they eat all the flesh raw, as some do imagine, and as James Quartier (Cartier) himself doth write, for they always carry, going through the woods, a tinder-box before their breasts for to make fire when hunting is done, or where night doth force them to tarry."

*   *   *

As with other native Americans, it was the custom of the Souriquois (Micmac) women "to do the hardest share of the work after a moose or other animal was killed; the chief hunter returned to the cabins and told where it was lying in the woods. So with no other information than this, they would go to the place, flay (skin) the ellan, the deer, stag or other game and bring it home. Then, as long as they had meat they feasted well. Although he that hunted and killed the creature had the lesser share. For," goes on Lescarbot, "it is their custom that he must serve the others... As long as winter lasts they lack none of it. There hath been some savages that in a hard season hath killed fifty of them for his part, as I have sometimes heard."

The same year that the French came to Port Royal they planted corn; and Lescarbot says that every plant planted in Paris yielded but one or two ears, and the grains were very scanty; while one grain planted at Port Royal yielded four, five and six ears, and every ear, one with another, above two hundred grains, "which," he says, "is a marvellous increase. After it was harvested, the people laid it up in the ground, in pits, usually in the side of a hill so that the water would drain off. The pits were lined with mats. Then the corn was quite out of the way of rats and mice." Lescarbot quotes Cartier as saying that the natives of Hochelaga and Canada tilled corn, peas, pumpkins, cucumbers and beans, "but that since their furs have been in such demand, they can get in return for them bread and other victuals without any other pains, they are become sluggish, as the Souriquois (Micmac) also, who did formerly addict themselves to tillage at the same time."

This is most interesting, since it refutes the statement made by some modern historians that corn was never grown by the Micmac people.

Lescarbot also tells us that the natives had "excellent hemp, higher, finer, whiter and stronger than that of France. But that of the Armouchiquois had a pod at the top of the stock filled with a kind of cotton, like silk, which contains the seed. This cotton, or silk," he asserts, "is a thousand times more excellent than feathers, and softer than common cotton."

*   *   *

"The Indians," he says, "have great store of tobacco, most precious to them. The smoake of which they sucked up with a pipe. After they have gathered the herb, they lay it to dry in the shade, and have certain small bags of leather, hanging from their necks, or at their girdles, wherein they always have some, and a tobacco pipe as well, which is a little pan hollowed at one side, and within which is a long quill or pipe, out of which they suck up the smoake. They will," he goes on, "sometimes suffer hunger eight days, having no other sustenance than this smoake; and our Frenchmen, who have frequented them, are so bewitched with this drunkenness of tobacco that they can no more be without it than without meat and drink. The Indians say that God took tobacco. The brain and the stomach is warmed by smoake, and the humidity of the breathing apparatus dried up."

Nicholas Denys says that the Souriquois made the stem of their pipes out of willow in this wise: They pare down one end of the stem disclosing the pith, then, with the pith between their teeth, they slowly rotated the stem, and gradually withdrew from it the whole of the pith.

*   *   *

"Our savages," continues Lescarbot, "although they be naked, are not void of those virtues that are found in men of civility (civilisation); for every one (saith Aristotle) hath in him, even from his birth, the principles and seeds of virtue. Taking then the four virtues in their spring, we shall first find that they anticipated much of them. For first concerning fortitude and courage, they have thereof as much as any nation of the savages. I speak of the Souriquois and of their allies—allies in such sort, that ten of them will always adventure themselves against twenty Armouchiquois, not that they be altogether without fear. They are too revengful and in that they put their sovereign contentment, which inclineth them to bruitishness. As for their liberality; when they visit one another, they give mutual presents one to the other. And when some French Sagamos (captains) cometh to them they do like with him, casting at his feet some bundles of beavers, or other furs, which be all their riches—and so they did to Mons. de Poutrincourt, *but* he took them not to his proper use, but rather put them into M. de Monts storehouse."

Membertou thought himself as good as any king (European) and thought cannon should be fired off when he arrived, as was done when the French captains came.

"They have humanity and mercy towards their enemie's wives and little children, whose lives they spare, but they keep them to serve them, according to the ancient right of servitude throughout all the nations of the other world. But as for the men of defence, they spare none but kill as many as they can catch." (Lescarbot evidently means those who refuse to surrender, for he later tells us they (the Souriquois) had one male prisoner at Port Royal.

Commenting on their justice, Lescarbot says: "One must not offend another, so they have quarrels relatively seldom, and if any such thing chance to happen, the sagamos quieteth all, and doth justice to him that is offended, giving some bastinadoes (blows) to the wrong-doer, or condemning him to make some presents to the other, for to pacify him." This refutes the statements of some modern writers that the chiefs exercised no control over other members of the tribe. "If it be one of their prisoners who hath offended, he is in danger to go to pot (killed), for after he is killed no body will revenge his death."

"One day an Armouchiquois woman, a prisoner, who had caused a countryman of hers (a prisoner) to escape, and to the end to travel and pass on the way; she had stolen from Membertou's cabin a tinder box and a satchel. When it came to the ears of the savages, they would not proceed on the execution thereof near us (French), but went to cabin themselves four or five leagues[99] from Port Royal, where she was killed; and because she was a woman, our savages' wives and daughters did execute her. *Kinibecheoech,* a young maid of eighteen years of age, fair and well spotted with colours, gave her the first stroke in the throat, with a knife; another maid of the same age followed on, and the daughter of Membertou made an end. We reproved them for their cruelty, whereof they were all ashamed. And this is their form of justice. Another time, a man and a woman, prisoners, went clean away, without tinder box or any provisions of meat, which was hard to be performed, as well for the great distance of the way, because it behooved them to go secretly, and to take heed from meeting with any savages. Nevertheless, these poor souls peeled off the bark of a certain tree, and made a little boat (canoe) with the bark of them, wherein they crossed the bay *Francois* (Fundy), shortening their way above one hundred and fifty leagues;[100] and got back into their country of the Armouchiquois.

"Our savages, says Lescarbot, "have not any salutation at departing but only the *Adieu* which they have learned from us. They are to be commended for their obedience they yield to their father and mother, to whose commandments they obey, do nourish them in their old age, and defend them against enemies.

*   *   *

"They cover themselves with a skin tied to a latch or girdle of leather, which passeth between their buttocks, and joineth the other end of the said latch behind. And for the rest of their garments, they have a cloak of otter or beaver on their backs made with many skins, whether they be of otter or of beavers; and only one skin, whether it is of ellan or stag's skin, bear or lucerne; which cloak is held upward with a leathern ribband (thong), and they thrust commonly one arm out; for being in their cabins they put it off, unless it be cold. And I cannot better compare them than to pictures that are made of Hercules, who killed a lion and put the skin thereof on his back; notwithstanding they have more civility in that they cover their privy members. As for the women, they differ only in one thing, that is they have a girdle over the skin they have on; and do resemble (without comparison) the pictures that be made of St John Baptist." (Nicholas Denys says the men tied their cloak across the front of the body with latches, and the women theirs at the side.) "But in winter," continues Lescarbot, "they make very good sleeves (of beaver) tied behind, which keep them very warm. And often after this manner were the ancient Germans clothed, by the report of Caesar and Tacitus, leaving most part of the body naked.

99   20-24 km.

100   725 km.

"Our savages, in the winter, going to sea, or a hunting, do use great and high stockings like to our boot-hosen; which they tie to their girdles, and at the sides outward. There is a great number of points without taggs. Besides their long stockings, our savages do use shoes, which they call *mekizen* (moccasins) which they fashion very properly, but they cannot endure long, especially when they go into watery (swampy) places, because they be not curried nor hardened, but only made after the manner of buff; which is the buff of an *ellan* (moose).

"As for their head attire, none of the savages have any unless it be that some of the hither lands truck their furs with Frenchmen for hats and caps; but rather both men and women wear their hair flittering over their shoulders, neither bound nor tied, except that the men do trim them upon the crown of the head some four fingers length, with a leather lace, which they let down behind."

Lescarbot informs us that the Souriquois did not tattoo their bodies. But he gives an interesting picture of their ornaments: "Our savages content themselves to have *matachias* (ornaments) hanging at their ears, about their necks, bodies, arms and legs. Now as with us, so in that country (Canada) women do deck themselves with such things, and will have chains that will go twelve times about their necks, hanging down upon their breasts and about their hand-wrists, and above the elbow. They also hang long strings of them at their ears, which come down as low as their shoulders. If the men wear any, it will only be some young man that is in love. In Port Royal, and in the confines thereof, and towards Newfoundland and at Tadousac, where they have neither jewels nor vignols, the maids and women do make *matachias* with the quills or bristols of porcupines, which they dye with black, white and red colours, as lively as possibly may be, for our fearlets have no better lustre than their red dyes; but they more esteem the *matachias* which come to them from the Armouchiquois country, and they buy them very dear; and that because they can get no great quantity of them, by reason of the wars that these nations have continuously one against another. There are brought unto them from France *matachias* made with small quills of glass mingled with tin or lead, which are trucked with them and measured by the fathom for want of an ell. They also make small squares of sundry colours sewed together, which they tie behind on the little children's' hairs. The men do not much care for them (but) our Souriquois do wear some jollities: half-moons of bones very white, without excess. And they which have none of that, do commonly carry a knife before their breasts, which they do not for ornament, but for want of a pocket, and because it is an implement which at all times is necessary unto them. Some of them have girdles made of *matachias* wherewith they serve themselves, and make them brave. The *Aoutmoins* or soothsayers do carry before their breasts some sign of their vocation. In days of solemnity and rejoicing among them, and when they go to the wars, they have about their heads, as it were, a crown made of very long hairs of an *ellan* or stag, painted in red, pasted or otherwise fastened to a fillet of leather of three fingers breadth, such as James Quartier (Cartier) saith he had seen with the king (so doth he call him), and lord of the savages which be found at Hochelaga."

Speaking of marriage, Lescarbot says "It is necessary for the male lover to get the consent of the girl's parents, and prove that he is a good hunter and able to support her.

As for dowry, there is no mention of it. Also, when there is any divorce the husband is bound to nothing; and although there is no promise of loyalty given before any superior power, nevertheless, in whatsoever the wives keep chastity, and seldom is any found that breaketh it. As for the widows, they stain their faces with black, when they please, and not always; if their husband hath been killed, they will not marry again, nor eat flesh, until they have seen the revenge of his death. Thus it was that when the husband of Membertou's daughter was killed in the war against Armouchiquois she, being revenged by the death of so many of the enemy, married again.

"Sometimes," says Lescarbot, "our savages, having many wives, will give one of them to their friend, if he hath a desire to take her in marriage, and shall thereby be much disburdened.

"I never saw amongst them any unseemly gesture or unchaste look, and I dare affirm that they be less given to that vice than we in these parts (France). I attribute the cause thereof partly to their nakedness, and chiefly to their keeping their head... This is to be noted, that they keep three degrees of consanguinity in the which they are not used to contract marriage, that is to wit of the son with the mother, of the father with his daughter, and of the son with his sister."

*   *   *

"When the winter is too mild, or at the latter end of the same, for then they have neither venison nor fish, they are often constrained to feed upon the barks of trees, and eat the parings of skins, and on their dogs, which, upon this extremity, they do eat. Truth it is that at Port Royal, there is always shell fish, so that in all cases they cannot die there for hunger. But yet they have some superstition that they will not eat mussels; and they can allege no reason for it, no more than our superstitious Christians which will not be thirteen at table, or which fear to pare their nails on the Friday... They have this mutual charity which hath been taken away from us, since that mine and thine hath come into the world... Everyone hath a dish made with the bark of a tree, and a spoon as deep as the palm of one's hand, or more. And there is to be noted, that he which entertaineth the others doth not dine, but serves the company, as very often the bride-groom do here in France. The women who are in another place apart do not eat with the men. They spread a skin on the ground, where they eat their meat, and sit on the ground. They do not wash themselves at (before) meals, unless they be monstrous foul, and not having any use of linen, when their hands are greasy they are constrained to wipe them upon their hairs or upon their dogs' hairs.

"Our savages," says Lescarbot, "have no base exercises, all their sport being the wars or hunting and dancing. They make bows, and arrows long and straight with only a knife or a stone. The feathers are of an eagle's tail because they are firm and carry well in the air; and when they want them they will give a beaver's skin, yea, twain, for one of these tails. They also make wooden maces, or clubs, in the fashion of an abbot's staff, for the wars, and shields which cover all their bodies. Our Indians get fish lines from the Frenchmen, as also fishing hooks to bait for fish; only they make with guts bowstrings and rackets (snowshoes) which they tie at their feet to go upon the snow hunting.

"In the country where they do tillage, as in that of the Armouchiquois and farther off, the men do make an infinite number of earthern pots, like in fashion to a night-cap, in which they do seethe their meats, fish, beans, corn and pumpkins. Our Souriquois did so anciently, and did till the ground, but since the Frenchmen do bring them kettles, beans, peas, biskit and other food, they have become slothful, and make no more account of these exercises."

Lescarbot gives us another exercise of the Souriquois: "Their play at hazard, whereunto they are so addicted that some times they play out all they have. They put some number of beans, coloured red and painted on one side, in a platter: and having stretched out a skin on the ground, they play thereupon, striking with the dish upon this skin, and by that means the beans do skip in the air, and do not all fall on that part (side) that be coloured; and in that consisteth the chance and hazard; and according to their chance they have a certain number of quills made of rushes, which they distribute to him that winneth to keep the reckoning."

This is the well-known game known as the "bowl or platter game", played by many Algonkian tribes, even to the far northwest of Canada. The Souriquois, or Micmac, call it Altestakum Omkwon.

The Maliseet or St John River Indians play the same game, but their dice are round, and about the same size as a twenty-five-cent piece, and about the same thickness. They are generally made of a moose bone, but I have seen one, picked up at the site of the old Medoctec village, which was made of slate stone. The bone dice contained what I took to be the gold-thread flower, the petals painted red; the stone had the same number of petals, but they had been etched on it with stone sharp implement, such as a flinty rock. The Maliseet call the game *Al-tes-tug-in-uk*.

I am especially happy that Lescarbot speaks of the vessel employed in this game, as a platter; for it proves that the Souriquois made such, as did the Maliseet.

Lescarbot tells us: "When the winter doth approach, the women prepare that which is necessary to oppose themselves against this rigorous adversary, and make mats of rushes, wherewith they garnish their cabins, and others to sit down upon, and all very artifically, yea also colouring these rushes, they make partitions (patterns) in their works, like to them our gardeners do make in their garden knots, with such measures and proportions as nothing is found amiss. And because that the body must be cloathed, they curry and supple the skins of beavers, stags and otters, as well as can be done here (France) If they be little they sew many together, and make cloaks, sleeves, stockings (he means leggings) and shoes (moccasins), upon which all things they make works (patterns) which have a very good grace. Item: they make panniers (baskets) of rushes and roots, for to put their necessities in, as corn, beans, peas, flesh, fish and other things. They also make purses of leather, upon which they make works worthy of admiration, with the hairs of porcupine quills, coloured with red, black, white and blue, which be the colours that they make, so lively that ours seem as nothing to be comparable to them; also dishes of bark to drink from, and put their meats in, which are very fair according to the stuff. Item: scarfs, necklaces and bracelets which they and the men wear, which they call *matachias,* are of their making. When the barks of trees must be taken off in the springtime or in summer, therewith to cover their houses, it is they which do that work; as likewise they labour in the making of canoes, and small boats when they are to be made. They do painting, carving, and do make pictures of beasts, birds and men as well in stone as in wood, as prettily as good workmen in these parts (France). And yet, notwithstanding all their labours, they love their husbands more than (do) the women of these parts (France). For none of them are seen to marry again upon their graves; that is to say presently after their decease, but rather do they tarry a long time. And if he hath been killed, they will eat no flesh, nor will condescend to second marriage until they have seen the revenge thereof made: a testimony of true love (which is scarce found among us), and also of chastity. There is seldom divorcement but such as are voluntary. And," goes on the enthusiastic Lescarbot, "if they would be christians, they would be families with whom God would dwell and be well pleased. as it is meant it should be so for to have perfect contentment, for otherwise marriage is but torment and tribulation."

After speaking of their fishing, Lescarbot says with ready Gallic wit: "And in this exercise did Mark Anthony, the son of the emperor Severus, delight himself very much; notwithstanding Plato's reason, who, forming his commonwealth, hath forbidden his citizens the exercise of fishing, as ignoble, and illiberal, and fosterer of idleness, wherein he did grossly equivocate, specially where he chargeth fishermen with idleness, which is so evident that I will not vouchsafe to refute him. But I marvel not of that which he says of fishing, seeing that with the same he rejected hawking upon the same reason. Plutarch saith that it is more laudable to take either a hart, a roebuck, or a hare, than to buy them, but he wadeth not so far as the other."

And the quaint, whimsical philosopher goes on: "And I find by my reckoning that Pythagoras was very ignorant, forbidding in his fair golden sentences the use of fish without distinction. One may excuse him, in that fish, being dumb, hath some conformity with his sect, wherein dumbness (or silence) was much commended. I would fain demand of such a man, if being in Canada he had rather die of hunger than to eat fish. So many anciently, to follow their own fancies, and to say there be we, have forbidden their followers the use of meats that God hath given to man, and some times have laid yoaks upon men that they themselves would not bear. Now whatsoever the philosophy of Pythagoras is, I am none of his."

And so I take leave of this delightful Frenchman, with only this observation: I wish it were possible to wheel back the centuries for a few hours, and I be privileged to sit at table in the Habitation at Port Royal, with him, the Baron de Poutrincourt, Champlain and the other members of *The Order Of Good Cheer*, and listen to their talk while the flames in the great fireplace leaped up the broad chimney into the Acadian night.

And thus, as our lawyer-poet-philosopher, of the kindly and understanding heart, ended his book with these words: "Praise be to God," so do I echo them in this.

APPENDIX 3

SOMEONE BEFORE US:
TECHNICAL CAPTIONS FOR ARTIFACT FIGURES
DAVID W. BLACK

Explanation: The technical captions below provide modern assessments of the archaeological artifacts shown in Figures in this edition of *Someone Before Us*. Artifact size is indicated by a scale or measurement on each Figure. Individual artifacts are designated by lower case letters adjacent to them on the Figures. For each artifact, four pieces of information may be included: 1) a classification and/or description of the artifact; 2) an assessment of the material from which the artifact is made; 3) the location where the artifact was found (when known); and 4) an age estimate for the artifact (when warranted). Occasionally, further information on specific artifacts is included in parentheses. Abbreviations are introduced when the abbreviated term is first used. Definitions for technical terms used in the captions may be found readily on the internet. Most Prehistoric artifacts in GFC's collection were made from materials acquired locally; however, source areas for some stone materials believed to have been acquired from outside New Brunswick are suggested. Age estimates take the form of conventional culture-history periods designated for northeastern North America. An age range, expressed in radiocarbon years before present (BP), is included at the first use of each culture-history designation; ages in radiocarbon years are similar to, but not exactly the same as calendar years. Age estimates are based on current knowledge, are probabilistic and are deliberately broad.

Figure 2: Three ground stone gouges: a) large short-channelled gouge, dark grey-green slate, near White Rapids, Main Southwest Miramichi River (MSWM); b) small short-channelled gouge, green laminated metamorphic, Three Brooks site, Tobique River (TR); c) large short-channelled gouge, green laminated metamorphic, St John River (SJR), opposite the mouth of the Eel River; all date to the Late Archaic period (4500–3800 BP).

Figure 5: A large flaked stone bifacial preform, grey-green flow-banded volcanic, Meductic Flat, SJR; probably dates to the Terminal Archaic–Early Woodland period (4000–2200 BP).

Figure 6: Eight flaked stone artifacts: a) retouched flake, dark variegated chert, SJR; b) side-scraper on a flake, obsidian, New Mexico, USA (note that this artifact was acquired from an American collector, not from the New Brunswick archaeological record); c) corner-notched projectile point, dark green volcanic, SJR; d) oval-pointed biface, bull quartz, the Forks, Juniper, MSWM; e) retouched flake, Ramah chert from Labrador, Lane's Creek, SJR, dates to either the Late Archaic period or the Late Woodland period (1400–400 BP); f) triangular biface, bleached fine-grained volcanic ("bleached" refers to natural loss of colour and structure due to acidic soil, acidic groundwater and/or exposure to sunlight), Wapske, TR; g) oval-pointed biface, bull quartz, the Forks, Juniper, MSWM; h) corner-notched/expanding-stemmed projectile point, dark volcanic, Meductic Flat, SJR; c–d, f–h) probably date to the Woodland period (3000–400 BP).

Figure 7: Eight metal artifacts, Meductic Flat, SJR, Historic period (500 BP–present): a & b) locks, c) hinge, d) hasp, e & h) knife blades, f & g) hand-wrought nails; all are ferrous metal except h), which is brass.

Figure 9: Four artifacts: a) ground stone knife blade or projectile point, serpentinite, Grand Lake, York County, St Croix River (SCR), Late Archaic period; b) ground stone knife blade, banded slate, SJR, Archaic period (9000–3000 BP); c) flaked-and-ground stone axe blade, grey-green metamorphic, the Forks, Juniper, MSWM, Early Woodland period (3000–2200 BP); d) bi-pointed biface, bleached green felsite, Shiktahawk site, Bristol, SJR, Early–Middle Woodland transition (2500–1800 BP).

Figure 10: A large notched weight or axe blade preform, grey-green volcanic, Phillips Flat, SJR, opposite the mouth of Eel River; probably dates to the Archaic period.

Figure 12: Metal artifact, Meductic Flat, SJR, early Historic period: door bolt, ferrous metal, set onto paper-board backing.

Figure 13: Metal artifacts, Meductic Flat, SJR, early Historic period: escutcheons, ferrous and non-ferrous metals, set onto foam block.

Figure 14: The base of a stone fireplace measuring 2.13 m by 1.37 m, uncovered by GFC near the northeast corner of the cemetery at Meductic Flat in May 1964, immediately before the New Brunswick Electric Power Commission prevented him from conducting further excavations. GFC believed that the fireplace was located in the priest's house or in the old chapel, dating to about AD 1717 or earlier. The view is from the upstream end of the feature toward the south (see pages 18, 62–63, 66–67, in Caywood, Louis R. 1969. *Excavations at Fort Meductic, New Brunswick.* Parks Canada Manuscript Report Number 123. Ottawa: National Historic Parks and Sites Branch, Department of Indian and Northern Affairs).

Figure 15: GFC beside the excavated base of the stone fireplace at Meductic Flat, May 1964. The view is upstream toward the northeast.

Figure 16: Thirteen scrapers: a) large end-scraper, bleached fine-grained volcanic, the Forks, Juniper, MSWM; b) large end-scraper, Tobique rhyolite, the Forks, Juniper,

MSWM; c) large end-scraper, red mudstone, SJR; d) medium end-scraper, Munsungun chert from Maine, TR; e) thumbnail scraper, Minas Basin/North Mountain chert from Nova Scotia, Meductic Flat, SJR; f) medium end-scraper, red Washademoak chert, Tobique Narrows, TR; g) medium end-scraper, grey banded mudstone, location unknown; h) thumbnail scraper, bull quartz, the Forks, Juniper, MSWM; i) medium end-scraper, Tobique chert, Wapske, TR; j) large bifacial scraper, bleached fine-grained volcanic, TR; k) medium end-scraper, waxy variegated chert, location unknown; l) thumbnail scraper, grey Washademoak chert, SJR; m) bifacial scraper, Tobique chert, Wapske, TR; all probably date to the Woodland period.

Figure 18: Three flaked stone artifacts: a) lanceolate oval-pointed biface, Tobique Narrows, TR, probably dates to the Woodland period; b) large irregular lanceolate biface, Noddins Flat, SJR; c) large triangular biface, Shiktahawk site, Bristol, SJR, probably dates to the Early Woodland period; all are made of bleached fine-grained volcanic materials.

Figure 19: Six flaked stone bifaces: a) oval-pointed, concave base, two pieces refitted by GFC, dark volcanic, McGuire site, SJR; b) oval-pointed, concave base, red-and-white flow-banded rhyolite, Grafton, SJR; c) bi-pointed, green felsite; d) bi-pointed, maroon mudstone; e) bi-pointed, green felsite with white inclusions; f) bi-pointed, green felsite with white inclusions; c–f) Shiktahawk site, Bristol, SJR; all date to the Early–Middle Woodland transition.

Figure 20: Two large contracting-stemmed projectile points from the Shiktahawk site, Bristol, SJR: a) two pieces refitted by GFC; b) whole; both are made of grey-green felsite with white inclusions; both resemble stemmed projectile points from the Midwestern United States dating to the Early–Middle Woodland transition.

Figure 21: Two artifacts: a) ground stone axe blade, dark green volcanic, Nictau, TR, probably dates to the Woodland period; b) contracting-stemmed projectile point, grey-green felsite, Shiktahawk site, Bristol, SJR, resembles stemmed projectile points from the Midwestern United States dating to the Early–Middle Woodland transition.

Figure 22: A large oval-pointed biface, two pieces refitted by GFC, bleached green felsite, Shiktahawk site, Bristol, SJR, Early–Middle Woodland transition.

Figure 23: Four flaked stone bi-pointed bifaces from the Shiktahawk site, Bristol, SJR: a) two pieces refitted by GFC; b–d) whole; all are made of grey-green felsite; all resemble preforms for "turkeytail" projectile points from the Midwestern United States dating to the Early–Middle Woodland transition.

Figure 24: Seven flaked stone artifacts: a) triangular biface, two pieces refitted by GFC, green felsite, SJR; b) side-notched projectile point, red flow-banded rhyolite, TR, Archaic period; c) bi-pointed biface, green felsite, Shiktahawk site, Bristol, SJR, Early–Middle Woodland transition; d) bi-pointed biface, grey banded mudstone, Shiktahawk site, Bristol, SJR, Early–Middle Woodland transition; e) oval-pointed biface, two pieces refitted by GFC, green felsite, TR; f) small bi-pointed biface, bleached fine-grained volcanic, location unknown; g) knife blade with convex base, Hinkley Point metasediment from Maine, Shiktahawk site, Bristol, SJR, Terminal Archaic–Early Woodland period.

Figure 25: Sixteen flaked stone projectile points from various sites: a–f, i–k, m–n & p) corner-notched; g & h) side-notched; l) stemmed; o) triangular, straight-based biface; a, c–e, i–k, m–n & p) the Forks, Juniper, MSWM; b) provenance unknown; f) TR; g) Tobique Narrows, TR; h) Meductic Flat, SJR; l) Upsalquitch River; o) Miramichi River (MR). All are made from fine-grained volcanics or cherts; all date to the Woodland period.

Figure 26: Nine flaked stone artifacts: a–e & g) side-notched projectile points, bull quartz, MR; f) stemmed projectile point, bull quartz, SJR; h) large biface, grey quartzite with red-brown banding, Charles and Carter Edgar Collection, Three Brooks, TR; i) triangular, indented-based biface, translucent chert, provenance unknown.

Figure 27: Three artifacts: a) short-channelled pecked-and-ground stone gouge, blue-green metamorphic, Pokiok Stream, SJR, Late Archaic period; b) irregular oval-pointed biface, bleached fine-grained volcanic, the Forks, Juniper, MSWM; c) irregular oval biface, bleached fine-grained volcanic, Smith Flat, TR.

Figure 28: Four examples of prehistoric pottery: a) pottery vessel rim, alternate notch impressions, five sherds refitted by GFC, Big Clearwater, MSWM; b) pottery vessel rim, zoned cord-wrapped edge impressions, the Forks, Juniper, MSWM; c) pottery vessel rim; d) pottery vessel rim, two pieces refitted by GFC; c & d) cord-wrapped edge impressions with row of punctates, Meductic, SJR. All are grit-tempered ceramics; all date to the Woodland period.

Figure 29: Large flanged and grooved axe or maul head, bleached granular stone, the Forks, Juniper, MSWM, probably dates to the Terminal Archaic period (4000–3000 BP).

Figure 30: Six ground stone artifacts: a) small grooved axe blade, two pieces refitted by GFC, bleached metamorphic, Big Clearwater, MSWM; b) semi-faceted plummet, fine-grained metamorphic, the Forks, Juniper, MSWM; c) ground stone eccentric, fine-grained metamorphic, Shiktahawk site, Bristol, SJR; d) small axe blade, fine-grained metamorphic, Three Brooks, TR; e) semi-facetted plummet, granular metamorphic, opposite Florenceville, SJR; f) grooved cobble, granular metamorphic, opposite Florenceville, SJR. All probably date to the Archaic period except c & d), which may date to the Early–Middle Woodland transition.

Figure 31: Four cut-and-polished stone artifacts: a) bar pendant, single bi-conical perforation, black slate; c) rounded rectangular gorget, double tubular perforation, banded grey-green slate; d) double-notched, grooved spear-thrower weight ("butterfly bannerstone"), partially reconstructed by GFC, banded grey-green slate; a, c & d) Grand Lake, York County, SCR; c & d) resemble artifacts and materials from the Midwestern United States; b) rectangular gorget, single bi-conical perforation, two pieces refitted by

GFC, grey-green laminated slate, Big Clearwater, MSWM; all probably date from the Late Archaic period (4500–3800 BP) through the Middle Woodland period (2200–1400 BP).

Figure 33: Two ground stone tools hafted by GFC: a) large short-channelled gouge, Phillips Flat, SJR; b) grooved axe blade, Meductic Flat, SJR; both date to the Archaic period.

Figure 34: Eight flaked stone artifacts: a) expanding-stemmed broadpoint, flow-banded rhyolite, Tobique Narrows, TR; b) triangular biface, three pieces refitted by GFC, bleached felsite, Big Clearwater, MSWM; c) triangular biface, bleached flow-banded rhyolite, Wapske, TR; d) stemmed projectile point, bleached felsite, Wapske, TR; e) side-scraper, concentrically banded chert from the Midwestern United States, Big Clearwater, MSWM; f) oval-pointed biface; g) bifacial scraper; h) triangular biface; f–h) bleached felsite, TR; a) Terminal Archaic period; b–d, f–h) probably date to the Early or early Middle Woodland period (3000–1800 BP); e) this artifact may be very old, possibly dating as early as the Late Paleoamerican (Paleoindian) period (ca. 10,000 BP).

Figure 35: Three artifacts: a) oval-pointed biface made on a very large flake blank, bleached fine-grained volcanic, Tobique Narrows, TR; b) ground stone pendant, single bi-conical perforation, ochre-stained metamorphic, Meductic Flat, SJR, dates from the Late Archaic to the Middle Woodland period; c) two perforated strips of gold-coloured non-ferrous metal, Big Clearwater, MSWM, Historic period.

Figure 36: Three bifaces: a) broken or unfinished preform, bleached fine-grained volcanic, Shiktahawk site, Bristol, SJR; b) broken or unfinished piece, grey quartzite, Three Brooks, TR; c) broken triangular biface, two pieces refitted by GFC, differentially bleached chert, Red Rapids, TR.

Figure 37: A large double-grooved, ground stone axe blade, granular metamorphic, Wapske, TR, Archaic period.

Figure 38: A large bifacial preform, grey-green flow-banded volcanic, Wapske, TR, probably dates to the Terminal Archaic–Early Woodland period.

Figure 39: Polychrome image of a bird, painted on the cortex of a discoidal cobble: red, green, white and black pigments on grey-green volcanic stone; found in a ploughed field near the Rosedale Road, north of Woodstock; probably dates to the Historic period.

Figure 40: Objects carved by Dr. Peter Polchies, healer, artist and stone carver, Woodstock reserve (now Woodstock First Nation); a, c & d) animal figurines; b & e) stone pipe bowls.

Figure 41: Various objects from GFC's collection: a & b) prehistoric woven fabric fragments, Sunny Corner, Northwest Miramichi River, probably date to the Woodland period; c) stone pipe bowl, Meductic Flat, SJR; d) stone pipe bowl, provenance unknown; e & f) European clay tobacco pipes, Meductic Flat, SJR, Historic period.

Figure 43: Three artifacts: a) large pecked-and-ground stone eccentric, possibly an unfinished gouge or maul head, green laminated metamorphic, Odell Flat, TR, Archaic period; b: flaked-and-ground stone axe blade, bleached volcanic, Crooked Rapids, MSWM, Early Woodland period; c) end-scraper on a large flake, Tobique rhyolite, Gulquac, TR, probably Terminal Archaic–Early Woodland period.

Back Cover: Eight translucent chert artifacts (photographed using transmitted light): Top Row. Left: triangular bifacial end-scraper, TR; Middle: unifacial end-scraper, Wapske, TR; Right: large flake, Three Brooks, TR. Middle Row. Left: large bifacial end-scraper, Three Brooks, TR; Middle: small lanceolate oval-pointed biface, Wapske, TR (scale: length = 7.8 cm); Right: small triangular biface, provenance unknown (writing indecipherable). Bottom Row. Left: large flake, Three Brooks, TR; Right: bifacial core, provenance unknown. All probably date to the Woodland period.

SOMEONE BEFORE US, HALF A CENTURY LATER: AN AFTERWORD

DAVID W. BLACK

Department of Anthropology, University of New Brunswick–Fredericton

Someone Before Us was the first book-length publication devoted substantially to the Prehistoric (pre-European Contact) archaeology of New Brunswick. Dr. George Frederick Clarke (GFC) undertook his archaeological work at a time when there was little other such research being conducted in the province. His period of active field research, from the mid-1920s to the early 1960s, fits almost perfectly between the demise of 19th-century, natural-history-style archaeology around 1914 and the development of national and provincial heritage regulations (marking the advent of cultural-resource-management archaeology) during the 1960s. GFC collected and excavated at some of the most widely recognized Prehistoric archaeological sites in New Brunswick—for example, Meductic Flat, the Shiktahawk site and the Three Brooks site—and many of the sites he investigated were subsequently inundated by waters ponded above hydro-electric dams constructed on the St John and Tobique rivers. For these reasons alone, GFC's work occupies an important place in the history of archaeological research in Eastern Canada; his publications, notes and artifact collection warrant consideration in the context of modern archaeological research and in light of on-going and proposed developments in the central St John River Valley.

My purpose here is to briefly review GFC's contributions to the developing discipline of archaeology in New Brunswick and Canada. In 2007, the Clarke family donated GFC's artifact collection and associated notes and records to the University of New Brunswick (UNB). A few years later, UNB named the George Frederick Clarke Archaeological Teaching Laboratory to commemorate his contributions to the discipline. At that time, I asked a group of senior undergraduates in the Anthropology program to create a poster about GFC's archaeological work to be displayed outside the door of the lab. I challenged them to construct it around a quote from one of GFC's publications that they felt epitomized his attitude toward archaeology. (To see the poster, go to: (http://www.unb.ca/fredericton/arts/departments/anthropology/pdfs/dwblack/pilgeretal2012poster.pdf.) This is the quote they selected:

> "Fundamentally, the archaeologist is a romantic. If he weren't he wouldn't be an archaeologist." (GFC, SBU, pg. 6)

The students' choice was prescient, since his romanticism is the thread that Mary Bernard employed to tie together GFC's disparate interests and accomplishments in her biography, *The Last Romantic* (Chapel Street Editions, Woodstock, N.B., 2015). This romanticism linked him back to 19th-century archaeology as it was practiced before the First World War. But his romanticism was maintained in uneasy balance with his scientific sensibilities: GFC frequently adopted a sceptical stance toward received wisdom, the point of departure for any scientific investigation; he scoffed at romantic interpretations of the meanings of Aboriginal place names, and even argued *against* romanticism in his polemic on the Red Paint People (about which more below).

GFC remains a liminal figure in New Brunswick and Canadian archaeology, spanning the gulf between non-professional and professional archaeology. He was, in modern parlance, an avocational archaeologist; but—more important—he was a creative writer first, with a writing and publication career that spanned the first six decades of the 20th century. GFC was necessarily self-educated in archaeology, because he was anchored to the Woodstock area both by inclination and by the need to make a living as a dentist, and no formal education in archaeology was available anywhere in New Brunswick before the 1960s. I suspect that GFC did most of his background reading in archaeology early in his archaeological career; the books he quoted most frequently in *Someone Before Us*—for example, Lord Avebury's *Prehistoric Times* (1865), John W. Dawson's *Fossil Men and their Modern Representatives* (1880) and Henry F. Osborn's *Men of the Old Stone Age* (1914)—are products of the era before 1914. Thus, it is not surprising that GFC's archaeological work, in various ways, harked back to 19th-century practices.

But his work also reflected developments in archaeology during the first half of the 20th century. GFC established avocational archaeology in New Brunswick as something more than curio-collecting, in part by recognizing the importance of recording and disseminating the knowledge that he acquired. As Mary Bernard shows in her biography, GFC intended to contribute to the archaeological literature with a monograph detailing his research and finds. He wrote it during the 1940s, but it was never published, through a series of unfortunate circumstances described in *The Last Romantic*. Apparently, the manuscript no longer exists. GFC incorporated portions of the monograph into *Someone Before Us*—as shown by the regional archaeological literature he most frequently cited (books and articles by Warren K. Moorehead, William A. Ritchie and Frederick Johnston, among others, all dating between the First and Second World Wars)—but, in preparing the manuscript for *Someone Before Us*, he did not update his references to include work published after 1950.

GFC's work sometimes foreshadowed developments in the late 20th and early 21st centuries. For example, one of his most important contributions involved promoting local archaeology and public education in archaeology. In the mid-20th century, the term "archaeology" most often conjured up images of Egyptian pyramids and Greek temples in the public imagination. GFC's message to the public, in his own words, was:

> "An archaeologist doesn't have to go to Egypt. There's plenty of good digging right here in New Brunswick..." (GFC, quoted by Ian Sclanders, in "2000 Arrowheads," *Telegraph-Journal* [Aug. 16, 1948], New Brunswick Parade #21).

GFC devoted considerable effort to convincing his fellow citizens, especially young people, that archaeology was not just an esoteric practice conducted in the far corners of the world: it could be undertaken in their own backyards. This made him, for several decades, the go-to person for those seeking information about New Brunswick archaeological objects, at a time when there were no resident professionals to fill that role.

GFC saw artifacts as information, rather than as mere objects, and went far beyond what most avocational archaeologists attempt with their collections. He recorded the locations of many of his finds, made maps of sites and excavations, refitted broken artifacts (see, for example, Figs. 22, p 69, 23 a, p 128, and 31 b, p 135), reconstructed incomplete artifacts (using, I suspect, tools and materials he was familiar with from his dental practice; see, for example, Fig. 31 d, p 135), and experimented with preserving metal artifacts (Figs. 12, p 37 and 13, p 38). He displayed items from his collection in public places, adopting techniques similar to those used by museums at the time (see, for example, the display case in Fig. 32, p 219). He even experimented with hafting ground-stone tools (Fig. 33, p 220) and cutting meat with flaked stone tools.

32 Roy Polchies, Peter Paul and GFC looking at artefacts in GFC's den, 1949

Roy Polchies holds a stone adze hafted by GFC (33a, p 220) and wears a pendant (31 a, p 135) on a rope. Peter Paul holds a gouge in his right hand (2 c, p 55), and a large pipe, probably made of wood, in his left; round his neck is a perforated plummet on a string. GFC is holding a maul (29, p 133). There are several large implements on the lowboy; above them on a box is an Adney model Shuswap-Chilkat spruce-bark canoe (45 d, p 143). On the mantel shelf is a wood salmon spear. Leaning against the mantelshelf is a rock-maple paddle decorated by Dr Peter Polchies (42, p 142). The case of artefacts on the floor in front of the lowboy looks very like the ones in which GFC displayed a selection of artefacts that he lent to the L.P. Fisher Library. He probably borrowed the case to include in the photograph.

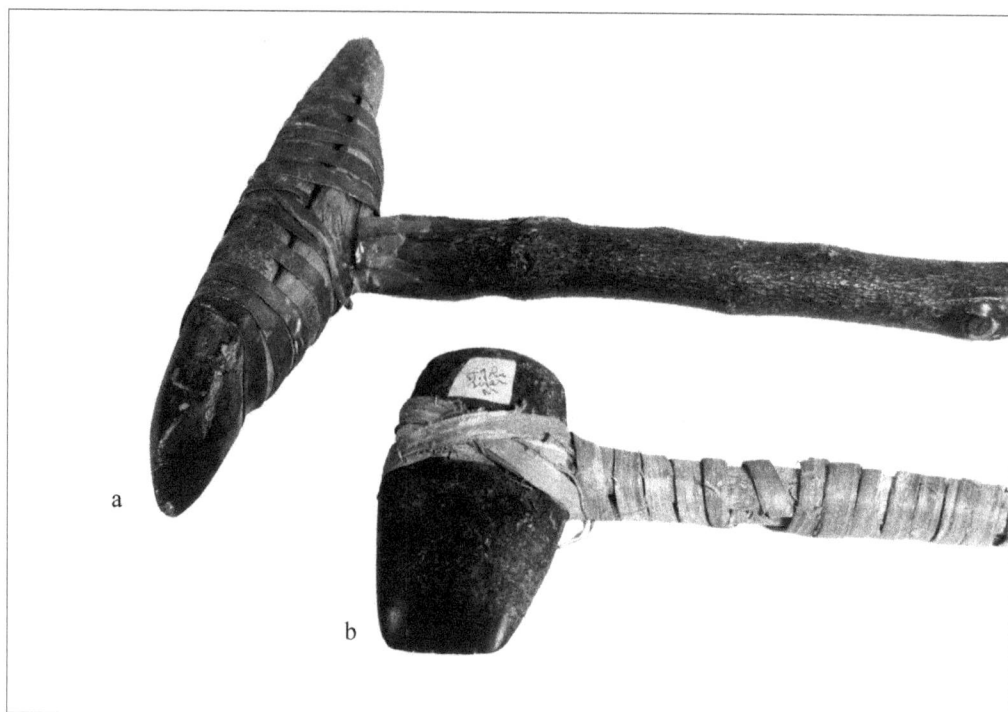

33 Adzes hafted by GFC. a. Phillips Flat, opposite Eel River; b. St John River

As a citizen scientist, GFC continued and extended the inventory science aspect of archaeology begun by such 19th-century scholars as Abraham Gesner (New Brunswick Provincial Geologist), Loring W. Bailey (UNB Natural Sciences) and George F. Matthew (Natural History Society of New Brunswick). GFC's work was conducted during what Gordon R. Willey and Jeremy A. Sabloff (in *A History of American Archaeology,* 1993) called the Classificatory-Historical Period, 1914–1960. In the United States, during that period and especially during the Depression years, archaeological excavations were conducted on a large scale as make-work projects, sponsored through the Works Progress Administration among other agencies. In Canada, no comparable initiatives were undertaken. In the Maritimes, in particular, archaeological research conducted by public institutions very nearly ceased altogether. GFC did much to keep archaeology alive in New Brunswick.

The small amount of professional archaeology conducted in the Maritimes at that time was undertaken by archaeologists based in Upper Canada and the United States—for example, William J. Wintemberg (National Museum of Man, now the Canadian Museum of History), Walter A. Kenyon (the Royal Ontario Museum) and Wendell S. Hadlock (the Robert Abbe Museum)—all of whom GFC met and cooperated with during their forays into the New Brunswick archaeological record. As is often the case for avocational archaeologists, his relationships with professionals in the discipline were frequently strained. Late in life, however, he developed a close relationship with David Sanger (then Atlantic Provinces Archaeologist at the National Museum of Man).

GFC set the precedent of involving Wolastoqiyik (Maliseet people), for example, Tom and Noel Moulton, in recovering their ancestors' past, long before this became a routine practice of professional archaeologists. His lifelong fascination with Aboriginal cultures, lifeways, and technologies, and his friendships with Dr. Peter Polchies, Noel Polchies and Peter Paul, among many others, led him to promote the rights of the Wolastoqiyik in contemporary society, embroiling himself in legal cases involving treaty rights, and supporting individuals by commissioning traditional craftworks from them. His respect for Aboriginal culture went well beyond his interest in artifacts to encompass studies in ethnohistory, linguistics and folklore. In addition, GFC's political activism in resisting the Mactaquac hydro-electric project, and his concerns with conserving the archaeological record, attest modern outlooks and preoccupations.

Like many avocational archaeologists, GFC's approach to finding artifacts tended to be intuitive rather than systematic. He believed that he could enter into the mental states of people of the past, replicate their thought processes and find artifacts and sites on that basis. His haphazard approach to archaeological fieldwork and the speed with which he conducted excavations reflected earlier norms in the discipline, although, to be fair, GFC's field methods were often constrained by the brief periods he could take away from making a living and from his other interests. The influence of antiquarianism can be seen in GFC's emphasis on complete and finished artifacts, especially stone tools. He rarely collected debitage (pieces resulting from the manufacture of stone tools) and was sometimes derisive of professional archaeologists who did so. He collected Prehistoric ceramic sherds, but barely mentioned them in *Someone Before Us*, and did not illustrate any (an oversight remedied in this edition, see Fig. 28, p 132).

That said, the aspect of GFC's thought that tied him most directly to the earlier phase of archaeology was his adoption of a short chronology for human habitation in New Brunswick. GFC was aware of Euro-American myths about the origins of Aboriginal peoples, and discounted them. He accepted the evidence of an ultimate Asian origin for the original inhabitants of the Americas. (Indeed, his comments about the role of boats in the peopling of the Americas presaged the theory popularized in archaeology by Knut R. Fladmark's [1979] "Routes" article, published in *American Antiquity*, which has stimulated much subsequent research on the west coast of North America.) And GFC understood that some time would have been required for ancestral people to spread from the Pacific Northwest through the American continents as far as Atlantic Canada.

GFC was sceptical of the assertions of professional archaeologists, especially with respect to the age of artifacts. Associations between stone tools and the bones of now-extinct Pleistocene (Ice Age) animals had been established in the southwestern United States by the mid-1920s, when GFC began to focus a significant portion of his attention on collecting and excavations. He must have been aware of this evidence, but it seems not to have influenced his beliefs about the Prehistoric chronology of the area where he worked. In the context of New Brunswick and the Maritimes, GFC did not believe that archaeologists had found evidence for any group of people culturally distinct from and chronologically earlier than the recent ancestors of the Wolastoqiyik and Mi'kmaq

(Micmac). And he believed that the migration of ancestral Wolastoqiyik into the St John River Valley occurred "not earlier than two thousand years before the coming of the French and English" (GFC, *SBU*, pg. 118).

At the time when GFC was writing up his archaeological research, the main archaeological construct for an earlier culture was the Red Paint People, identified primarily from graves containing distinctive ground-stone tools in patches of ochre-stained soil, but generally lacking preserved human remains. GFC was sceptical that these archaeological features even represented graves, and he completely disbelieved the interpretation of the Red Paint People as a distinct culture that preceded recent Native American cultures. He devoted an entire chapter of *Someone Before Us*, probably lifted directly from his 1940s monograph, to refute the concept. His argument, reduced to its essentials, consisted of two points: (1) that the use of red ochre paint was widespread, world-wide and among Native American cultures, and thus could not be used to characterize a specific time or culture in the past; and (2) that he had uncovered evidence showing that the supposedly early ground-stone tools had in fact been manufactured by inhabitants of the St John River Valley right up to European Contact. As it turned out, GFC was wrong on both counts: (1) the particular way that red ochre was used— in what archaeologists now refer to as Late Archaic period mortuary and ceremonial features— was distinctive in the coastal Northeast; and (2) the artifact associations he referred to were the result of mixing of earlier and later Prehistoric assemblages. GFC was on the wrong side of history in this, but, in the time before radiocarbon dating, his skepticism was at least understandable, if not justified.

A couple of years before his death, and a couple of years after the publication of *Someone Before Us*, GFC visited David Sanger's 1970 excavation of the Late Archaic cemetery at Cow Point on the Grand Lake–Maquapit Lake thoroughfare. In notes he made after that visit, GFC complimented Sanger's field methods, but there is no indication he accepted the possibility that the Cow Point features represented an earlier Aboriginal culture, dating to a time when the ancestors and predecessors of the Wolastoqiyik and Mi'kmaq did not make ceramics, or birchbark canoes, or use bows and arrows. This is doubly ironic given the truly spectacular Late Archaic artifacts that are part of GFC's collection (for example, Figs. 2, p 55, 9 a, p 60, 27 a, p 131, and 31 a, p 135). Radiocarbon dates had been measured on New Brunswick sites by the early 1960s and G.F. MacDonald's suite of radiocarbon dates, showing that the Debert site in Nova Scotia was occupied before 10,000 years ago, was published in the same year as *Someone Before Us*. Even though the last two decades of GFC's life coincided with the first two decades of the radiocarbon-dating revolution in archaeology, *Someone Before Us* remained effectively in the pre-chronometric era.

GFC's adoption of a short chronology for New Brunswick's past constrained his perspective and distorted his work in several ways. He never dug very far into the ground when searching for artifacts, probably because he did not believe that archaeological evidence could be deeply buried. He recognized and sometimes recorded stratification in the sites he studied, but never made much of it, perhaps because he never developed a conception of cultural change outside the context of European Contact (and, even in the context of the Historic period, his interests were narrowly focused on the early French occupation). GFC's description of excavations at Meductic Flat show that he understood the principles and sometimes recognized the effects of natural and cultural mixing of earlier (Prehistoric) and later (Historic) archaeological assemblages, but he did not apply these insights to identifying sequences of Prehistoric assemblages.

Because they largely represent the concerns and thinking of the 1940s and before, the interpretations that GFC presented in *Someone Before Us* were anachronistic when they were published in 1968. The impression of the Prehistoric past that he created is that of a static backdrop against which the actions of the Early Historic period were carried out by Native Americans and by European explorers, soldiers, clergymen and settlers. In this sense, GFC was out of step with the dynamic, long-term sequences of Prehistoric cultural change that were developed by North American archaeologists during the Classificatory-Historical Period. Nevertheless, the archaeological information that he presented in *Someone Before Us* was fresh and unique and remains important today.

THE LIVING MEMORY OF ANCIENT THINGS
A PUBLISHER'S AFTERWORD

BY KEITH HELMUTH

The past is never dead. It's not even past.
William Faulkner

Not everyone is interested in the story told by ancient artefacts, but those who are, are *really* interested. George Frederick Clarke was interested in almost everything and exploring the buried history of human settlement along the St. John River Valley was a calling he could not but answer.

The echo that rises from the title of this book – *Someone Before Us* – is itself a miniature story. For those with imaginations drawn to this story, Clarke's archaeological memoir is a both a telescope and a mirror. As a telescope, it helps us travel deep into the human ecology of the past; as a mirror, it reflects back and enhances our interest in such things. We are thus brought to a heightened awareness of the story of human settlement within the St. John River watershed of central New Brunswick.

In his classic book on human adaptation to Earth's ecosystems, *Soil and Civilization*, Edward Hyams writes;

> There is no peculiar merit in ancient things, but there is merit in integrity, and integrity entails the keeping together the parts of any whole, and if those parts are scattered throughout time, then integrity entails a knowledge, a memory, of ancient things.

There is something about archaeology, something about the calling to discover and assemble the scattered parts of the human story that is driven by this sense of integrity, a sense of how the human story hangs together in all its parts over vast reaches of time and landscape. The ecology of the human-Earth relationship, the story of human settlement, livelihood, and adaptation to various environments is a grand narrative.

The magic of unearthing long buried stone tools, their careful study, and public display creates a connection with the arc of the human story that is not obtained in any other way. This connection draws us close to the soil and to the hands of those who crafted such tools. And it may be that in drawing close to the soil and to the reality of the lives of those who have come before, we can achieve a more fully rounded understanding of what it means to be a dweller in this land.

The development of the historical sciences was never simply a matter of curiosity. In particular, archaeology, physical anthropology, and human ecology have always had an interest in what their findings reveal about patterns of human adaptation within particular environments. The story of the human-Earth relationship, of ecological adaptation, can often be read in the artefacts that remain and in the traces of land use that can still be seen.

Up to the time George Frederick Clarke began his life-long search for evidence of past settlement of the St. John River watershed, most settlers of European descent would have subscribed, consciously or unconsciously, to the ideology of assimilation. This view saw Western Civilization and the supposed superiority of its economic and technological prowess as the only future for human development. Indigenous peoples were expected to get on board for their own good. The alternative was extinction. Facing this situation from the indigenous point of view, it's hard to see the difference. Fortunately for us all, a subtle but persistent resistance to assimilation set in, and a "comeback" of indigenous cultural flourishing is now emerging.*

Although George Frederick Clarke was culturally in tune with the ethos of the British Tradition, he came to know members of the Woodstock Maliseet community as friends and colleagues. His archaeological work was thus connected to the living descendants of the ancient way of life for which he was uncovering the evidence. Some of his Maliseet friends joined in his archaeological work. He, in turn, took a great interest in the elements of Maliseet culture that were still a functional part of their way of life. This interest, of course, included the skills of hunting and fishing and especially the technology of the birchbark canoe, but it extended as well to the subtleties of the Maliseet language and to the way his Maliseet friends felt their relationship to the river, the woods, and to all the animals that made up the great commonwealth of life around them.

This connection, this feeling for the living elements of a cultural tradition thousands of years old, is what makes *Someone Before Us* an unusual book. As important as the more rigorously structured books on archaeological findings are, there is something about Clarke's memoir and storytelling account of his work that gives his book enduring appeal for the general reader.

When Clarke sat down to write *Someone Before Us*, the conservation ethic had already been central to his mission for a long time. But more than this, the ecological worldview was brimming up in his assessment of what modern technology and economics were so thoughtlessly doing to the integrity of the environment. By the time this book was published, he had poured his best, and at time vociferous, efforts into stopping the construction of the Mactaquac dam. Only he, and a few others, understood and cared about the ecological destruction the dam would visit on sixty miles of the St. John River. His feeling for the river valley included not only sites of archaeological importance, but also places "of haunting spiritual significance" that would be lost.

---

* See John Ralston Saul *The Comeback* (2014) and *A Fair Country: Telling Truths About Canada* (2008).

Clarke's sense of "spiritual significance," which emanated from both his experience of the beauty of Earth and from his awareness of deep-rooted human habitation, seems to have been innate. A story from childhood has him knocking on neighbours' doors and bidding the housewives who answered to come out and see an extraordinary sunset. One woman thought him dotty; another complained that he had woken the baby.* The boy was undeterred.

Years later, when he walked the shoreline and explored the interval flats of the St. John River with spade in hand, ready to make a dig where he thought it likely an ancient campsite might have been, he was still thought a bit strange. The behaviour of the boy calling citizens to view the sunset and that of the man searching for beautifully crafted stone tools were of a piece; they both came from a whole-hearted response to whatever he encountered and whatever he was moved to do. This same whole-hearted response made him a master storyteller and storytelling writer.

When he came to write *Someone Before Us*, he employed his story telling skill in the service of integrity as characterized by the quote from Edward Hyams. The artefacts of the ancient Wolastoqiyik that he found were scattered in both geography and in the horizons of time through which he dug. Writing this book, telling the stories of his discoveries and reflecting on his findings, was his way of bringing together "the parts of a whole," his way of creating "a memory of ancient things."

The impulse of integrity that George Frederick Clarke served does not stop with unearthing the story of ancient tools. It attaches to the deeper cultural story of ecologically sound adaptation as well. Clarke was well aware that this deeper dimension of the human-Earth relationship was an intuitive attribute of his indigenous friends. He made it a central motif in his two books of Jimmy-Why stories for children.** It fuelled his fight to save the St. John River from the Mactaquac dam. It is interwoven through the whole of *Someone Before Us* and is the legacy he offers to us, his readers, and to the future.

Keith Helmuth
Chapel Street Editions

---

* See *The Last Romantic: The Life of George Frederick Clarke, Master Storyteller of New Brunswick*. Published by Chapel Street Editions, Woodstock NB, 2015.

** See *Jimmy-Why and Noël Polchies: Their Adventures in the Great Woods*. Published by Chapel Street Editions, Woodstock NB, 2016.

INDEX

Page numbers in bold type refer to illustrations